A HISTORY OF CANBERRA

Designed as an 'ideal city' and emblem of the nation, Canberra has long been a source of ambivalence for many Australians. In this charming and concise book, Nicholas Brown challenges these ideas and looks beyond the clichés to illuminate the unique, layered and often colourful history of Australia's capital.

Beginning with Aboriginal occupation and European settlement of the region, Brown covers Canberra's selection as the site of the national capital, the turbulent path of Walter Burley Griffin's plan for the city, and the many phases of its construction. He surveys citizens' diverse experiences of the city and the impact of the Second World War on Canberra's growth, and explores the city's political history with insight and wit.

A History of Canberra is informed by the interplay of three themes central to Canberra's identity: government, community and environment. Canberra's distinctive social and cultural history as a centre for the public service and national institutions is vividly rendered. Brown analyses the city as a symbol of suburban modernity and highlights its emergence as a regional centre of influence.

Illustrated with maps and photographs, this book offers insight into the enduring dynamic between Canberra, its community and the country.

Nicholas Brown is Associate Professor in the School of History, Australian National University.

Also published by Cambridge University Press

Geoffrey Blainey, *A History of Victoria* Second Edition
Raymond Evans, *A History of Queensland*
Beverley Kingston, *A History of New South Wales*
Henry Reynolds, *A History of Tasmania*

A History of Canberra

NICHOLAS BROWN

CAMBRIDGE
UNIVERSITY PRESS

CAMBRIDGE
UNIVERSITY PRESS

Shaftesbury Road, Cambridge CB2 8EA, United Kingdom

One Liberty Plaza, 20th Floor, New York, NY 10006, USA

477 Williamstown Road, Port Melbourne, VIC 3207, Australia

314–321, 3rd Floor, Plot 3, Splendor Forum, Jasola District Centre, New Delhi – 110025, India

103 Penang Road, #05–06/07, Visioncrest Commercial, Singapore 238467

Cambridge University Press is part of Cambridge University Press & Assessment, a department of the University of Cambridge.

We share the University's mission to contribute to society through the pursuit of education, learning and research at the highest international levels of excellence.

www.cambridge.org
Information on this title: www.cambridge.org/9781107646094

© Cambridge University Press & Assessment 2014

This publication is in copyright. Subject to statutory exception and to the provisions of relevant collective licensing agreements, no reproduction of any part may take place without the written permission of Cambridge University Press & Assessment.

First published 2014

Cover designed by Anne-Marie Reeves

A catalogue record for this publication is available from the British Library

A Cataloguing-in-Publication entry is available from the catalogue of the National Library of Australia at www.nla.gov.au

ISBN   978-1-107-64609-4   Paperback

Reproduction and communication for educational purposes
The Australian *Copyright Act 1968* (the Act) allows a maximum of one chapter or 10% of the pages of this work, whichever is the greater, to be reproduced and/or communicated by any educational institution for its educational purposes provided that the educational institution (or the body that administers it) has given a remuneration notice to Copyright Agency Limited (CAL) under the Act.

For details of the CAL licence for educational institutions contact:

Copyright Agency Limited
Level 15, 233 Castlereagh Street
Sydney NSW 2000
Telephone: (02) 9394 7600
Facsimile: (02) 9394 7601
E-mail: info@copyright.com.au

Reproduction and communication for other purposes
Except as permitted under the Act (for example a fair dealing for the purposes of study, research, criticism or review) no part of this publication may be reproduced, stored in a retrieval system, communicated or transmitted in any form or by any means without prior written permission. All inquiries should be made to the publisher at the address above.

Cambridge University Press & Assessment has no responsibility for the persistence or accuracy of URLs for external or third-party internet websites referred to in this publication and does not guarantee that any content on such websites is, or will remain, accurate or appropriate.

Aboriginal and Torres Strait Islander readers are respectfully advised that images of deceased persons appear in this book and may cause distress.

CONTENTS

Illustrations	*page* vii
Acknowledgements	ix
Introduction	1
1 Ngunawal country and the Limestone Plains	6
2 Not like any other	37
3 A document of Australian immaturity	62
4 Unreal city	96
5 Moving up, and moving in	122
6 Quiet revolution	159
7 You're on your own	192
8 Feel the power	222
Conclusion	247
Notes	252
Index	282

ILLUSTRATIONS

IMAGES

1	The McKeahnie family at Well Station, circa 1880s	page 21
2	Wool from the Limestone Plains, for loading at Queanbeyan station	27
3	Yarralumla Station at the end of the 19th century	32
4	Nellie Hamilton, Bobby Deuamonga and their children	34
5	A group of children and their teachers outside the school tent, Cotter Dam, circa 1917	49
6	Marion Mahony Griffin's elevations of the first-prize winning entry in the Federal Capital Design Competition, 1911	54
7	Prime Minister W.M. Hughes in discussion with C.S. Daley and P.G. Stewart	66
8	Thomas Weston and Mrs Gipps at a tree planting ceremony, around 1926	71
9	The first group of 12 cottages built on Ainslie Avenue, circa 1921	74
10	Workmen at a quarry on Capital Hill, circa 1928	75
11	Working men's married quarters at Westlake, circa 1928	76
12	The Prime Minister's Lodge, circa 1930	78
13	Parliament House from Mount Pleasant, on the eve of World War II	97
14	Women workers having lunch in the sun during World War II	111

15 Werners Linde's painting for the 1950 National
    Citizenship Convention   126
16 The Stud Book   128
17 Civic Centre in 1958   132
18 Two men in front of the Russian Orthodox Church,
    Kingston, mid-1950s   138
19 Woden Town Centre, Health Centre, Library and office
    tower, late 1970s   166
20 WEL – ACT members holding a children's party in
    front of Parliament House in 1974   181
21 Megalo International Screenprinting Collective postcard 205
22 Patricia Piccinini's *Skywhale*, afloat over Canberra,
    2013   248

MAPS

1 Canberra, the Australian Capital Territory and
   surrounds   2
2 Canberra in 1950   124
3 Canberra in 1960   151
4 A formulation of the 'Y-plan'   164

ACKNOWLEDGEMENTS

By virtue of its particular status, Canberra has never lacked for historians, and a concise history such as this relies heavily, and all too selectively, on their work. A rich seam of local history, reflection and memoir already runs parallel to accounts of national government – politics and administration – and to another strand of commentary in which 'Canberra' figures as a cipher for all kinds of discontents often loosely associated with the place, its people and its functions. In preparing this book I have been conscious of this daunting span of experience, reflection and scholarship and of the need to balance the familiar with the little known in a story to which many readers will bring a version already close to their hearts. I have also wanted to place the city in the context of a land that has its own diverse narratives, and in relation to the patterns of a wider national story. I am indebted to all those who have explored Canberra and its significance before me. My hope is that I can contribute at least a fresh perspective to the conversation started by previous narratives about some classic themes in Australian history – among them, what does it mean to 'make a place', what should we seek from 'nation building', and what defines a sense of 'community'?

I am grateful for the support provided through periods of research and writing by the Research Centre at the National Museum of Australia (NMA) – my thanks especially to Peter Stanley, Anne Faris and the NMA's excellent library and librarians. I appreciate also the interest and curiosity shown for this project by my colleagues in the School of History, College of Arts and Social Sciences, Australian

National University. The great resources of the National Library of Australia, and the facilities, staff and research culture of its Petherick Room, were vital to this project. Librarians at the Australian Institute for Aboriginal and Torres Strait Islander Studies and the ACT Heritage Library were quick in response to my vague requests. I drew heavily on the wealth of the Canberra and District Historical Society, both in its archives and in the dedication of its officers, especially Helen Digan, Nick Swain, Marilyn Truscott and Kay Walsh. Alison Alder, Esther Davies, Val Emerton, Mary Hutchinson, Megan Kelly, Chris Monnox, Nicolas Peterson, Gina Pinkus, Gail Radford, Alan Roberts, Marian Sawer, Biff Ward and Susan Mary Withycombe were among the many people who offered guidance and enthusiasm at many points. I am deeply thankful to Patrick Troy, Stuart Macintyre and anonymous referees for pointing out what more (or less) should be said; to Philippa Whishaw, Jessica Pearce, Jodie Fitzsimmons and Tara Peck at Cambridge University Press for patience beyond belief; and to Lily Keil, for closer attention than I deserved, as copy editor.

Canberra – and what came before it – is in my family's bones. My father, Bill, was of the place; my mother, Bet, embraced it. My brother and sisters were born there, as were their children and grandchildren. And so was my wife, Susan Boden, and our two children, Imogen and Naoise. Sometimes it has seemed foolish to seek the necessary distance to write about a city so much a part of our lives. Sometimes it has seemed a disqualification, when the image popularly held of Canberra is one of artificiality and impermanence. Clearly, that is not my experience. This book is a gesture of thanks to a nurturing place, and to those who continue to nurture me – especially Susan, Imogen and Naoise; and to generations past and present for what we can learn from them about making a better future.

INTRODUCTION

On 11 May 1861 James Brown died in a paddock on one of the land grants taken up in the early decades of settlement on and around the Limestone Plains. In 1834, aged 19, he had been convicted of assault and theft in Edinburgh. Sentenced to transportation and seven years' labour, he arrived in Sydney and was assigned to James Wright at Lanyon, now a heritage listed property from which the spread of Canberra's newer suburbs is kept only just out of sight. But at the time Brown arrived, Lanyon was at the further edges of pastoral expansion in New South Wales, and was described by an early visitor as 'one of the most picturesque places I have seen in the colony' even before 'art' contributed to its 'improvement'. That 'art' was essentially convict sweat, and Wright was for a time infamous for his fastidious attention to the punishments that kept his workers at their tasks. Enduring this regime, receiving a ticket of leave in 1839, and declared free in 1842, Brown stayed on as an overseer at Lanyon, which was sold amid drought and an economic slump. A Scottish banker, Andrew Cunningham, bought it in 1848, but it was on Cunningham's other, nearby choice of 'cold, wet and sour country' at Congwarra, that Brown was killed by a falling tree. His burial was the first recorded in the district after compulsory registration – but his grave remains unmarked in Lanyon's small cemetery. He was, Cunningham lamented, 'my oldest and most trusted employee'.[1]

Down the line the Browns stayed in the district, first as pastoral workers before, in the third generation, gaining land for themselves

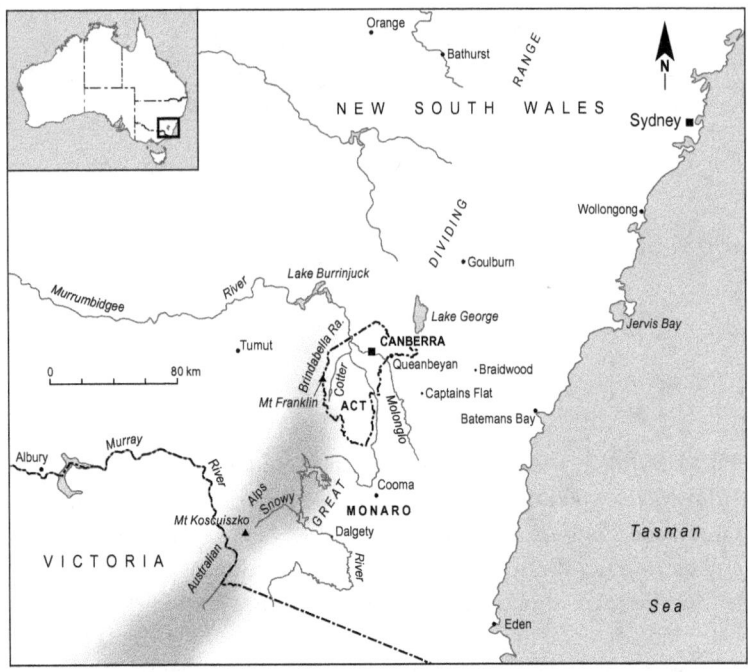

Map 1: Canberra, the Australian Capital Territory, and the main surrounding rivers, landforms, towns and cities (map by Peter Johnson)

at Bulga Creek, further down the Murrumbidgee River – and only then because the previous owners were not prepared to stay once their freehold was resumed for lease under the conditions of the new Federal Capital Territory, declared in 1911. It was on that property that my father, born in 1920, grew up. He proved bright at Canberra's first convent school, where the nuns pressed him to complete his leaving certificate and sit an exam to join the Commonwealth public service – a favoured path, then, of advancement for Catholic boys. In 1938, he became a clerk in the Department of the Interior, which controlled Canberra's development, although his section dealt with the alarming thinning of the life-blood of British migration to Australia. Following the outbreak of World War II, he fought with the 3rd Battalion of the militia, heavily recruited locally, in Papua and New Guinea before returning home and transferring to the newly established Department of Immigration – that testament to the postwar surge in nation building.

There he met my mother, who had come from Hobart to work in the typing pools serving Canberra's expanding ranks of men in suits. They married and built a house on the graceful curve of a street that had survived relatively untouched from Walter Burley Griffin's final plan for the city, before he was effectively dismissed from the project. That street marked just one of the boundaries that came to matter so much in the allocation of status in Canberra's tight bureaucratic world. To live, as we did, on the high side in Griffith, named after a 'father of federation' was one thing; to be in Narrabundah (a name drawn from the Ngunawal language, and carried over from a colonial parish designation) was – the pun went – a social blunder.

This brief autobiographical diversion, I hope, is not too indulgent, but one way of viewing the history of Canberra, and one which inevitably shapes my narrative. Canberra – the planned capital, the city without a soul, the good sheep station spoiled – is often presented as without a past. But Paul Daley's concept of Canberra as a 'continuing city' is personified in the lineage of James Brown, the Scottish-born loyal convict servant, to Bill Brown, a proud public servant, posted in the late 1950s to Athens and then Rome to bring back 'New Australians'. It is easy to focus on the moments of Canberra's invention: the decision to build a new capital, to select a site, to choose a plan and to assemble the expertise, authority and interest needed to create the kind of city required, in itself and for the nation. But those moments – interventions from beyond the place – need also their local context, a host of lives, a landscape, patterns of impact and adaptability, that made that invention possible. My goal is to strike a balance between these two elements: the local continuities, in which the story of the Limestone Plains connects to broader aspects of Australian experiences of colonisation, settlement and development, and the ideals and interventions of personnel, policy and politics that produced a new city, a bold exercise in urban design and an attempt to symbolise a nation and its government.[2]

There is no current single volume, general and concise history of Canberra. Nor is there any recent work on the city and its region that offers the span in coverage and reflection on scholarship that I attempt here. This book is carried on the shoulders of many other studies and students of Australia's capital and what came before it. In relation to those works, my claims to originality must be thin, and my account far from comprehensive. But there is, I hope, in what follows, a synthesis with a value of its own, in making this survey and in seeking this balance. Of its nature, Canberra has never been lost for words, nor for people whose stories and achievements are important, intriguing and expansive. Perhaps the best claim I can make is that my synthesis, of course highly selective, seeks to listen to as many of them as possible, whether convict labourer or typist, public servant or prime minister, and not to take for granted any one idea of what frame 'Canberra' – such a loaded term, at least among Australians – puts around the meaning we might attach to their experience. If, inevitably, much of what follows has elements of familiarity for many readers, my intention has been to present it in ways that, if only for a moment, prompt a rethinking, a revisiting, a reflection both on Canberra as a subject and the uses – as capital, planned city, politics or paperwork – to which it has been put.

To enhance the coherence of this synthesis, I have adopted three guiding themes: environment, government and community. These themes arose from core questions which emerged through my research. How did the environment into which Canberra was placed, and which it also created, influence the history of the city? How was Canberra defined by, and how did it contribute to, the practices of government in Australia so closely associated with it? And for all the attention given to the making of a new *city*, what kinds of *communities* developed in Canberra, and what influence did they have over the capital project, and in terms of its significance for the rest of the nation?

Each theme, importantly, seeks to push beyond the perimeter of the city itself into the landscape, the institutions and the mobility and ingenuity of people which are vital to Canberra's story. 'Environment' includes the country surrounding the city, at once the setting (often idealised) for its urban forms and identity as well as being a resource transformed by it, and with an agency of its own. 'Community' reflects the patterns of life – in arrivals, settlement, suburbs, workplaces, conflicts, movements, associations, families and friendships – that have evolved in the sometimes halting, sometimes rapid, transitions in Canberra's progress. And inevitably, as national capital, Canberra offers a sharp perspective on the practices and cultures of Australian 'government' as they, too, have evolved with the business of the national parliament, the functions of the national bureaucracy, the cultures of journalism, lobbying and political protest, and the role of many national agencies. Always, there is a dialectic between how the theme has defined Canberra, and how Canberra has defined the theme. And each theme has its continuing relevance, in terms of issues of sustainability, inclusiveness and political representation that find their focus in, and have their own meaning for, our purpose-built capital.

These themes are intended to function as points of reference in what remains a chronological narrative, to provide frameworks within which to balance a local and continuing history with interventions from beyond, and to suggest terms in which we might reflect on the historical significance of a place which, as eminent Australian architect Philip Cox declared, is 'inherently unnatural'. The narrative and the themes might together prompt answers to enduring questions. To what is Canberra accountable? Whose place is it? Former speechwriter for Paul Keating – Prime Minister of Australia from 1993 to 1996 – Don Watson, reflecting on the remark by his one-time employer that the capital was 'a great mistake', conceded that Canberra could seduce residents into complacency. But he also judged that it 'is like no other Australian town or city, yet no other Australian town or city is more Australian'. And as Jeanne MacKenzie noted before Watson, 'it is not like Australia and yet it could not be anywhere else'. This paradox drives what follows.[3]

I

Ngunawal country and the Limestone Plains

A GOOD SHEEP STATION SPOILED

For a city preoccupied by its own becoming – its destiny as a peerless national capital – Canberra sits in a landscape of layered, often lost histories. The future has always beckoned the city, even taunted it. 'I have planned a city that is not like any other', Walter Burley Griffin declared in 1912: 'a city that meets my ideal of the city of the future'. That aspiration set the tone for visions of Canberra's perennial making – laments at provisional structures, transient populations, or urban forms unravelling across the landscape (as novelist Tom Hungerford saw it) like 'a mad woman's knitting'. Over a hundred years on from the inauguration of the capital on 12 March 1913, a familiar story contains a wealth of gestures towards a time yet to come. But the perpetual 'time will tell' verdict too easily obscures a past on the Limestone Plains that has a significance of its own.[1]

The derision of Canberra as a 'good sheep station spoiled' allows that it had first to be a sheep station, and a good one at that. Let the borders proclaimed in 1910, to mark the surrender of the Federal Capital Territory from New South Wales to the Australian Commonwealth, blur back into their mountain ridges, watersheds and train lines, and then the landscape reveals other meanings and purposes and displays a history connecting with wider patterns of experience. Throughout the 19th century, and long before, the site of the future capital was a microcosm of phases of adaptation to the environment, of work, movement, authority and community. Those layers of endeavour and belonging never entirely disappeared beneath the experiment to come.

As an environment, Canberra's landscape blends out into the undulating, open bushland of the New South Wales southern tablelands, up onto the spare plateau of the Monaro, and edges into the high country of the Australian Alps. Its geology is defined by three dominant north–south running fault lines dating back to major tectonic shifts between 480 and 360 million years ago, and marking the break between two topographical formations and vegetation associations. To the east is a network of plains, tilting away at between 900 and 600 metres above sea level, dominated by savannah woodlands and grasslands. Tussock and kangaroo grasses predominate, with Eucalyptus species – red gum, apple box, red and yellow box – spread among them. To the west the land abruptly grows mountainous, rising from 1500 to over 1900 metres, with denser forests and rugged terrain, sprawling south towards Australia's highest peak, Mount Kosciuszko (2228 metres). Scribbly gum, Argyle apples and wattles are prominent species, along with ribbon gums, alpine ash and snow gums and a scattered understorey of grasses and herbs. The plains offered prospects of a journey, but these ranges call a halt, or hesitation, as trees gather closer and the undergrowth thickens in cooler, higher air.

These two landscapes – the grasslands and the mountains – are each emblematic of aspects of Australian human settlement, framing cultures and identities. In deeper time, the Canberra region was once under the sea, covered in sediments washed from the continent then rising further to the west. An intense period of volcanic activity produced dominating rift systems as the land began to lift and the sea retreat. It has become almost ritual for journalists and school excursion leaders to note that evidence of those shifts – the violent 'unconformity' in rock profiles revealed in road cuttings of the 1970s – can be found in close proximity to the national parliament, with its own pattern of slips, twists and contortions. The parallel is neat, but scarcely comprehends the magnitude, or legacies, of these much earlier processes.[2]

Emerging in a sequence of uplifts and glaciation, this country was exposed from the start to sustained erosion. In 1929, geological advisor to the Commonwealth government W.G. Woolnough offered a dramatic account of the 'structure' of the region:

For hundreds and millions of years, this particular part of Australia existed as dry land. At intervals it became ridged up into higher mountains. These were worn down to their very roots by the gnawing tooth of time...they were raised up again, and worn down...twice, at least, thrice in all probability, they were covered in sheets of ice.

Debate still surrounds aspects of the region's geological sequence, but Woolnough's account retains a power of evocation. The 'beautifully rounded summits' that characterise Canberra – Majura, Ainslie, Black Mountain, Red Hill, Mugga Mugga and Stromlo – are the worn 'residuals' of those tumults. The valleys are the scars of related processes of attrition, as rivers cut deep into soft rock or proceeded in pools across the surface, depositing little sediment and leaving ridges further exposed to denudation. To the west, mountains offer more 'spectacular' evidence of such rifting, crushing processes. The landforms bequeathed are old, weathered and lean.[3]

What became, then, for Griffin and many others, a 'city beautiful', a landscape of trees – introduced to link and soften suburbs, infusing civic virtue and amenity – was laid over an environment that did not naturally support such a profusion or variety of vegetation. The microclimates of frost-hollows and thin, acid soils set the scene for an unusually close juxtaposition of mountain, woodland and grassland habitats, all at relatively high altitudes, often in rain shadows and with low rainfall relative to surrounding areas. The climate produced, naturalist Ian Fraser notes, was 'more markedly seasonal than much of the country', and to it a remarkable diversity of animals adapted in all their 'ancient, teeming and subtle life'. It would prove, however, testing for human habitation.[4]

Canberra's human story begins with the movement of Aboriginal people in from the west, as the waning of the Last Glacial Maximum around 21 000 years ago began to make the barren, cold and windy 'high plains', if not the ranges, marginally more attractive for at least seasonal occupation. To the east, the coastal strip still stretched to a far horizon, 'dry, sparsely vegetated and subject to widespread dust storms'. A gradually warming, wetter climate induced less sporadic excursions and then more permanent occupation. By around 5000 years ago expanding populations on the now more salubrious coast were causing some groups to move back inland. Analysis of the Birrigai rock shelter in Namadgi National Park, south of Canberra, offers a rare perspective on this phase of mainland, highland Aboriginal prehistory. It suggests that at least by 3000 years ago there began a more constant, intense occupation of these high valleys.[5]

Working with this environment, Aboriginal people usually lived in small groups or 'bands' within larger regional populations. Rivers provided a focus for camps, with durable and comfortable shelter, ample access to fish, birdlife, fruits, berries, tubers and rhizomes, honey, and proximity to stone quarries for tools. Several old trees still standing in Canberra show the scars of having large slabs of bark cut away for canoes, roofing or carrying utensils; other sites show grinding rocks; and several granite overhangs in Namadgi bear rock paintings. Kangaroo and possum skin cloaks, stitched with sinew, kept people warm in winter on the plains; in summer, small groups followed kangaroos and emus to higher ground. Each year there was a journey into the mountains to feast, over three to four months, on the Bogong moths that migrated from the heat of the north and the inland to aestivate, a low-energy existence similar to hibernation, in rock shelters until autumn. These feasts – not signs of nomadism, archaeologist Harry Lourandos insists, but of 'more sedentary practice, organised settlement and behaviour, and complex inter-group relations' – gathered well over one thousand people to harvest the protein-rich, nut-tasting moths for roasting or keeping in smoked cakes, for shared ceremonies, including initiation rites, cultural exchange and trade.[6]

Inter-group ties reached well beyond the immediate area, including the maintenance of close links to coastal groups, if less easy relationships with those further inland. (The 'Yass blacks', early white settlers noted, were particularly feared by Limestone and coastal people.) The boundaries and appropriate naming of local groups remains a matter of dispute, on account of the profound impact of the arrival of Europeans on the mobility of the Aboriginal groups, and the more recent pressures to resolve the claims of traditional ownership. But, in general, it is accepted that the area had a permanent population now most often identified as Ngunawal and Ngambri (or Kamberri), and, as a language group, most recently classified as Kurrmal. Many locations around Canberra still bear the traces of clan names: the Namwitch of the country rising to the south, now Namadgi; the Biyaligee of the river flats now known as

Pialligo; the Toogoranoongh of the Tuggeranong valley; the Cumbeyan of Queanbeyan.[7]

In the 1820s, another human narrative begins, part of those processes of white 'mastery' which, as environmental historian George Main describes, claimed an expansive country for white settlement and Empire. The first European sighting of the plains, at the end of 1820, was by a small party including an illiterate ex-convict, Joseph Wild, and a police constable, James Vaughan. Wild was employed by Charles Throsby, a surgeon turned settler who had been 'discontented' by the colony's early political turmoil. Throsby was a 'persistent' defender of Aboriginal people from abuse. A proud, sensitive man, Throsby committed suicide in 1828 under the mounting strain of personal economic uncertainty. In the 1810s, however, he had been one of the first to move into the Illawarra, on the coast south of Sydney, and then urged the claims of land past Moss Vale and Marulan on the governor, Lachlan Macquarie. 'The finest country as ever was', Throsby reported, lay beyond the road he had been contracted to oversee in construction to the Goulburn Plains. It was land 'fit for any purpose, either for grazing or agriculture'.[8]

Enticed – as much perhaps by the prospect of easing the already entrenched power of large landholders by offering small, usually ex-convict farmers a chance – the governor travelled as far as Lake George in October, was struck by the 'beauty and fertility' of the country, and allowed for 'temporary expansion' into 'the new country'. Commissioner Bigge, sent out from London to check such flights of expansion, was a surly companion on this journey: the further he went from the coastal escarpment, the less he could see to warrant investment. Yet water as well as land remained irresistible, and when told that Aboriginal people spoke of a big river further south, Throsby's nephew, Charles Throsby Smith, went in search with Wild and Vaughan. On 7 December, after travelling through 'barren and scrubby country', they descended onto 'a very extensive plain' with 'plenty of grass' and a 'beautiful river'. This was the smaller Molonglo, not the Murrumbidgee mentioned by the Aboriginal people, but the party's identification of what appeared to be 'immense quantities of limestone' near its banks locked the place into a new history.[9]

Further exploration over three years, including by Throsby, located the Murrumbidgee and reached further south onto the 'downs' of the Monaro. These were not 'epic' journeys, environmental researcher Stephen Dovers argues, but expeditions aimed at 'filling out the maps and assessing a country' already embraced for enterprise. The hoof tracks of one party through soft grasslands – often on paths established by Aboriginal people – were sometimes still visible to the next group of explorers. Good reports went back to Sydney of open 'park'-like country, of, as historian Bill Gammage emphasises, a landscape already fashioned and carefully managed by Aboriginal practices of burning. When the Governor of New South Wales, Sir Ralph Darling, proclaimed the 'limits of location' in 1829, to bring a pretence of control to the spread of pastoralism spurred by such reports, the Limestone Plains were just within his authority, the border at the time running along the Murrumbidgee River. Sir George Gipps, a successor to Darling, observed in 1840 that it was 'as well...to confine the Arabs of the desert within a circle, traced upon their sands, as to confine the graziers of New South Wales' – and by then the Limestone Plains were well and truly claimed by such settlers, who had also transgressed the limits out of ambition, adventure or necessity. In his book *Heartland*, Main quotes the daughter of one pioneering family who moved past Darling's boundaries with the view that it 'was a simple enough matter' to establish a station further west, 'after one had reached a desirable place to squat, providing, of course, one got a passport from the blacks'.[10]

With the 'Yass blacks' and beyond, that passport would be negotiated in violence, as colonists were met with concerted opposition. 'The Wiradjuri were not easily subdued', Peter Read records of the Aboriginal peoples whose land began to the north-west of the Limestone Plains: martial law was proclaimed around Bathurst in 1824 in an attempt to end the guerilla tactics of Aboriginal resistance across an expansive frontier. On Limestone, however, the relatively lower population densities on both sides, and local patterns of Aboriginal land use, did not support such action. In any case, other factors were at work. 'Limestone natives', an early observer judged, 'are a fine, stout, athletic race, men and women well-proportioned', yet even when they were first seen by Europeans it was apparent that a 'passport' was being transacted with them more in disease than in blood. Much later, Canberra's first chroniclers used this point to smooth the path of their destiny. As Frederick Watson wrote in 1927, 'the aborigines disappeared rapidly before the advance of civilization...about Canberra'.[11]

'Civilisation' hung in the air over Canberra's first white settlement. The 'irresistible urge' of pastoralism, as Stephen Roberts argued, had pushed south-west from Sydney as soon as it could, and the Limestone Plains was early in its path – at least until the 'Great Unknown' of central western New South Wales gave way to the triumphal age of squatting after 1835. Meanwhile, Limestone was defined by a transitional phase. In an almost feudal fashion, a few wealthy men began sending their employees and usually convict labourers to take up the best land, marking time between the closed convict colony and pressures for expansion. And, cradled in its skein of valleys, something about the Limestone Plains soon prompted reflection on a particular kind of future. Dr Johann (John) Lhotsky, an Austrian-born naturalist, travelling south in 1834, was struck there by a 'heavenly sky' under which 'Italian-like scenery' extended towards the 'colossus' of the Australian Alps. This could be, Lhotsky perceived, 'one of the most important spots as far as the political economy of the colony is concerned': a site for a 'fine town', a point of convergence between metropolitan influence and 'a whole continent of immense extent'.[12]

Equally, however, Lhotsky feared that 'with regard to Limestone this is now too late'. He lamented that, even in so short a time, large portions of land had been given to only a few settlers in an 'inconsiderate disposal' of what might have contributed to the *general* welfare' of the colony. This volatile, plaintive scientist, a cosmopolitan, outspoken venturer, would have successors in his view of what was possible yet forsaken on these plains, just as he would in his reverie at the landscape itself: the grace of the valleys and the sublime blue of the ranges beyond.[13]

So soon into the story of Canberra, then, some themes are already evident: the qualities of the landscape, the vision of a common wealth, but also one of the slate too readily wiped clean. Just before arriving at Limestone, Lhotsky grandly invoked providence, writing of the 'warnings to future Governments' his reflections might provide on the consequences of parsimony and opportunism. But other, less portentous impressions also came as he paused in the heat of late January into February. He gathered samples of rock, noted plants and animals, wondered why the plains were 'altogether destitute of trees of any kind', and recorded sudden vacillations in the weather ('what is stable and uniform in Australian nature?'). He took the comforts to be had 'as it were at the end of the world' while brushing away the moths clustering around his candle. He observed the eccentricity of one of the area's first pioneers, whose delusions in this remote setting had a kind of comic grandeur. Lhotsky's account captures a sense of place, of paradox, of ease and unreality, of sophistication in a potentially bold venture, thrown into relief from this almost arbitrary margin, in ways that will echo through Canberra's history.[14]

THE GREAT RESORT OF OUR GRAZIERS

Those 'entire dukedoms' of alienated land of which Lhotsky despaired on the Limestone Plains in 1834 had prosaic origins. A decade earlier, John McLaughlin, an ex-convict overseer employed by Joshua John Moore, then clerk to the judge-advocate in Sydney and holder of several grants near Liverpool and Goulburn, followed the explorers' path south. With two assigned convicts, McLaughlin established a 'stock station' on a loop in the Molonglo. Named 'Canberry', an adaptation of the local Aboriginal word for the place, it consisted at first of rough slab huts. By a 'ticket of occupation', Moore acquired a claim to the land, but did not move to purchase the 1000 acres (405 hectares) he 'possessed' until 1826, and not until 1836 did he pay the fee of a shilling an acre. Moore never lived on the property. Nor was he recalled as playing any role in the affairs of the district – although he continued to acquire further outstations on the Monaro. And despite the relative depth of Canberry's alluvial soils, under Moore's inattention the property 'failed to do well'. But with him came the first stamp of the 'servant' and 'the squatter', and of the ad hoc, on Canberra's tangled mix of environment, community and government.[15]

Settlers who followed showed more commitment and success. In 1825, James Ainslie was employed by the wealthy Sydney merchant,

Robert Campbell, to take delivery of 700 sheep from government stocks held at Bathurst, in compensation for his loss of a ship. While overlanding that flock in search of pasture, Ainslie fell in with 'a camp of blacks' and was guided by a young Aboriginal woman to suitable land. There Ainslie stopped and settled what became 'Duntroon' (named after the Campbells' Scottish ancestral home), by the 1840s a fine estate. A strict disciplinarian in handling convicts, it was Ainslie who Lhotsky observed to be prone to 'irritability and excitement', especially when drunk, on account (it was said) of a head wound inflicted while serving with the Scottish cavalry at the Battle of Waterloo. But he was a 'fine fellow' in consolidating his flock and bringing wealth to his employer. His name was not given to the daughter he fathered with that Aboriginal guide before returning to Scotland, to alcoholism and suicide in 1835. It endures, however, in the peak that rises highest above the Limestone Plains and would later shoulder Burley Griffin's vision.[16]

Unauthorised squatters were joined by settlers who received land in recognition of services to the colony, or of wealth invested in it. By 1829, the district had been mostly mapped, but grants were not formally surveyed until 1832, a year after regulations replaced free grants with the sale by auction of 640-acre sections. A patchwork of elongated blocks was laid across or against the creeks and rivers, and began extending from the Molonglo into neighbouring valleys: Tuggeranong (or Isabella Plains) to the south, west to abut the Murrumbidgee, north to Ginninderra. Drought throughout 1825–28 pushed settlers further out, and it was tacitly accepted that landholders would roam wide beyond their own, and the colony's, boundaries to take advantage of any 'grassy, well-watered plains' in higher country. Garrett Cotter, a Cork-born Irishman, charged with insurrection after a skirmish with British troops in 1820, sentenced to transportation and assigned to a station near Lake George, was among the first to take the cattle in his care across the Murrumbidgee, and also advised by Aboriginal people on where to find pasture. After being effectively banished for feuding over a horse and evading arrest, Cotter, and his free-roaming herd, would later shelter beyond the 'limits of location', in lonely communion with the river that would eventually carry his name and make Canberra itself viable.[17]

Entrepreneurs as much as pioneers, these men consolidated their holdings – and even if they didn't, they claimed the country. Sheep steadily replaced the cattle, which had often been 'the small man's stock' and which – it was noted – could not survive on pasture close-bitten by sheep. And sheep brought other dynamics of their own. Coming to land near the Limestone Plains, and seeking to eradicate scab mite from his flocks, Edward John Eyre adopted the practice of treating infected stock, then selecting a new run some 30 kilometres away to which the sheep were sent to keep them 'clean', and so the sequence went:

> Of course the forming [of] a new and distant sheep station where huts had to be built, hurdles taken, supplies provided and other arrangements had to be made, all involved a large additional expenditure, but as long as we kept charge of the sheep we were determined to spare neither cash nor exertion to cure them if possible.

Within two years Eyre determined that he would never recover his investment and sold his property in the area, recording 'the complete...failure of our unlucky speculation'. Yet his station had increased nearly fourfold in value during that time, simply in rudimentary improvements and in forging paths of expansion over country reduced literally to 'sheep walks' or, more appropriately, 'runs'.[18]

Not only – as Eyre's account suggests – was the best land quickly taken in large portions, but it also demanded hard labour: clearing ground, ringbarking and felling trees, cutting logs, tending crops, shepherding large flocks in the absence of fences, penning them at night against dingos, washing and shearing. Convicts, along with 'lags' at the end of their sentence, provided by far the majority of this workforce. Their labour was often exacted under the threat, and practice, of flogging, and (if unrepentant) of return to chain gangs. The 1828 census counted 19 people at Duntroon, 10 at Canberry, and – at three stations established over the previous two years – 14 at Ginninderra, seven at Jerrabomberra and three at Quinbean (later the site of the township, Queanbeyan), which was run by an ex-convict, Owen Bowen, who had himself been successively moved on from land granted to Moore. Within 10 years over 30 assigned men were labouring under James Wright at Lanyon, just south of

Tuggeranong – who disturbed officials with his practice of closely inspecting the work of the flogger at nearby Queanbeyan, to ensure there had been no lenience in the punishment of his men.[19]

Even given the imbalances of the colony's demography at that time, the scarcity of women (two white women appeared in that 1828 count) and the absence of children made these clusters a gross distortion of 'community'. Those in charge of stations often fought an 'unsupportable loneliness', marked by a chasm of sociability separating them from workers, whom they judged 'led rude and rough lives...wanting entirely the disciplinary influences of civilisation'. Sly grog was endemic – or so masters said – and isolation placed a premium on capacities to 'hold dignity and authority' by insisting on order, discipline and distance. From early on, and for a long time, the district had its convict 'bolters' – men who simply fled their masters – and bushrangers, who returned to rob and assault. Mount Tennant, to the south, was named after one bushranger who, from 1827 into 1828, hid on its slopes until captured with the aid of Aboriginal trackers and dispatched to the privations of Norfolk Island. Stories like this added to a sense of menace and isolation among settlers, but could also spur a certain romanticism among those who also felt themselves ground down by 'dukes'. In 1913, when the capital was proclaimed, this convict past was still familiar enough to prompt Thomas Kinleyside – a local radical – to observe:

> Well on Canberra's plains long gone by
> Was waged a far different fight
> When the triangle, the cat and the flogger were here
> And it was not a capital sight.[20]

Steadily, however, prospects improved. By April 1832, the *Sydney Gazette* was directing the government's attention to 'two points of the interior' where roads were urgently needed to service the prospects for expansion: 'Bathurst, our great interior wool country'; and the Limestone Plains, described then as 'the great resort of our graziers, and, for wheat, the best soil in either of the colonies'.[21] Such boosterism was wide of the truth, but through that decade the district began featuring regularly in Sydney's press: in classified advertisements that charted the extension of itinerant services and commerce around Limestone; and in reports of the personalities and fluctuating fortunes which characterised society there. Getting as far as Goulburn by a coach service, en route to Limestone in 1838, a correspondent to the Sydney *Colonist* protested at having to share the cabin with 'beasty-drunken individuals': surely better services were needed for such a promising area? Schemers looked for alternative connections. By 1840, settlement at Broulee, on the south coast, was boosted as offering the 'only shipping harbor for the immense produce brought down from Manaroo, Molonglo, Limestone Plains and the entire south and eastern district of the Colony' – a prospect only dependent on the completion of a road reaching over the escarpment to Braidwood and on the capacity of politicians to break the hold of Sydney over the business of the colony, which never happened.[22]

Visiting in 1844, as the official Protector of Aborigines, George Robinson was struck by settlers' boasts that more land in the Limestone district had been simply given by government grants to 'private individuals of money' than had been sold in the opening up of Port Phillip – noting equally that even then that this land was often heavily mortgaged, reflecting the risks of speculation and the costs inherent in what were still remote ventures. But as the first resident landholders arrived, a greater sense of order and propriety emerged. Already keen to shake off the taint of 'squattage', at Duntroon the Campbells began recruiting free labour, preferably from their native Scotland, in place of convicts. They hoped to create small 'frugal and industrious' villages, to raise 'the physical and moral condition of our working classes'. Each worker and their family were allowed a plot of ground, usually to keep a cow and grow vegetables: potatoes, pumpkin and corn. Under contract to the Campbells, in 1856 it took the Shumack family, Anglican immigrants from County Cork, three weeks to travel from Sydney on a dray pulled by nine horses over the rough track that still served as the route to the plains. The then six-year-old Samuel Shumack recalled that the Campbells 'treated their servants well', albeit relative to conditions on other stations. But throughout his life in the district Samuel noted that boundaries between owners and 'toilers' never disappeared.[23]

Within that distinction others developed. By the early 1840s, the prevalence of Scotch Gaelic around Duntroon was matched at Terrence Aubrey Murray's Yarralumla, at the other end of the plain, where, as historian Patricia Clarke notes, an Irish-Catholic 'enclave' developed. Murray was County Limerick born, an imposing, well-educated figure. He came with his father to the colony in 1826, and in 1835, aged 25, inherited extensive land holdings around Lake George. Despite 'impeccable revolutionary credentials' stretching back to the Battle of the Boyne, he served as police magistrate for the colony's southern districts. The pressure of a second drought in the late 1830s, when there was not even enough fat on his sheep to warrant boiling them down for tallow (a practice first adopted at Yass), brought Murray to Limestone, looking for pasture. Yarralumla became one of several stations he acquired in his push south-west, extending into the Brindabella and over the Snowy mountains.[24]

By then, Murray calculated that up to two-thirds of the flocks of most large landholders were 'without the boundaries' at any time, whether recognised by pasturing licences or not. But Yarralumla, a particularly 'pretty place', became his 'headquarters', and Murray another relatively benevolent master on the plains. He also proved 'a good friend to the Blacks' who gathered around his yards and huts, taking occasional work and rations. In 1843, Murray was elected unopposed to represent three southern counties in the New South Wales Legislative Council – Australia's first form of representative government – and was relatively liberal in his causes. He opposed heavy government licence fees on squatters, especially given that little security came with that tenure, and drew on the civil and religious liberties precious to an Irish patriot in calling for an end to convict transportation and for a program of free immigration – if in the hope that it would exert pressure on high wages and bring more regularity to the attitudes of labour. In this objective, at least, there was common cause with the Campbells, although not to the extent that Murray would also consider importing 'Coolies' as cheap workers.[25]

By 1841 – the year in which convict assignment ended – the district's population had risen to 451, of whom 92 were women and 180 convicts still under sentence. At Yarralumla, 108 people were 'in residence', 100 men, eight women, 56 'free' and 52 still in 'bond'. At Duntroon, the numbers were 84, 60 men and 24 women, and 22 still serving time. At Lanyon, where James Wright at last began turning to the inducement of rations rather than flogging to extract labour, there were 59 people (49 men, of whom eight were married, and 10 women, of whom five were single), with 31 in some form of assignment. Slowly, however, 'lags' became less prominent among workers, and large landholders began to lease out portions of their estates to smaller settlers and their families. So, in 1841, 25 children under 14 were recorded at Duntroon, six at Yarralumla, and 19 at Palmerville, an estate established in 1826 on Ginninderra Creek to the north.[26]

The landscape also changed, if at the margins. Small timber-slab or rubble cottages and cultivation paddocks for barley, oats, wheat and corn appeared among flocks. So did patterns of labour, as hands alternated between their plots and their masters' tasks, and small-scale free settlers took seasonal work on stations to make ends meet. Most agricultural produce was for local use and was processed nearby, including at a few windmills grinding grain. Distance made both the import and export of perishable produce risky and expensive, and while orchards, vegetable plots, poultry, dairy cows and pigs helped alleviate the costs of buying food for settlers, they could never provide an income, or support a market in themselves.[27]

Amid these changes, it soon became evident that the growth of the colony was bypassing that potential fusion of 'political economy' Lhotsky had foreseen for Limestone: it was not so much becoming a 'point of convergence' as a dead end. Better prospects were luring people further afield, and geography itself closed Limestone off at the 'Alps'. After 1836, Braidwood, 100 kilometres to the east, served as the administrative headquarters for the 'squattage district' extending further into the Monaro. Closer by, and also better positioned on the tracks of colonial expansion, Queanbeyan, with a population of 50, had been gazetted as a township in 1838, anchoring a more balanced community around an inn, post office, police magistrate and doctor. Well into the 20th century, despite being three or more hours away by horse and cart, Queanbeyan would remain the nearest source for most household and farm supplies for Limestone residents. The gold rushes of the 1850s – around Majors Creek (near Braidwood) and later Kiandra (on the western fringe of the Monaro) – accentuated Limestone's marginalisation, even prompting the Wrights at Cuppacumbalong to 'procure... five

Chinamen' to take the place of shepherds who 'flew' to the diggings – and who proved 'not half bad' as workers.[28]

The 'cultural pockets' of the large stations became more insular in these circumstances, and society more stratified in the absence of dynamics for change. The first church on the plains, St John the Baptist, was erected by Robert Campbell (who turned to the Church of England as the colony's 'establishment' was formalised) and consecrated in 1845. For decades St John's had the only resident clergyman in the district, other faiths relying on visiting priests or lay preachers and makeshift places of worship. Now managing Duntroon, Robert's son and Charles' brother, George 'the Squire' Campbell gave his workers a Saturday half-holiday in 1856, so that they could attend to domestic chores and have no excuse to not attend services on Sunday. Other landholders were said to disapprove of his leniency, and its effects in establishing social as well as religious authority. William Davis at Ginninderra only conceded a half-day if his labourers were playing in a cricket match. Yet a more general bitterness would spread when Campbell then denied Presbyterians the use of St John's schoolhouse for worship, dismissed the teacher for insult to his authority, and was said to drive the children from their desks with his whip handle.[29]

More staunch than the Campbells, the proud McKeahnies had arrived as assisted immigrants in 1838, working briefly for Moore at Canberry and by the 1860s establishing a cattle station at Booroomba, to the south. Even that relatively high country did not salve Elizabeth McKeahnie's longing or pride in the independence of 'brave Scottish covenanters' in upholding the principles of their faith:

> O give me a brace aw heather clad
>   And farewell to Australia's waving grass
> Wha can love like a Highland lad
>   Wha so leal as a lowland lass.

Many of those who settled, not far from Booroomba, behind Mount Tennant on the Naas River – named after a town in Kildare, the site of an early revolutionary battle – were equally vehement, and accented, Irish.[30]

Figure 1: The McKeahnie family at Well Station, circa 1880s: Archibald and Mary McKeahnie, seated, arrived in 1838 and became successful landholders at Booroomba and Blythburn, south of the Limestone Plains, and Gunghalin, to the north. (Reproduced with permission of the Canberra and District Historical Society)

Whatever this mix and tension of identities, there was a common interest in the enterprise of the land, and an awareness of its changes. The tall 'waving grass' that impressed first settlers soon lost out to shorter native forms that proved more resilient to the hard-hoofed grazing of sheep and cattle. Even through them, however, the compacted wagon trails and bullock tracks wore quickly into gullies, especially after rain. John Gale, who arrived in Queanbeyan as a Methodist missionary and settled as a journalist and keen local historian, wrote eloquently of the losses to the natural profusion of plant and animal life he witnessed on that 'stretch of magnificent country' which he first saw in 1855. Not least among these impacts was that of 'man and his death-dealing tube', and many pioneers' accounts offered a staggering, routine enumeration of the birds, kangaroos, wallabies, dingos, koalas and possums shot for pleasure, fur, food or as pests. The impact of overstocking in good years was graphically evident to another Polish explorer-scientist, Paul Strzelecki, who – also travelling to the Alps, in 1841 – observed on the Monaro the 'prejudicial practice' of exposing soil to 'innumerable flocks and axes'. The cumulative effect was of 'enervating the surface and assimilating its best parts to the rest already sterile'.[31]

The perennial gamble with stock and land, and of adjusting to the environment, was brought to bear in the successive droughts that marked the early decades of settlement. Drought on the plains, Davis Wright recalled, was 'a truly dreadful affair', with 'thousands of suffering animals all round, gaunt, staring-eyed spectres'. What would now be identified as an El Niño weather pattern sat over the colony in 1837–39 and 1841–43, bringing 'the worst years that anybody could remember'. Workers' wages were cut severely, rations reduced to bad Chilean flour, and bankruptcies threatened or fell on even the most settled property owners. Thomas Macquoid named the station he purchased in 1835, to the north of Lanyon, 'Waniassa' after the Javanese coffee estate he had managed for the East India Company. He envisaged – like many – a different kind of empire by the Murrumbidgee. Yet failure in the drought of the coming years drove him to suicide, leaving a son to pull family and honour together. Joshua Moore was forced to sell Canberry, which was added to the Campbells' holdings. James Wright sold Lanyon, which went next to Andrew Cunningham, a Scottish banker, and the beginning of another, more successful, local pastoral dynasty.[32]

Eventually rain returned, and, in 1851 and 1852, with a vengeance that contributed to another of the more enduring transformations of the landscape. Early explorers and settlers remarked that the rivers on the southern tablelands had a distinct form: they were often 'a chain of ponds', characterised by a slow flow through deep pools, surrounded by reeds, good alluvial soil and swampy flood plains. These ponds provided distinct habitats, held water through drier times, and had their own beauty. Even the Murrumbidgee, Davis Wright noted, although 'a fine and generously flowing river', had gentle banks and deep pools from which 'good fishing' was assured. But the flood of June 1852 – which swept away much of Gundagai, further downstream – 'was indeed disastrous' also around Limestone. Soils hardened and laid bare by grazing accelerated the rush of water and debris into river channels. As the flood subsided, Wright 'grieved' to see the Murrumbidgee transfigured into 'a coarse stream between unfertile banks', scoured into a 'wasteful flow'. These 'alterations' seemed both 'rapid and large', and were recorded also in smaller rivers and creeks as they were carved into channels and gullies, the timeless erosion of the prehistoric landscape being accelerated in full human view. Even at the time, settlers grasped the extent to which pastoral practices had an impact on such events. For the 'sad and sorry community' on Limestone, the flood of 1852 offered graphic evidence of how deeply they already depended on their remade landscape.

AN AIR OF PECULIAR SOFTNESS

In 1834, Lhotsky recorded, with dramatic irony, that the name 'Kembery' came from 'local natives who are no more!' The invisibility of the Aboriginal population around Limestone perhaps served his point about a pervasive indifference among settlers, but did not reflect reality. In 1832, the surveyor Robert Hoddle placed a group of Aboriginal people at the centre of his painting of 'Limestone Hill', the expanse of the plains in the background, and apparently unconcerned by a stockman riding towards them. Perhaps he, too, had a point to make about the approach of civilisation, although his several watercolours completed around Ginninderra record similar combinations of farmer, stock and Aboriginal people hunting or at repose around a fire. And by the mid-19th century, settlers such as Davis Wright were still observing the seasonal coming together of large groups of Aboriginal people. The dances at such corroborees, as Eyre recorded during his time in the district in the mid-1830s, were 'graceful' or 'wild and exciting, some lascivious'. Others observed the 'careless elegance' with which skin cloaks were worn, and the 'affection and care' characterising personal relationships among these groups. Local Aboriginal people, it was noted, spoke among themselves with 'an air of peculiar softness': they were 'untroublesome'. Yet, while these ceremonies might have impressed European observers, even providing a subtle prompt (to those who saw it) of the extent to which the people assembling among them had lost traditional meeting grounds, consciences were less stirred by the more usual Aboriginal 'camp', described by Wright as comprising up to 30 people who followed an 'uneasy flitting from one spot to another, living on the animal, grub and plant life and moving on as they exhausted each place'. At this level, colonists showed little awareness of the impact of their having taken the land that remained the most basic resource for Aboriginal survival.[33]

That disjunction ran deeply through relationships. Wright, born at Lanyon in 1841, recalled growing up at Cuppacumbalong, further up the Murrumbidgee River, as 'an unlimited out-of-doors' existence, shared with 'blackfellows, who to my childish brain seemed to me to be in number as the stars'. Aboriginal beliefs, customs, ceremonies and even the structure of traditional authority were sufficiently present to Wright to generate awe and 'a very healthy respect'. A Ngambri 'chief' such as 'Hong Kong' (Onyong) seemed a 'terror' to him as a child, if more a curiosity to adults. Wright would have known the story of the young Aboriginal woman who ran more than 20 kilometres to tell his mother, Mary, that the party including her parents and six brothers had stopped for the night near Duntroon and would be with her next day. Such sentimental constructions of relationships could foster respect, but also breed their own blind spots in understanding the impact of colonisation. Reflecting in 1923, Wright lamented the steady 'despoilation' of Aboriginal life due to the impact of disease, from influenza and measles to smallpox and syphilis. Such 'contamination' was, however, only one dimension of the impact of colonisation. Even while they noted the waning of traditional practices, early settlers respected the skills of Aboriginal people as stockmen, in bushcraft, buckjumping, hunting, and in assistance in the tracking of bushrangers. But it was also noted that it was hard to hold them to labour, an observation highlighting concerns with regularising the management of the land while also indicating an alienation of Aboriginal people from the emerging economy of pastoralism, with its own supply of more readily disciplined workers.[34]

No white deaths at the hands of Aboriginal people were recorded around the Limestone Plains. Occasional friction at the sexual predation of white men on Aboriginal women reflected an Australia-wide pattern of dispossession. On Limestone, for all the aspects of the place and its peoples already noted, more concerted resistance perhaps seemed futile. Onyong, for example, seems to have calculated what might be gained from working with European settlers in preserving what remained of his authority among rival groups. Even that bargaining was seasoned by experience. He had been shot and wounded while spearing a cow by Henry Hall, 'a good all-round rough and ready farmer', who settled Charnwood, to the north of Limestone, in 1833, in the kind of leap-frogging opportunism that brought many early settlers to the district, and made them trenchant in hanging on to what they had. There were strict limits to the kind of tolerance a figure such as Hall would extend – and a propensity, too, for settlers to exaggerate the 'native threat' when it suited them. But relationships of striking intensity could still endure. In 2013, the Palmer-Woods family donated to the Canberra Museum and Gallery an Aboriginal reed necklace, given to Minna Close Palmer, granddaughter of pioneering Ginninderra settler, on the occasion of her marriage in 1862 – the gift being all the more remarkable in that it was delivered to her personally, at night, by a local leader, Jimmy the Rover, who was being pursued by police.[35]

The dating of Aboriginal campsites and stone tools found in higher country to the south indicate that traditional practices continued there at least into the 1850s. Permanent retreat from the life on the plains, however, was not sustainable. From 1834, the names recorded in the official lists of blankets issued to help Aboriginal people through the winter kept a sombre track of the processes of dispossession. In 1841, Governor Gipps quibbled at the request for 170 blankets to be distributed from Queanbeyan, seeing no need to issue them 'gratuitously' to any 'native' who 'is able to obtain one by working for it'. Over the coming decades, working as labourers or maids, or even, after 1870, on whatever land Aboriginal people might have been eligible to claim, did little to maintain visibility or recognition, but could still provide points of resilience that would endure into the next century.[36]

A PERMANENT HOME

Into the second half of the 19th century, Limestone's small community consolidated, but remained at best – as evoked by Frederick Watson – 'a tiny straggling village'. Around the modest stones of

St John's spread 'a few largish stations, long established and prosperous... and a substantial sprinkling of small farmers, tenants or freeholders'. That prosperity reflected the rapid expansion of the wool industry in the eastern colonies. On Lanyon, for example, under the shrewd eye of Cunningham, new breeding and business practices were producing prize-winning fleece by the end of the 1860s. But Limestone had become progressively more distant from the dynamics evident elsewhere in colonial rural development: those 'rough edges' of frontiers to the west, where the growth of the wool industry was most pronounced, with associated conflicts between 'master and servant', or the surges of gold fever. 'Probably no area of Australia', Watson observed, saw 'fewer changes over an extended term of years' than did Limestone in its 'quiet and conservative epoch' from 1851 to 1911. To a large extent it was that isolation that made the area available for a very different pace of development.[37]

The village Watson described might have 'no official status', not even a name, but it still benefited from the gradual extension of basic services: a police station; a few small schools – reliant at first on privately provided rooms, local initiative and subsidy, and jobbing teachers. A postal service and a telegraph office opened in Queanbeyan in 1864. And steadily came the railway: to Goulburn from Sydney by 1869, Bungendore by 1885, Queanbeyan in 1887, then down towards Cooma past Tuggeranong and Lanyon stations. No line, however, seemed warranted onto the Limestone Plains, although its effects were evident: in a clearer division between town and country, and in regional specialisation – cheaper and better wheat came in; more wool moved efficiently out. No doubt the quality of life improved with these connections, and in the ease with which at least the wealthier families could link to the better schools, 'seasons', circles and influence of the metropolis. But Limestone also slipped a little further into relative insularity.[38]

At lower ranks, settlements around the district were steadily transforming from raw, predominantly masculine clusters into more balanced villages, often characterised by chains of family migration and tight networks of marriage and association. Those who followed the evangelistic Thomas Southwell, who arrived at Parkwood in 1840, transformed 'a perfect hell' of disorder into a respectful and

Figure 2: The golden fleece: 10 ton of wool from the Limestone Plains, for loading at Queanbeyan station, late 19th century. (Reproduced with permission of the Canberra and District Historical Society)

respected community. At Queanbeyan, gatherings for horse races might last for 'three or four days, with dancing on the green and a ball every night'. Ploughing competitions, held across rural Australia, were valued locally for 'exerting a spirit of emulation, industry and neatness in husbandry', despite agriculture falling further from prominence as a local industry. Cricket was the most popular sport in the district. Davis' Ginninderra team was famously strengthened by three 'star' Aboriginal players – Jimmy Taylor, Johnny Taylor and Bobby Deumonga – but at least once in 1861 the proud Duntroon team refused to play against such 'common blackfellows'.[39]

At Gundaroo, to the north-east, spurred by its own small gold rush, a Mutual Improvement Society was holding regular meetings by the 1860s, the town also hosting a procession of pubic speakers, concerts and touring performers. Several neighbouring villages around Limestone developed equivalent public cohesion around pubs and shops. But not Limestone, where the baker and blacksmith worked from their homes and large landholders opposed the first granting of a liquor licence in 1876 (they were unsuccessful at first, but the licence lapsed in 1887 due to lack of custom). Growing up in the Brindabella valley to the west, the novelist Miles Franklin recalled her home amid a beloved 'wilderness' which nonetheless 'boasted the quintessential markers of colonial respectability: a piano brought up by bullock dray'; 'a Singer sewing machine on which, with the aid of the latest patterns, [her mother] made the family clothing; and an enormous perambulator, apparently never used'. While, as Franklin put it, 'at the edge of Empire', settlers made the best of the resources to hand, and the connections they built.[40]

Campaigns for colonial political reform in the second half of the century also came to Limestone, adapting to the scale of the settlement and its prevailing interests. In 1861, legislation designed to 'unlock the lands' still held by squatters was introduced into the New South Wales Parliament. Settlers were enabled to 'select' up to 320 acres from properties leased by squatters, and to purchase that land at a fixed price, paid in full over three years or with interest beyond that, on condition that their blocks were 'improved'. All around Limestone there was enthusiasm for assisting 'the permanent occupation of the land by industrious settlers', and for challenging the sprawl and power of sheep and cattle associated with large pastoral stations, with the cultivation of the soil and rewards for independent labour. In the local electorate created for the Legislative Assembly in 1856, the battle between the candidate for the 'moneyed class' and 'the toilers' intensified around these issues, further challenging the prevailing pattern of pastoralists dominating electoral contests, and intimidating servants and tenants into support. Even after 15 years, the architect of those 1861 laws, Sir John Robertson, was still assured of a rousing welcome when he visited Queanbeyan, where many continued to rally to the cause of 'affording opportunities for the great mass of the people to . . . settle down'.[41]

The reality of undertaking free selection was no easier around Limestone than anywhere else. The skills, capital and endurance required to make even good land support a family were sorely trying. But first came – as historian W.K. Hancock observed of the Monaro – the 'embittering struggle for ownership' as large leaseholders resisted the incursion of selectors.[42]

In itself, the 'sprinkling' of small farms on Limestone reflected that relatively little good land remained available for selection. Also, while many local labourers welcomed Robertson's reforms, their employers did not share their enthusiasm. On Lanyon, Cunningham – like many station owners – resorted to 'dummying', getting workers to select land in their name but under his control. Further up the Murrumbidgee, Leopold de Salis – an experienced pastoralist and descendant of European aristocracy who bought Cuppacumbalong in 1856 – did the same, comparing tactics with Cunningham and systematically 'defending his run' by exploiting bureaucratic processes and using family members, loyal employees and 'jackeroos' down from the city to claim land in portions that made it difficult for others to find viable blocks. Those who agreed to act as 'dummies' entrenched patterns of deference to such 'dukes'; those who defied them – such as Garrett Cotter's son, who selected portions of de Salis' land south of Cuppacumbalong – had to tough out various forms of intimidation. Shumack's father was promptly dismissed when he informed William Davis, for whom he had worked since 1858, that he intended to take up a block at Weetangera, and his family was repeatedly taunted with the certainty of their failure. At Duntroon, Charles Campbell gave employees a choice: give up their selection or their job.[43]

This choice itself might seem obvious for those who saw at last 'an object in life – to establish a permanent home', but the consequences were tough. Clearing, fencing, grubbing and ploughing variable land was daunting, as was taking the chances of sowing and reaping through hard seasons. Drought came again in the mid-1860s, and there was also the sudden, legendary severity of local wind and hailstorms that could destroy crops and stock in an hour. But for those who took up selections, like the Shumacks at 'Springvale', pride came in independent 'bush work' instead of in following someone else's sheep. Still, selectors, like tenant farmers, needed to earn money to get by, often labouring on those large stations when they could, and seeking whatever might earn cash or barter – poultry, milk, some tobacco, or raising geese for feather mattresses. Overall, the results were mixed, even despite the vigorous agitation of the local branch of the Free Selectors Protective Association, which looked beyond the 'squatters' dominance of land to consider also their power in offices such as the magistracy. With understated insight, in 1871 a visitor noted the contrast between the enduring affluence of stations such as Lanyon and 'the abodes of a struggling peasantry or thriving selectors' spread around it.[44]

The conflicts of land reform ran deep, and endured. Selectors continued to try their luck, heading into harder, cattle or horse country in the mountains. Limestone's crude roads saw a series of confrontations between selectors such as the Southwells and wealthy landholders – Davis, Campbell, Cunningham and Crace at Gunghalin – who fenced off pathways across their land, frustrating customary routes of access for smallholders. If the courts usually held for those alleging trespass, it was at the expense of the general push to end the 'hideous ravening' of the wealthy upon hard-working men and their families.[45]

Such tensions also emerged over the conditions of work itself. When unionism began to rally shearers through the 1870s, local station owners were earnest in response. Frederick Campbell, the next in the dynasty (and born at Duntroon), had bought Yarralumla in 1881; soon he was urging fellow pastoralists to form a 'counter-union'. Cunningham, at Lanyon, also assembled a committee to coordinate resistance to unionism. Their enthusiasm, however, seemed out of proportion to the immediate threat. The interdependencies, and the simple proximities, of the local economy put a brake on the extent to which smallholders, reliant on earnings during the shearing season, could embrace the union cause, and the district was not on the main route of travelling, unionised shearing teams. While 'disturbances' were reported in local shearing sheds, readers of the Queanbeyan *Age* – a paper generally sympathetic to labour – were advised that such accounts were 'exaggerated', reflecting 'the good deal of unpleasantness [that] existed between the squatter and men' elsewhere in the colony. Itinerant unionists were rumoured to be throwing non-unionists into creeks around

Limestone, frustrated at their lack of solidarity with the larger cause. In 1887, Cunningham refused on principle to submit to union rules, even though shearers judged his terms 'very liberal'. In the standoff that followed, union members walked off. But within three days Cunningham had 'a full board' of 25 men in his shed, needing the work.[46]

In Limestone's valleys, then, white people at least had to learn to live together, despite tensions of labour, class and faith among them. By the close of the 19th century, the dance held to mark the end of shearing held at Tuggeranong – run by Cunningham's son, Jim, since 1874 (and with a mechanised shed after 1889) – offered supper at midnight, and sets, songs and recitations until dawn, to a gathering that included shearers and shed hands. Such occasions raised funds for the local charities and causes championed by station-owners' wives: a hospital for Queanbeyan, for example. At Yarralumla, Campbell – who stood apart from the 'high society' of Duntroon – similarly hosted annual picnics for the children of nearby schools. But such benevolence was premised on roles and relationships dominated by the economy of sheep stations. The vigorously democratic E.W. O'Sullivan, as local Legislative Assembly member from 1885 to 1904, boasted of 'converting the young farmers of the district' to a range of reforms, including uniting unionists and selectors in the cause of the working man. But he was perhaps more effective as New South Wales Minister of Works in overseeing a program of bridge building aimed at diminishing the chronic isolation of the district, and making sure its wool got to market.[47]

In 1878 a visitor – in a good season – described the Limestone Plains as a valley of 'flourishing and peaceful little farms' in 'an unbroken tract of verdure'. That 'verdure', like that 'peace', was carefully managed, and on closer inspection showed the stamp of modernisation. Resuming land once leased to tenants, Frederick Campbell assiduously consolidated Yarralumla, increasing it from an 8000- to a 20 000-acre freehold in less than a decade. He took what had remained under Murray and his successors 'poor sheep country' – 'wet, flukey, cold flats and gullies covered with scrub and bad timber' – and cleared, drained and fenced it. Yarralumla became

Figure 3: Yarralumla Station at the end of the 19th century: the big house, the assembled community, the bend in the Molonglo and a scarred landscape. (Reproduced with permission of the Canberra and District Historical Society)

a 'model station'. Around it, selectors with fewer resources dug out dams or dug in sheep manure in an attempt to increase their own viability. The imperative of 'improving' the land took many dimensions. The most graphic was the widespread practice of ringbarking trees, and their bare skeletons would mark the landscape for decades.

Equally profound was the impact of another import. Noted first in the 1860s, by the 1890s invasions of rabbits and hares – 'a great gray moving mass', as Shumack recalled of one plague – wore away grasslands, crops and soils. Their impact, too, would endure.[48]

None of these transformations were peculiar to the Limestone Plains: they were part of what Dovers has termed a late colonial phase of 'shuffling boundaries and learning the land'. One local adaptation was distinct, however, and made its own wider contribution. William Farrer, a Cambridge science graduate who arrived at Duntroon as a tutor in 1870, married Nina de Salis in 1882 and pursued his ambition to breed a rust-resistant wheat at Lambrigg, a property excised by his father-in-law from Cuppacumbalong. Success came with the 'Federation' strain, released in 1901. Farrer's triumph, however, stood in contrast to Leopold de Salis' failure: however skilled in managing land, and defending his interests, the Count went bankrupt with the return of deep depression in the early 1890s. A prolonged drought, coming later in the decade, and extending into the 20th century, reflected the fact that it was still possible for the dukedoms of the district to fall – although the drought's weight, again, fell heaviest on smallholders and selectors.[49]

The flux of settlers' opportunities was nothing in comparison to the experience of local Aboriginal people. Larger stations continued to employ a few Aboriginal men as workers and tolerate the gathering of groups on the fringes of their land. The lives of Ngambri men Harry Williams and Dick Lowe, both working as stockmen through the latter 19th century, provide examples of a determination to find continuity in place, and to keep connections to country alive. But most families were increasingly fractured. Necessity drove some to move to the Christian missions established from the late 1870s, even as far down the Murrumbidgee as Darlington Point, or – in the 1880s – to government-created Aboriginal Stations such as Brungle, near Tumut. Aboriginal people also settled on the periphery of towns such as Yass or Blakney Creek, to the north, in fragmented kin and community groupings, or leased small farms made available to them by government, where a few sheep and crops were supplemented by seasonal labour, fencing, domestic service or trapping. In these conditions, Aboriginality could be hidden, or unspoken, if not forgotten; they at least avoided the verdict passed on 'traditional' people. In the early 1860s, Queanbeyan's residents noted the 'last', 'motley' gathering of a sizeable group of Aboriginal people in the town, and in 1889 they souvenired the local 'extinction' of the race in recording the death of the last 'full-blood'. But at least that figure 'Queen' Nellie Hamilton was remembered by John Gale as defying their hypocrisy – 'Yah, yah! I don't think much of your law, you come here and take my land...leave me starve' – with a vehemence that was 'proof positive of her superior intelligence'.[50]

The 1891 census recorded 6522 people living in the district, around a quarter of them likely to be in the area that was increasingly being referred to as Canberra, but still had no official

Figure 4: Nellie Hamilton, Bobby Deuamonga and their children: an Aboriginal family enduring the loss of their country. (Reproduced with permission of Neil Gillespie)

designation: 27 were Chinese and 20 were identified as Aboriginal people. There were also over 4000 horses, 22 000 cattle and 603 000 sheep. In this small population, several figures had become almost part of the landscape. 'Short-tempered, strictly honest, and straight-forward in all his actions', Reverend Pierce Galliard Smith served as Rector of St John's from 1855 to 1906, often on horseback, in presiding over personal and parish affairs while also dispensing simple medicines and scattering seeds for pines, elms and oaks from his saddlebags. Long-serving doctors and teachers, as well as familial dynasties, exerted similar influences and were associated with permanence. The feudal gave way to the patrician – although new causes were in the air.[51]

As local member, O'Sullivan kept up democratic causes, hoping in 1888 to raise politics above the level of 'parish vestry solicitations', by posing the question: if the Australian colonies really had 'broad minded statesmen... why are we still without federation?' Once the idea of forming an Australian nation gained traction through the 1890s, the Limestone district – like many others – rallied to the cause. The citizens of Collector and Gundaroo, for example, staged a debate on federation; politicians visited many local centres in their campaign, the local press largely supporting the cause of nationhood. The electorate was enthusiastic in voting for a delegate to attend the inter-colonial convention to draft a federal constitution (a 60 per cent turn out in 1897, the New South Wales average being 54 per cent). But it proved a resilient pocket in voting against federation in the referendum of 1898 (48 per cent 'yes' to union – around the median level of support within New South Wales' 125 electorates) and 1899 (44 per cent). Why? There were local concerns about what of its wealth and interests New South Wales might forfeit, as the 'mother colony', to the nation, and perhaps an identification with the anti-federation view that prevailed in Sydney in an area still lacking a strong sense of its own regional interests.[52]

Despite these reservations, by 1899 neighbouring centres – such as Yass, or Bombala to the south – were forming Federal Capital Leagues to lobby for consideration as prospective sites for a national capital, once it became clear that neither Sydney nor Melbourne would concede the honour to the other and that a compromise in regional New South Wales would prevail. Observing this process, O'Sullivan enthused in May:

As there are splendid prospects of getting the capital at Goulburn, or somewhere near Lake George, Federation will operate like a goldfield, by bringing a large number of people in or near our electorate, and will constitute a splendid market for all time for our farmers, dairymen, selectors, graziers, etc., and create many good positions for the young people of the district to fulfil.

In October the townspeople of Queanbeyan and local pastoralists finally met to urge their own claims. Their submission was considered, alongside 45 others, by a royal commission appointed to begin the process of selecting a site. The Limestone Plains were central to Queanbeyan's claim, and in early November Alexander Oliver, the appointed royal commissioner, toured Tuggeranong, Lanyon and

Duntroon, offering assurance also that 'he had "done" Queanbeyan on a more extensive scale than any other place he had been to'. Yet even with the short-term lifting of the drought, the site did not rank highly for this first of many officials, sent to exercise an eye for the future. The relative isolation of the Limestone Plains counted against it in Oliver's ranking. With the coming of a new century, and a transition in ideals of environment, community and government that would inform the choice of a site and a vision of the capital, its prospects would greatly improve.[53]

2

Not like any other

THE MIRROR OF THE NATION'S TASTE

A national capital presupposes a nation, and can be expected to reflect something of whatever it is that draws people towards political unity. More particularly, the capitals of federations have a role in creating that spirit out of a range of pre-existing and contending loyalties. In the long debates, over more than two decades, leading towards Australian federation in 1901, such differences were clear, but a common spirit also developed. Recently, Australian historians have contended that these debates were a 'high point in Australian history', drawing together causes of political reform, of faith and destiny, to be championed by social movements and expressed in the popular election of delegates to drafting conventions that embodied the 'sovereignty of the people'. But the issue of a capital was far from central to agenda that related primarily to the balance of interests between the colonies, and to what kind of constitution – what concepts of representation, inclusion or exclusion, what rights and powers – should characterise the nation to sit over them. Ideas for the capital itself would only gradually emerge in the fray. The realisation of that project would always be weighted by the past and shadowed by ambiguity and ambivalence.[1]

Pragmatism eventually prevailed in those federation conventions, where any suggestion that either of the dominant colonial cities might be elevated to pre-eminence was at best a taunt to be ridiculed. 'St Kilda!', 'Mount Gambier!' or 'some place in Tasmania!' were among delegates' responses to the goading proposition that Sydney, as the 'mother' city, was the obvious choice to become the national capital. Instead, it was agreed that the constitution would allow the new national parliament to choose its own home, albeit with clear constraints. A reluctant vote for federation was won from New South Wales with the condition that the nation's 'seat of government' must be in that state, and no less than 100 miles (160 kilometres) from Sydney. For Melbourne, the compensation was that the Commonwealth parliament would sit there until that permanent home was secured. Both vying states had reasons to delay a solution given the concessions of land sought from New South Wales and the influence gained by Victoria.[2]

Beyond political strategy, and still in schemes more than practical plans, ideas were already massing around what that 'seat' should comprise as a necessarily *new* city. Even the usually sardonic Sydney *Bulletin* enthused in 1905 about a capital capable of giving 'Australia a national heart whose pulsing throbs will be felt throughout the six States'. Much was inspired by cities overseas. In a formulation taken from the model of Washington, the constitution established that the capital was to be within a territory of at least 100 square miles (259 square kilometres) to be 'granted to or acquired by the Commonwealth...without any payment therefor'. This provision was to ensure that the management of city itself was not open to the influence of a neighbouring state. The kind of city to be built within that territory also galvanised imaginations. Similarly drawn from North American and European ideas were the 'City Beautiful' principles to guide the planning of the capital. These ideals are summarised by the urban historian Karl Fischer as aiming at 'engendering in every citizen...a feeling of aesthetic appreciation and thereby of civic pride'. In 1900 Alexander Oliver, a polymathic, vigorous public servant, appointed the Royal Commissioner to begin the process of identifying sites, defined his goal in these terms:

The City which is to be the seat of power, the nerve centre of the Commonwealth, and, in the future, the focus of its intellectual activities and the mirror of the Nation's taste, will depend in no small measure upon its situation. This will govern also, to a large degree, the comfort, health and happiness of all its residents.

With similar enthusiasm, a congress of engineers, architects and surveyors in Melbourne in May 1901 argued that 'a perfect design' for the capital, defined by 'dignity' rather than 'zig-zag' opulence, could only emerge from deliberations that were properly handled by 'experts'. By 1906, J.D. Fitzgerald, a prominent reformer in law, politics and municipalism, added that the 'conscious ordering of cities' was a crucial field in which to express a new national ethos.[3]

These formulations, integrating themes of environment, community and government, were not mere glosses. If they revealed understandable ambitions to secure influence over what must be a major, defining undertaking – unprecedented for Australia – they also reflected syntheses of ideas that would substantially define the Canberra project. Meeting in 1899 with those who pushed for Queanbeyan's consideration, for example, Oliver declared that 'climate' above all else guided his quest for what must be a 'sanatorium' as well as a political centre. Such a concept of public health encompassed influences on citizens' character, outlook and ethics as well as fitness. Few coastal centres formed committees to urge their claims – few, perhaps, had land they were prepared to cede to a new government, or were keen for the heavy hand of state-driven development. But a turn inland meant that access to reliable, unpolluted water figured highest of all on Oliver's search for a viable city – and that imperative, too, steadily drove the search into more remote areas. Overall, it was a feature of the designed capitals of modernity – a company in which Canberra would figure alongside New Delhi and Brasilia – that they were purposely distanced from trade and commerce for the sake of cultivating a purer form of nationalism. So when Oliver declared that the 'depressing influences associated with moist sea breezes' were 'enervating' and unsuited to 'the various classes of the body politic' who would need to make the capital their home, the nation their object, and accordingly thrive in a more suitably 'bracing' air, this was no archaic asceticism. It was a reflection of the mix of purposes the capital, and its people, were to serve.[4]

Limestone did not find early favour in this search – neither among the pragmatists nor the idealists. Its ultimate success would reflect a process neatly summarised by John Reps: Canberra proved 'a city conceived in controversy, born in competition, and nurtured in conflict'.[5]

WHERE MEN CAN HOPE

In his first cull of prospective sites to be offered the new Commonwealth, Oliver sought proximity to existing population centres for reasons of economy and access – as well as 'hygiene'. On this basis, contenders in the north of the state were excluded (and, in any case, Oliver judged Armidale 'too low with regard to the surrounding country' to command 'distinction'). To the west, he was most impressed by the soils and climate of Orange, although noting that Bathurst had proved 'especially beneficial to cases of pulmonary disease'. To the south-west, Yass appealed, given that land could be acquired there more cheaply than around larger centres such as Goulburn. But it was to the far south, and especially at Bombala – a small town serving a wool and mixed farming district – that several of the attributes he sought came together. The town was high, its air clear, and it had the advantage of the Snowy River as a source for hydroelectricity for lighting, tramways and rail. It also had ready links to Twofold Bay, at Eden, as a port, and so for maritime connection to the rest of the nation. In October 1900, Oliver declared Bombala the best site, followed equally by Orange and Yass.[6]

These three sites were duly offered by New South Wales to federal parliament, occasioning the first of many rounds of lobbying. In these rounds, again, practical interests as well as ideals were at stake. Tasmania's redoubtable King O'Malley – a once peripatetic, mischievous insurance salesman turned politician – began his colourful embellishing of 'a cold climate' city as one where 'men can hope'. Most likely an American by birth (which, if true, would have made him ineligible for parliament), O'Malley sought to avoid Washington's fate of being confined on the 'faultline' between America's northern and southern states, and tyrannised by fears of 'big government'. Australia's capital, he argued, needed a territory 10 times as large to ensure that it could begin afresh in upholding 'human freedom, human justice, and human rights'. Amid these debates, a party of Senators visited potential sites in what some derided as 'picnics' but which nonetheless meant representatives from all States experienced the contending landscapes, and appreciated the issues they raised. They toured in the depths of drought, prompting an observation in Yass that the objective was to see the district, not eat its dust, while early winter chills at Bombala and Dalgety left many unimpressed by such 'bracing' air. Those who advised them, such as the surveyor Charles Scrivener, steadily maintained that the hard numbers associated with the cost of engineering works must inform any judgements based on the visual attractions of sites.[7]

Still undecided, in 1903 the Commonwealth convened its own royal commission, now focused on eight sites and a tighter evaluation of accessibility, water supply, price of land, climate, soil productivity and the general suitability of surrounding districts for a city projected to serve around 20 000 people. Rivalries resurfaced: preferences for Albury on the Victorian border were suspected as a southern ploy for the loyalty of the capital. New contenders emerged, such as Tooma in the far south, which had produced, the New South Wales Premier noted, an abnormal number of robust centenarians and people over 6'1" (1.9 metres). After a cumbersome series of ballots, Tumut, on the western foothills of the Snowy Mountains, was endorsed by the House of Representatives. The Senate, however, stuck with Bombala. In a young and still unsettled parliament, Alfred Deakin, mindful of expense and doubting the need to draw politicians and public servants together for more than four months each year, wondered whether some basic premises of the exercise needed to be rethought.[8]

Debate resumed in mid-1904, leading to a compromise agreement on the settlement of Dalgety in the Commonwealth Parliament's first *Seat of Government Act*, largely on the grounds of cheap land for a designated territory of 900 square miles (2330 square kilometres). Never having offered that site, the New South Wales government was unimpressed, and declared 200 square miles the most it would make available anywhere, pointedly leaving Dalgety off its revised list of options. Stalemate endured for over four years. The attention of political leaders gradually returned to the case made by Queanbeyan, where a rail connection to Sydney already existed, the climate was less severe, and no significant vested interests had to be conciliated or negotiated, given its relative remoteness. To overturn the 1904 Act, however, required another round of ballots in which contenders again rallied their factions. But once it was realised that no other site would gain sufficient support, a 'Canberra-Yass' ambit claim edged ahead by default. In November 1908, a new *Seat of Government Act* settled on that district.[9]

Inevitably, this compromise had its detractors, the *Bulletin* declaring the area 'a handful of hovels in a howling wilderness'. Scrivener was speedily despatched to end such carping by identifying a site suitable 'for a beautiful city, occupying a commanding position'. He had his own reservations, ruling out the northern parts of the district because they would compete for the water needed for irrigation further down the Murrumbidgee, and being sceptical about reliable supplies to the south. Working intensively, by February 1909 he had selected the Limestone Plains, albeit in valleys sheltered from prevailing winds rather than triumphant over the landscape. His team then marked out a territory of 1015 square miles (2630 square kilometres), defined by rivers that would ensure sufficient water – for, as one surveyor, the young geographer Griffith Taylor, observed, a city in this location would be a welcome experiment in Australia's necessary adaptation to low rainfall. After some cavilling (New South Wales was not prepared to entertain Scrivener's inclusion of Queanbeyan and its river), 912 square miles (2358 square kilometres), now including the catchments of the Gudgenby and Nass Rivers, was 'surrendered' to the Commonwealth in a ceremony on New Year's Day, 1911, in Sydney's Centennial Park, at the place and on the 10th anniversary of federation. Such symbolism was elevating. Its pomp, however, contrasted to Scrivener's ongoing work, his party stationed in a rough hut and tents above the Molonglo River. Visiting this camp in 1910, a British journalist described the work there as a prelude to 'as interesting an architectural problem as has ever yet been propounded'.[10]

Scrivener's maps – marking the country as 'well-grassed', 'stony spurs', 'red-gravelly sand', 'open forest', 'poor shaley soil', 'good orchard land', 'land devoid of timber' – conveyed a bare site. His anticipation of impounding the 'sluggish' Molonglo to form an ornamental lake in itself underlined a prevailing sense of vacancy, and possibility. As Fischer puts it, 'the poverty of economic geography' was, ironically, what most recommended this site. And even the excision from New South Wales of a portion of Jervis Bay as a prospective port for the capital in 1915 had about it an arbitrary air, unlike the links envisaged between earlier sites and the harbour at Eden. Scrivener, again, surveyed a possible rail line to the bay, but it was never built. This city was not considered to need those kinds of connections.[11]

The Commonwealth's acquisition of this land did, however, enable it to act on one established ambition for its seat of government. Among the surge of ideas that fed into debates over federation – and in part in reaction to the 'inconsiderate disposal' of land that had marked first European settlement of the Limestone Plains – was that of land nationalisation. The American political economist, Henry George, had gained influence in the colonies by arguing that the monopoly of property ownership by the few was 'the root cause of inequalities in wealth'. Land, ran George's argument, should be owned only by the state, and leased for rents calculated according to its unimproved value. As a 'single tax', those rents would provide the state with sufficient and equitably raised revenue to cover the costs of its responsibilities. Many Australian political leaders saw in the prospect of a national territory an opportunity to avoid the colonial experience of speculator-driven boom-and-bust cycles. Edmund Barton, campaigning in 1901 as caretaker prime minister, and no radical, argued that as a 'business proposition' more than a political principle, the prospective national capital should be established on Georgist lines:

So far as the law of the land allows, land within the federal area will not be sold. Its ownership will be retained in the Commonwealth. The land will be let for considerable terms but with periodic reappraisal so that the revenues thus obtained will assist in the cost of creating the Commonwealth Capital.

The generation of funds aside, visions were built of the kind of laboratory the city might become. Senator Stanisforth Smith, Labour-aligned and from Western Australia, welcomed the chance 'to put to practical test many of the social problems exercising the greatest brains in the world'. 'Utilisers' rather than opportunists would benefit from a government-coordinated release of land, determining what was built on it, and citizens' access to services, amenities and leisure. Conservatives and liberals, free traders and protectionists alike endorsed what Victoria's liberal-aligned Hume Cook allowed to be 'a brand of municipal socialism': of presenting 'a spectacle the world has not previously seen – an entire city...owned and managed for the people of Australia'. As enshrined in the *Seat of Government (Administration) Act 1910*, a leasehold national capital promised a progressive future, at least on this measure.[12]

AN AREA OF EMPTINESS

For the first decade after federation, lives on the Limestone Plains were not much affected by, or interested in, these debates. The community was still defined by the 19th-century pattern of large estates, extended families, and some 200 smaller farming and grazing properties. Around 1700 people, a remarkably high percentage of them native-born – an indication of little flux – lived within the boundaries determined for the Federal Capital Territory, along with 8412 cattle and 224764 sheep. But those boundaries – largely of water catchments – were irrelevant to the community's established patterns of labour and often tight-knit sociability. While bicycles and motor cars had become more evident, horses (1762 of them) continued to provide most transportation. Private homes and homesteads provided most meeting places, including for the frequently large gatherings associated with dances and sports. An enterprising spirit was evident in the foundation of the Ginninderra Farmers' Union in 1906, which sought to 'advance' local pastoralism and agriculture, to send members away for further training, or simply to talk through issues in a spirit of fellowship. A similar support network existed for women in largely church-based groups that provided opportunities for meeting, friendship, support and philanthropy. The patterns for men, women and children remained essentially those of a small rural economy.[13]

If those patterns did not change with the declaration of the Federal Capital Territory, other aspects of life did. On 1 January 1911, adults within the territory were deprived of the franchise for any level of government, given that they were deemed too few to warrant independent representation. They similarly faced the end of their freehold rights. And in an ordinance passed by the Commonwealth in place of New South Wales law, O'Malley, as Minister for Home Affairs, forbade the granting of any further liquor licences in the territory, eliminating (so he hoped) the evils of 'stagger juice' from the prospect of 'a new Eden', and from the reach of its 'good, Christian government'.[14]

'Government', then, rode heavily into the new territory. The Labor Party, in its first federal majority after April 1910, placed the capital project amid its nation-building enterprises – like the Commonwealth Bank, an Australian currency and postage stamps. O'Malley personally relished placing his authority in opposition to 'the rot' of municipal populism. Others were equally quick to begin projecting onto the site and its unsuspecting residents their own visions, expertise and ambition. The fervent Sydney journalist-inventor, George Taylor, saw the capital expressing the best of 'the virile white race which is building a nation great in the Southern Seas'. Other modernist, progressive, transformative projects also attached themselves to the place – although the ties could seem fragile, even at the time. In 1913 the adventure novelist, Sir Henry Rider Haggard, came to the district, travelling as a member of a British Royal Commission appointed to assess the scientific, trade, commercial and resource opportunities that might draw all the dominions closer together. Pausing at Canberra, Haggard remarked that he could 'imagine no site more fitted to become a future capital', warned that when he had recently called at New Delhi it was apparent that any budget for such a new city was at best rubbery, and quipped that when he was 'conducted to the exact spot on which will stand the Parliament House of Australia...it was occupied by two rabbits':

> I saw them both. And I could not help wondering which would be the harmful or harmless occupant of that mound – those two rabbits or the future legislators of Australia, whose eloquence will echo from this spot for generations to come.[15]

Polite laughter greeted these remarks as Haggard journeyed on to Yass. But the rabbits reflected real problems in planting modernity in the bush.

In November 1910, the *Pastoralist's Review* despaired at the impact the taxes of the 'present socialistic Federal Government' were having on the landholders of the Limestone Plains, but conceded that the more immediate curse was the 'rabbit pest'. It had, for example, reduced the carrying capacity of Frederick Campbell's improved Yarralumla from 40 000 to 25 000 sheep. Limestone, when declared the site for the national capital, was a hard-bitten, compacted and bare landscape. Scrivener's surveyors were alarmed at the degradation they observed, particularly given that ideals of the city to be mapped over these denuded grasslands included visions of splicing the high urban with the restorative pleasures of nature: woodlands, gardens and parks – and both, it seemed, would need to be created from nothing. Among the first officials dispatched to the site was J.C. Brackenreg, charged with eradicating rabbits by netting, digging, ploughing, poisoning or trapping them or unleashing dogs. There was also Charles Weston, a horticulturalist, tasked with remedying nearly a century's pursuit of (in Griffith Taylor's words) 'suicidal cutting and clearing of every inch of timber' on the plains. First visiting the site in 1911, and settling in 1913, Weston began establishing nurseries where he tested species for their capacity to endure bruising winters and the searing attrition of summer winds. The fact that, from the start, he often preferred gelignite to a spade in breaking the soil for trial plantings illustrates the challenges he and his team faced.[16]

Such arduous groundwork was accompanied by shifts in social foundations and structures. The first property to be compulsorily acquired by the Commonwealth – after dispute – was Acton in 1911, near the site of the first European settlement. It was designated to become the administrative centre for the city. Colonel David Miller, formal by temperament, occasionally pompous, but dedicated as Secretary of Home Affairs to the project of building the capital by his own lights, joined a small staff there as Resident Administrator in 1912. At the time, the only available housing for them was still tents. Yarralumla was next, acquired for £150 000 as a temporary residence for the Governor-General, but providing accommodation for other officials and purposes until 1927. While these self-contained and intent clusters of new arrivals must have seemed somewhat irrelevant to life as then lived at Limestone, their impacts were soon evident.[17]

Responding to these compulsory acquisitions, local landholders formed a 'vigilance association' to defend their rights. It was a remarkably inclusive group: 'a small-scale Catholic farmer' was elected president to lobby that land resumptions occur as quickly as possible, ending the uncertainty that would only strip value from all properties. The early pace of acquisitions was brisk – 51 properties by 1913, another 66 by 1916. Some early settlers, such as the Corkhills, who had been employed to run a dairy on Yarralumla, took pride in now having the opportunity to maintain the business, in their own name, as lessees from the government. But the loss of ownership was hard to accept for many who had worked long and hard to build their holdings. Even enthusiasts for the capital noted the 'serious loss of useful men and their families' who chose to go elsewhere, often with the bitterness of knowing that small settlers had scarcely the same capacity as the rich to inveigle a good price for their land. In 1913, St John's faced an alarming collapse in its parish funds as 'pioneering' families moved on. By 1916, the Ginninderra Farmers' Union was disbanded for lack of members.[18]

The Campbell family stronghold, Duntroon, having reverted to being run by absentee owners by the turn of the century, was in disrepair when it was acquired. Once the emblem of patrician order at Limestone, it was now to become a training school for military officers – a professionalised military being another component of the modern nation state, and seen as appropriately connected to the national capital. The Royal Military College, Duntroon, opened in June 1911, with 31 Australians and 10 New Zealanders its first intake. Envisaged by the Acting Minister for Defence as providing 'the intelligence and the soul' of Australia's citizen forces, under Brigadier-General W.T. Bridges as Commandant, it added its own discipline to the capital's unfolding laboratory – the first of many 'national' institutions reflecting changing associations and symbolism. As military historian Chris Coulthard-Clark argues, Bridges aimed at stripping away the civilian identities of those under his authority, promoting instead 'the national ideal of egalitarianism' and entrenching 'a protection against the rise of a military caste' in the new nation. This goal was augmented by spartan provision as the college began in provisional buildings hastily constructed around the old homestead. But these first cadets proved more congenial to some residents than a corps of administrators, engineers and surveyors: they danced, were upright and marriageable, and soon were destined to play their own role in the desired drama of nation-building.[19]

Yet the cadets, like the officials at Acton, felt their own displacement. Coming from far afield, they lamented (as soldier Tom Elliot – killed on the Western Front – noted in 1913) that 'one never sees a strange face' around the small community. They took advantage of whatever travelling entertainment came to treat 'the country yokels' among whom they had to mix. Much further down the evolving social order were the 'navvies' and labourers, who began arriving to lay the first foundations for the coming city. They built a railway line from the railhead in Queanbeyan; a dam on the Cotter River; a pumping station, pipelines and reservoirs to provide water; a brickworks; and a coal-fired power station to provide electricity – the first substantial building to rise above the paddocks. The engineering histories of these projects record significant elements of innovation, and in time recast the landscape: the famously sturdy Canberra red bricks were being fired by 1913; the first goods train travelled into the territory in May 1914; electricity was available by August 1915; and reticulated water by 1920.[20]

Each project's social history was equally significant. Labour, especially skilled trades, proved difficult to attract to sites at which – as Humphrey McQueen notes – 'living conditions were crude even by bush standards'. A local branch of the Railway Workers and General Labourers Association was formed in 1911, and among workforces, such as the 500 men at the Cotter by early 1914, industrial grievances built solidarity. The pace of building, however, meant that numbers fluctuated – in a few months the Cotter team was down to 200 – and nothing about 'the hide-bound bureaucracy' that drove construction schedules convinced workers that they were any better off under contracts to the state than to private bosses. Their camps, usually divided between 'married' and 'single men's' quarters, developed alongside these projects, often as little more than shanty or canvas towns, prey to the elements and supplemented by scrounged materials, but still needing basic facilities, including schools. Sites like these did little to evoke a coming city – but then that city was no more meant for these workers than it was for farmers. Still, their concentrated settlements generated their own

Figure 5: A group of children and their teachers outside the school tent serving the camp for workers constructing the Cotter Dam, circa 1917. (Reproduced with permission of the Canberra and District Historical Society)

rhythms, adding to the hierarchies of role and entitlement among the new arrivals.[21]

The camps for more skilled workers around the power station or the brickworks put down deeper roots, hinting at suburban development. At Acton, a bachelors' quarters and mess hall provided a space for games, recitations and musical performances. Gradually, after 1912, cottages were erected for married senior public servants; a two-storey residence was completed for Colonel Miller in 1913; also a temporary hospital. In such provision, status mattered: Weston, for example, might have had a vital job in 'reafforestation', but as a gardener he was entitled only to a two-roomed hut. His wife and daughters remained in Sydney. Still, new patterns of community within ranks replaced the extended-family based ties of the past. Officials coming from Melbourne brought Australian Rules to a largely Rugby Union district; Duntroon's cadets strengthened team and club-based competitions, even introducing a swimming carnival on the Molonglo. Amid such initiative and consolidation, H.M. Rolland, arriving at Acton as resident architect in 1912, was still overwhelmed by 'an area of emptiness', beyond which 'great mountain ranges seemed to approach in waves'. He relocated with his family to Queanbeyan.[22]

Whatever progress was being made, everything was still waiting. In April 1911, O'Malley formally announced an international competition for the design of Australia's national capital, with a closing date of 31 January 1912. Colonel Miller declared his determination to implement a plan on 'the most modern lines...as an example to the rest of the world'. That statement in itself reflected a tension. Whose plan, or project, would it be? Whose sense of 'modern lines'? Some decisions had already been made – provisional perhaps, but taking root nonetheless as practical men kept busy and determined in their choices. And there were the continuing debates among the relatively small group of Australian urban planners, among whom differences became personalised and competitive even if, as architectural historian Robert Freestone notes, within an overarching 'spirit of melioristic nationalism'. Should the new city be in a radial form, to break the monotony of urban grids? Should it encourage a variety in land uses through symmetrical rather than lineal alignments? Should it insist on a segregation of functions to foster a balance of work, home and leisure? Variations on these themes were intently discussed. Against such debate, in preparing the terms of the competition, Miller provided that 'the whole or any part of an accepted design may be used by the Commonwealth', on the expectation – as he advised O'Malley – that 'it is more than probable that no design will be adopted in its entirety'. And equally eschewing the complications of expert advice, O'Malley reserved to himself the final right of adjudication on what was to be 'the finest Capital City in the World – the Pride of Time'. This was already a sticky web.[23]

The materials prepared for prospective entrants made a handsome package, if dispatched in a rather rough-hewn box. Along with Scrivener's contour maps, rainfall and temperature statistics and other data, went a 2.5 metre watercolour 'cyclorama' of the site, depicting the 'pale tints' of cultivation and pasture, of haystacks and birds in flight, of smoke from cottage chimneys and a rather unlikely dusting of snow (the panels were dated 2 January 1911) on a distant Mount Bimberi, rising above 'sombre-toned' ranges. This gentle husbandry contrasted to the harsher landscape recorded in photographs and commentary of the time. The list of facilities to be included in plans for the 'official and social centre of Australia' included – in addition to official residences, parliament and the departments of government – an art gallery, a library, a city hall, a museum, a national theatre, a stadium, technical colleges, a university, a gaol, tramways and 'military equipment' – all to serve an assumed population of 25 000 people. Entrants were encouraged to consult the proceedings of the 1910 Royal Institute of British Architects (RIBA) conference for up-to-date 'utilitarian, architectural, scientific and artistic' theories. All of this was inspiring, and 1000 copies of the conditions were distributed internationally. But protests mounted against the terms of the competition, including O'Malley's prerogative and the meagre prizes: £1500 for first, then £1000 and £500. Responding to the concerns of Australian affiliates, the RIBA boycotted the competition, several other professional bodies conveyed deep reservations, and the press derided the predictably 'wild-cat' habits of a government, and a Labor government especially, in so constricting a search for the best ideas.[24]

Intransigent, O'Malley contended that if the old and staid stood aloof, then the young and vigorous would at last have their chance. The competition closed with 137 designs received: 42 from Australia, 41 from the United Kingdom, 20 from the United States, 12 from South Africa, six from France, four from Canada, three from New Zealand, and entrants also from Finland, Hungary, India, Italy, Mexico and Rhodesia. The discouragement of eminent bodies might have explained why few of the most prominent designers of the time had applied. Unconcerned – as the still anonymous submissions went on display in the ballroom of Government House, Victoria, before the judges, John Kirkpatrick (architect), James Smith (mechanical engineer) and J.M. Coane (surveyor and chair) – O'Malley declared the field 'marvellous'.[25]

On closer inspection, the standard of entries proved disappointing. Elements of eccentricity, excessive formality or irrelevance to the site characterised most. The field was narrowed to eight but then – as rumoured in newspapers – irreconcilable differences emerged between the judges. Coane opted for Number 10 as the winner, which proved to be the only Australian entry in that last cut. The work of a Sydney-based partnership, Charles Caswell, Robert

Coulter and Walter Scott, it offered an avowedly 'common-sense' solution: compact and 'utilitarian'. Kirkpatrick and Smith favoured Number 29, an entry inspired by geometry and artistry. No amount of bargaining could resolve the impasse, which extended to choices for the other rankings. Coane stood by practicality; Kirkpatrick and Smith for imaginative evocations: the bold, highly artificial formalism of Number 18 (from Eliel Saarinen, of Finland) and the confected elegance of Number 4 (from Alfred Donat Agache, of France). Adopting the ranking of the majority, on 23 May 1913 O'Malley opened the envelope that revealed Number 29 to be the work of 'Mr Walter Burley Griffin, architect (landscape architect)' of Chicago, Illinois. Griffin's was a 'wonderful design', O'Malley declared – although he remarked that the government would be justified in assembling a composite scheme from the wider field of entries: 'a park might be taken from one, a boulevard from another, and a public square from a third'. Controversy and competition were indeed about to pass into conflict as such patchworking began.[26]

MONGREL CITY

Born in 1876, Griffin was a product of Chicago as 'the first expression of American thought as a unity': a city that reflected the fusion of commodities and commerce, of space and technology, of (in environmental historian William Cronon's formulation) the 'first nature' of the 'Great West' and the 'second nature' of urban amenity and prosperity. Griffin had attended the World's Columbian Exposition of 1893, which drew more than 27 million people to Chicago's extensive 'White City' site, famously exemplifying principles of integrated, symmetrical design, landscaped urban parks, and the credo of the 'City Beautiful' movement. By temperament he was reflective and idealistic, stirred as a youth by botany and horticulture as well as by social reformers such as Henry George. The latter fed his vision of government kept 'as simple as possible, its functions restricted to those most necessary to the common welfare'. The former underpinned a reverence for patterns in his thinking. Emerging from education as an architect, from collaborative work at Chicago's inner-city Steinway Hall and then in Frank Lloyd Wright's suburban practice, he valued simplicity and organicism, showing – so contemporaries noted – 'a flair for systems', with an emphasis on order, function and symbolism. He had an 'incandescent' quality, alight with his own dreams, coupled to 'a thoughtful, placid' demeanour that concealed determination. His partnership in private practice, and after 1911 in marriage, to the 'fiery' Marion Lucy Mahony, among the first female graduates in architecture from the Massachusetts Institute of Technology, seemed at first unlikely. Yet her skills in drafting, and faith in him, provided a means to express their shared search for 'universality' in philosophy and form.[27]

Griffin had keenly awaited the competition for Australia's national capital. Like many progressively minded Americans, he admired what he saw as the Australian social experiment – its 'bold radical steps in politics and economics'. He saw a fit between that path and an architecture speaking 'a democratic language', not that of 'an aristocratic cult'. His plan for Australia's capital reflected aspirations to design a city which would (as evoked by architectural historian James Weirick) 'express in physical form the nature of the democratic experience', woven with the more esoteric symbolism of syncretic religious movements.

The core elements of the scheme he submitted were anchored by geometry: a system of bold axes – water, land and municipal – which lay with remarkable harmony over the site, working with landforms to achieve a spatial ordering and massing of the city's functions. In this plan, Weirick continues, 'everyday activities', along with the work of the state, 'were so arrayed in the landscape that by simply moving about the city ... the powers and responsibility of each individual would become manifest'. The design possessed an 'inherent perfection', its power owing much to its presentation in Marion Mahony Griffin's rendering. The bucolic panorama sent out to competitors had been returned by the Griffins as an uncompromising, integrated urban form, set with ease and authority on its site, and conveyed in a palette of sepia, gold and greys on linen and silk, at once seemingly intuitively Australian yet also tapping a wide fusion of early 20th-century aesthetics.[28]

Informed of his success, an elated Griffin declared that he had risked designing a city 'not like any other', adding that 'I have planned it not in a way that I expected any government authorities in the world would accept'. Under the conditions of the competition,

Figure 6: Marion Mahony Griffin's elevations of the first-prize winning entry Number 29 in the Federal Capital Design Competition, 1911. (Reproduced with permission of the National Library of Australia)

it was unclear what role he might have in the realisation of his 'ideal city'. It was soon evident that those who did have that role were moving to confirm his initial expectations. In November 1912, Miller advised O'Malley that a departmental board was unable to endorse any of the prize-winning plans. Griffin's design disturbed them on a number of counts. It extended across the breadth of the Molonglo valley, requiring a scale of construction that would be prohibitive in cost and exposing the city to the full force of prevailing winds. It exceeded the needs of the likely population. And it also required fashioning artificial lake basins that would involve shifting massive amounts of earth, as did cuts and fills required for the rail line to serve a central station to the north of the lake. The core urbanity of Griffin's plan – his envisaging of residential units that were essentially terrace-house precincts, to enhance 'that larger family, the neighbourhood group' – ran against the view of at least one member of the board, John Murdoch (a dour architect, who conceded that he 'never did enthuse over' the capital). 'The temperament of the average Australian', Murdoch held, was decidedly of a bungalow cast: nucleated and detached. The board presented O'Malley with a plan of its own – a modest affair, its centre sheltered on the southern side of the valley, below a lake meandering according to natural contours, and with Griffin's axes largely truncated into suburban crescents.[29]

Uncharacteristically demure – and reluctant not to seem to favour the 'Yankee' – O'Malley approved the board's plan, and on this basis the first moves were made to formally inaugurate the new city. On 20 February 1913, the minister drove in a peg to mark a proposed (and never completed) 'commencement column' on Camp Hill, a spur of the higher point – Capitol Hill – rising above the Molonglo River. On 12 March he returned for a ceremony of more enduring significance, at which Lady Denman, the wife of the Governor-General, officially named the future city 'Canberra'. As imagined by historian Ken Inglis, the day was a microcosm of the national story to that point. The clipped vice-regal announcement of 'Can/b'ra' was coupled to accents in speeches from the Scottish-born Prime Minister, the Welsh-born Attorney-General, and O'Malley's American flourish. Lady Denman had in fact taken counsel on her pronunciation, having been advised by the 'simple and nice' Labor men, with whom she and her husband felt most comfortable, that her first interpretation, with a rounded attention to all syllables, was too 'upper class'.[30]

Many of the 500 invited guests, 2000 mounted troops and 3000 observers had sheltered the previous night under tents. Inevitably, most attention centred on the announcement of the name, and, as a popular newsreel – among the first by pioneering filmmaker Raymond Longford – emphasised, that 'mystic word' was soon dispatched to the world in reports at the rate of 200 words a minute by government telegraphists, themselves in tents. Carried over from customary usage, if surrounded by debate over whether the word came from a local Aboriginal language, and if so what it meant, the choice was greeted with general relief given the range of over 700 suggestions received from the public in a process carefully guarded by the government but subject to intense speculation. Some names were serious contenders, such as 'Myola' (reputedly deriving from an unspecified Aboriginal language and meaning 'break of day', and already given to well-to-do suburban residences, sometimes to female children). Some names among them overly earnest were: 'Shakespeare', 'Democratia', 'Pacifica' or 'Empire City'. Many were frivolous: 'Swindleville', 'Gonebroke' or 'Holy City'. The Brisbane *Courier* took consolation in observing that if the 'business of the Commonwealth' must eventually be 'transacted away out in the wilds', such deliberations would at least be associated with a word that has 'a wholesome manly burr about it'. And the name soon served purposes of its own. Even while federal parliament remained in Melbourne, politicians began speaking of 'Canberra' imposing legislation on the nation; equally, it was proudly bestowed on commercial buildings, a coastal steamer, private houses, racehorses, and even an incubator for chickens.[31]

Such popularity contrasted to the derision with which the compromise of Griffin's plan was received. From Britain, the board's design was denounced as an amateur's 'Luna Park'; from America, a 'grotesque' exercise. Local responses were initially more accepting of its 'practicality', but steadily gravitated to the verdict of the recently retired New South Wales government architect, Walter Vernon. A 'desultory scheme', he argued, had replaced the dignity of the winning plan. Griffin, in alarm, wrote to O'Malley, offering to travel to Australia at his own expense and consult with the board. Miller advised his minister that his officers were 'thoroughly competent' in their work, and that 'it would be most unwise to interfere with them'. Not for the last time, a change of government in 1913 meant that different counsel, for a while, prevailed.³²

The incoming Liberal Minister, W.H. Kelly – Eton-educated and suave – responded to mounting petitioning regarding what George Taylor feared would become a 'mongrel city'. Backed by his Prime Minister, Kelly extended an official invitation to Griffin (already en route) and instructed Miller that once Griffin arrived he should be brought to Canberra to study the site 'without the presence of the Board'. This instruction was ignored. From the time the 'boyish' Chicago architect stepped ashore in Sydney in August – snidely described in the press as mannered like 'a sculptor, or a star violinist, or a tragedian' – he was shadowed by men who began with condescension towards him which soon became hostility. At Canberra, over six days, Griffin noted with concern the extent to which early developments such as the power station were at variance with his design. He also recoiled from the trenchant opposition of the board to most of the matters he raised with them. His first experience of the valley – which 'accentuated in an unexpected degree' his sense of its 'attractiveness due to clear atmosphere, bright sunlight, intense colours, and brilliant cloud effects' – made him even more restless in the face of their limited view of what could be achieved. He saw a city of 75 000; the board doubted the population would exceed 10 000. He saw the possibilities for a radical sewerage and wastewater system that could replenish the lake with purified water; they recoiled from such uncleanliness. And so it went on.³³

By October this impasse was so pronounced that Kelly moved to strengthen Griffin's powers to restore 'the integrity of his plan'. Disbanding the board, he appointed Griffin Federal Capital Director of Design and Construction, with responsibility 'to prepare designs, specifications, plans and documents' and 'generally direct the details and executions of works necessary'. It was an impressive title, coming with a handsome salary and conditions that could only humiliate the officials who until that point had effectively controlled all that Canberra was and could be. Yet in a farce of organisational reform, Griffin's new position still left him relying on the cooperation of those same men, in their continuing roles as surveyors, engineers, architects and administrators.³⁴

The frustration Griffin endured for over six years – his three-year contract renewed in 1916, extended on a monthly basis through to 1919 – are well documented in many accounts. On becoming Director, he agreed to revise his plan in response to concerns over its expense and soften its strict geometry. He proposed 'an initial city' for the south-eastern corner of the site, to be developed first and independently of the larger scheme. Even his most sympathetic critics argue that too much was compromised at the start in acceding to a form that 'tangled' the spatial relationships and 'ensemble planning' of his original design. Early on, then, began on paper a drift from his preferred urban concentration, with associated grids of commuter tramlines, to a 'dispersed suburbanism' that reflected more Australian 'garden city' enthusiasms. Throughout his tenure, while he fought to exercise control over the planning process, he was effectively undercut by the resistance Miller and others perfected in handling him, utilising strict bureaucratic procedures to block his access to staff, resources and information. This pattern was entrenched when another change of government in 1914 brought in as minister Labor's determined and direct W.H. Archibald. Soon impatient with 'that Yankee Bounder', as he termed Griffin, Archibald sided with officials who held sincere concerns about the extravagance of his plan, the intransigence of his positions and the abstractions of this thinking, and simply resented his ideals.³⁵

Nor was it helped by the new priorities and demands – especially the financial demands – that came with the outbreak of World War I. The rush to prove national destiny in combat saw commitment to Canberra as a city falter. On every indicator, progress effectively stalled. Government expenditure in the Federal Capital Territory went from £20 319 in 1910–11 to peak at £215 669 in 1914–15, then fall steadily to £3211 in 1917–18 and a mere £931 in 1918–19. Jobs and development followed the same path. The population fluctuated from 1988 in 1913 to 1829 in 1915, and from 2232 in 1918 to match the year itself in 1919. Land acquisitions similarly dropped from a peak of 86 625 acres (35 056 hectares) in 1912 to 6595 acres (2668 hectares) in 1917 and none in the next two years.

The combined impact of these factors was not simply a suspension of progress, but a corrosion of guiding principles.[36]

One early casualty was Griffin's initiation of an international competition for a parliament house. Announced in 1914, with some already arguing the field should be confined to Australian entrants, Griffin saw the competition as 'establishing an architectural standard...for a great new Democracy of scope, scale and modern advantages'. He sought a building to bring coherence to the 'government group' at the heart of his plan, and positioned in relation to his idea of paramount 'Capitol', as a pavilion of popular 'assembly and festivity'. The competition was closed with the outbreak of war, reopened for British architects only in August 1916, and indefinitely postponed by November. The decision taken then to construct only a temporary building at some point in the future, Griffin argued, risked setting a low standard that would inevitably prevail in the city as a whole.[37]

He similarly wrestled with the war-spurred momentum to construct an armaments factory in the Federal Capital Territory, together with a 'garden suburb' to house its projected workforce of married and unmarried men and boys. It was not only the inclusion of such industry that concerned him, but the distortion that its development, necessarily at some distance from the city centre, would bring to the overall concept of the capital. Again, the misfit in government imperatives, planning objectives, costs and processes, produced tensions that were unresolved when the coming of peace saw the arsenal scheme suddenly dropped. Similarly, an internment camp of austere huts was hastily constructed in 1918 on the margins of the projected 'initial city'. It was intended to house 3000 German nationals from China, but eventually accommodated only 200 Germans and Austrians in family groups brought from other camps in New South Wales. With the end of war, the camp at least demonstrated the ingenuity of the locals in adapting whatever came their way in materials and people to a variety of purposes.[38]

These were the contrasts of Canberra during World War I. The community itself experienced the war much as other Australian towns: 320 local men and women enlisted – a comparatively high proportion of the population – and served in the major campaigns, suffering in the same ways. Duntroon's first class of cadets, although only half way through their course, were made officers and sent to battle, with a zeal for 'adventure' that soon settled into the deeper registers of duty and loyalty. The adults of the territory were briefly enfranchised in 1916 and 1917 to vote in the referenda on conscription, which they favoured also in comparatively high numbers, reflecting the success of local campaigning on the part of the established patrician order. Leaving Duntroon to command troops in battle, Brigadier-General Bridges insisted that his men serve as a national corps rather than being dispersed among the British contingent. His death at Gallipoli, three weeks after the landing, and the return of his body for burial in Canberra, brought the rustic capital its first ritual and monument: the slow cortege proceeded along a 'dusty, rough track...cleared and scraped a few days earlier' – later named Anzac Parade; the grave Griffin was commissioned to design for Bridges achieved a simplicity and resolution he was unable to secure in any other aspect of his 'ideal city'.[39]

Others had more success in shaping their vision of the capital, none more so than Thomas Weston. By 1920, he had grown over 44 900 trees at a permanent nursery and arboretum in Yarralumla, determined to transform a ringbarked landscape into something more appropriate to a city. An advocate of Australian trees, he also experimented with exotic species, looking for those that would best accentuate the 'chief ornamental charms' likely to mark Canberra in spring and autumn, and to endure the hardships in between. Even Weston tangled with Griffin over the latter's desire to plant hills in uniform species, and to trial plantations of cork oaks and redwoods which struggled to survive. In time, Weston would triumph in his visions of a 'garden city'.[40]

The return of O'Malley as minister in 1915 did not solve the mounting obstacles Griffin faced, but at least enabled the convening of a royal commission into the accumulating controversies surrounding Canberra's progress. Gauging the depth of disharmony, the commissioner, Wilfred Blacket – a reform-minded lawyer – clearly sympathised with an architect whose role was being 'frittered away'. Blacket also diagnosed a more pervasive 'Canberra method', amounting to a 'want of thought' and meanness of initial provision, whether in meeting the needs of labour or coordinating works, which had produced 'excessive cost and lack of efficiency'. Humiliation, again, came to officials through this inquiry: but they would bide their time. O'Malley was gone again by 1917, and Griffin still more isolated.[41]

In all of these elements, patterns for Canberra's future were being set: a fraught balance between official pragmatism, governmental expediency, and an ideal acknowledged in occasional gestures but never honoured in full. 'There must be finality', Prime Minister Hughes informed Griffin in December 1920, terminating the government's association with him. Some, such as the then responsible minister, Littleton Groom, with no malice to any party, saw that there had always been a mismatch between the obvious talent of the architect and the practical challenges of overseeing the construction of the kind of capital Australians wanted, and in circumstances that war had made more demanding. In private practice, in Melbourne and Sydney, and in commissions to design Leeton and Griffith, Griffin saw more of his thinking realised before he and Marion Mahony left for India in 1935, where he died in 1937. Little, however, had been achieved on the site by the Molonglo when he ended his links with the city. But at least by then the laying out of a few main roads (if cut by rabbit gates), and of small residential and commercial centres on both sides of the river, intimated that the larger compass of his plan might still prevail. As Peter Harrison argues, it was testament to the power of its central geometry that Griffin's scheme almost resolutely imprinted itself on the landscape, proving 'adaptable to change without loss of its essential characteristics'. Concepts of government, environment and community at Canberra would continue to evolve around that ideal – but a hard pragmatism had won this formative engagement with aspirations for a capital, and a symbol of the nation.[42]

3

A document of Australian immaturity

A NORMAL LIFE

At the beginning of the 1920s Canberra had stalled to such an extent that, at this point more than any other, it might conceivably have been abandoned. No buildings associated with housing government on the Limestone Plains were yet on drawing boards, let alone on the ground. No officials charged with those tasks had moved from the comforts of Melbourne, and certainly no politicians. Members of Parliament, and their wives and children, were offered free railway passes and lodging to visit the site in the hope that this might help overcome their prejudices against it. In 1923 one aspiring political leader, then independent member for Kooyong, John Latham, determined to 'see the place for himself'. He returned (with specimens from the government nursery) conceding that it might be 'a beautiful site for a beautiful city', but the prospect of regular travel there was 'one of the most awful things that an Australian citizen could be asked to endure in the course of a normal life'. His sentiment may betray a Victorian bias. It still begged the question: could life in Canberra ever prove 'normal' for those to whom the city owed its existence?[1]

Carping had surrounded Canberra up until the outbreak of World War I, which in turn deadened appetites for an 'ideal city'. In 1920, the population of the Federal Capital Territory (1972) continued below its pre-war levels. Reassessments even surrounded the terms in which the capital was envisaged. In 1914, Walter Burley Griffin embraced working for a nation possessing, more than any other, 'an immediate advantage in the public control of public affairs'. By the end of the decade, 'public control' assumed other connotations, amid an intensification of ideological division, a scrutiny of excess in government, and a watch on the assumptions of national power that had expanded with war and needed to adjust to its legacies. Just as Canberra reflected a pre-war reformism – in the search for a healthy, improving environment and transformative concept of the city and its governance – so it became a testament to a new political contestation: still buoyed by modernity's promise, it would also be weighted by new trends of political wariness, economic uncertainty and social polarisation.[2]

June 1920 hinted at the transition. To rousing welcomes, Edward, Prince of Wales, toured Australia, thanking British subjects for loyal service during the recent conflict. He paused at Canberra on Kurrajong Hill to lay another foundation stone in what he tactlessly remarked was a city consisting of nothing else. This stone was for the Capitol, envisaged by Griffin as the culminating expression of organic democracy. Australians had always found this the most elusive of his concepts, so it is curious that it should be the building inaugurated by 'the digger Prince'. But the granite stone, suspended before His Royal Highness that afternoon, from a tripod under a tree, would not hold its status for long. It was soon removed, and rumoured lost for a time. The Capitol was never built. Instead, as the Prince moved on, critics calculated that nearly £2 000 000 had so far been spent in the Federal Capital Territory, but the only revenue accruing from its one asset, the rent of land, amounted to a mere £35 000 a year. When the Commonwealth was paying 6 per cent on the massive debt it accumulated in the lead-up to and during the war, many – especially in states that laboured under disadvantages of distance and development – openly contested the wisdom of continuing such a bad investment.[3]

Undaunted, Canberra's advocates pushed for action. Seven million bricks had been piled at the Yarralumla brickworks since the outbreak of war. To Austin Chapman – a protectionist liberal-aligned member for Eden-Monaro since 1901, and effectively the territory's Commonwealth representative – they symbolised the absurdity of not making good Federation's undertaking. Several parliamentarians disagreed, either with the 'huge joke' that Canberra had always been or with the probity of making commitments until 'we have reduced taxation to normality, and when the cost of labour is relatively normal'. Debate centred on how the priorities of national government should be defined. What might it mean, Labor's J.E. West asked, if politicians at last could 'all breathe the true Federal Atmosphere'?[4]

That atmosphere had several elements. Petty politics and inefficiencies in areas from tariff reform to meeting the impact of the influenza pandemic of 1919 suggested the need for a 'neutral' centre of national 'administration', observed the *Sydney Morning Herald*. Business, professional and local government leaders joined in a Federal Capital Progressive Association and a Federal Capital League to push for Canberra as a model for decentralised investment and growth, free from the constraints of other major cities. Amid debate over whether Australia's constitution itself needed revision to take account of rising agendas in areas such as welfare, interstate trade and industrial arbitration, W.M. Hughes' Nationalist Party edged Canberra back into discussion. Hoping the image of the capital might raise such issues above a prevailing tide of discontent, Hughes placed 'the transfer of the seat of Government to Canberra' on his party's platform for re-election at the end of 1922. 'The Federal Legislature', he declared, 'will never be a truly National Parliament, taking a broad national outlook, until it meets in its own house in Federal Territory'.[5]

Labor made no formal response to Hughes' commitment, harbouring ambivalences of its own about what the capital might represent in the new climate of postwar politics. But Hughes had flushed out new questions about the terms in which the project might go ahead. He promised that the city would proceed only 'with the early cooperation of private industry' – but even so, the Victorian Farmers' Union decried the implicit socialism within this 'scandalous Canberra movement'. The Associated Chamber of Manufacturers despaired of an addition to 'the colossal expansion of public debt' certain to follow from the venture. From Perth, the *Daily Mail* wondered whether Australia really needed 'a new Washington in the wilderness'. Noses sniffed keenly for any scent of indulgence, or advantage, drifting from the Limestone Plains.[6]

The Nationalists were returned – although much reduced and after an apathetic poll that made this the last federal election in which Australians were not compelled to vote (a duty of citizenship that would add its own tint to Canberra's accumulating aura). Hughes, however, was finished. In February 1923, leadership passed to Stanley Melbourne Bruce. This was generational change: the Fathers of Federation, and first shapers of policies and parties, were gone. Bruce brought relative youth and more experience in business than politics, more polish than populism, and an ethic of enterprise to government. Securing an anti-Labor coalition that would endure in an ambitious program of national development – a vision of 'a potent and integrated Australia, altogether capitalist and somewhat cooperative' – his government acted on Canberra more decisively than any predecessor. In 1927, Federal Parliament finally transferred from Melbourne, Bruce becoming the first prime minister to live in, and conspicuously identify with, the city. Each aspect of this transition set the terms in which the city's destiny would be debated until the outbreak of another war, and the structures within which its future would enfold even after that.[7]

'AS UNEMBARRASSED AS POSSIBLE'

As a sign of its intent, in 1921 Hughes' government created a Federal Capital Advisory Committee (FCAC) to review what had been achieved so far and determine the next steps.

The FCAC's 'advisory' role was a compromise with the executive authority sought by the Minister for Home Affairs, Littleton Groom. But it was a start, and had influence in the absence of any other source of ideas. Griffin declined to join it, not wanting to lose any of his remaining status among four other members, at least one of whom – Percy Owen, as Director-General of Works – had frustrated his progress to that point. In exchange for a knighthood, John Sulman, the revered 'father' of Australian town planning, was appointed from retirement in Sydney to be the FCAC's chair. The position gave Sulman an influence over the capital he had sought since 1908. In Griffin's place as an 'architect of distinction' was Herbert Ross, a man of 'sound practical judgement' on matters technical, certainly not a 'dreamer'.[8]

Figure 7: Prime Minister W.M. Hughes, left, a little demure in the expanse of the latent national capital in 1923, in discussion with C.S. Daley and P.G. Stewart. (Reproduced with permission of the Canberra and District Historical Society)

Sulman – crisply evoked by Robert Freestone as 'forceful, egotistical, decisive, tenacious but gentlemanly' – had long brought those qualities to 'garden city' advocacy. He looked to Canberra as a suburban model of 'convenience, healthfulness and beauty'. Griffin's artistry appealed to him, but not his gridiron emphases. Sulman declared in 1910 that 'the boulevard, as a public resort' was alien to Australians and would be 'unappreciated by them'. 'As to dwellings', he added, 'the Australian, of whatever degree, generally prefers...the "cottage"'. His 1921 treatise, *An Introduction to Town Planning in Australia*, noted 'practical defects' in Griffin's plan that might be excused in the cause of conveying 'the power and order which is at the root of all stable government'. But on assuming charge of the FCAC, Sulman put that allowance aside, and found support: Canberra was to be less about 'power', more about 'beauty'. As secretary to the committee, C.S. Daley recalled its members as 'absolutely sincere' in diagnosing inherent flaws in Griffin's scheme. It was inconceivable to them that Canberra would ever reach the population Griffin envisaged: 6000 rather than 15 000 seemed to them realistic. The modest city envisaged by the Home Affairs Departmental Board in 1912 again suggested itself as the model to adopt.[9]

Disturbed by this shuffle, and the mediocrity it suggested, Groom directed that Griffin's plan must provide the basis for the FCAC's work. That instruction would not determine practice, particularly once 'strict economy' and Hughes' and then Bruce's priority of transferring parliament and core administrative departments to the city 'as early as practicable' added pressure and expediency to the mix. The FCAC's tasks quickly gained some intensity, particularly in determining what priorities, timetables and limits should be observed. In addressing these questions, an early decision was taken that all 'works of a monumental character' would be deferred and 'utilitarian' calculations prevail. Confining itself to short-term provisions, the committee declared that it would leave the city of the future 'as unembarrassed as possible'. The effect, of course, was quite the opposite.[10]

A Parliament House must be the first requirement of that transfer strategy. Griffin's international competition for such a building had lapsed in 1916. The FCAC began fresh discussions about an appropriate type of structure ('temporary', of timber; 'provisional', of brick) and its siting. Some members favoured the dominant Kurrajong site, where the Prince had placed his stone – but it was too prominent for short-term use. By early 1923, a decision was made in favour of a provisional building, to be located in front of the site nominated by Griffin – and effectively frustrating what remained of his vision of an ornamental water feature, envisaged as bringing tranquillity to an assembly of government buildings. As always, much wrangling preceded this decision, but as Hughes urged now from the sidelines, the priority was to get something resolved, 'believing delay to be dangerous, and fearing that if the city is not established now it will never be done'.[11]

Commissioned to design the building, J.S. Murdoch, the Department of Works' chief architect, compounded an already austere brief with the conviction that Australians had no taste for 'those extremely elaborate structures to be found elsewhere in the world'.

With its restrained, functional elegance – heavy horizontal masses, white-finished, in the 'stripped classicism' that would define much public building in Canberra – Murdoch's plan commenced its own process of revision. The Public Works Committee increased its size by a third, raised its cost from £180 000 to £225 000, and the clock started ticking. The Commonwealth's ninth parliament, assembling in July 1923, declared that the 10th, in three years, should be summoned at Canberra.[12]

An adjacent series of timber pavilions was proposed as temporary accommodation for the officers who must attend the needs of parliament, with brick only for agencies and records 'deemed especially important' for preservation from fire. These barracks perhaps reflected the relatively low status then accorded to the Commonwealth Public Service, which had been found, in a series of postwar royal commissions, to be 'a cumbrous, costly, and ill-managed instrumentality'. By 1923, better counsel prevailed. Another competition was announced for a permanent, large administration building, although in the interim the FCAC worked on the premise that the capital could at first accommodate only a small 'secretariat' of around 160 essential officials, required to support their ministers, and needing only modest accommodation. Murdoch designed East and West Block, the former completed in 1926, to sit behind the parliamentary building and in the same style. Already in these calculations, assumptions were being made about the relations between political, ministerial and bureaucratic practice that would have enduring consequences for how Canberra functioned, and the boundaries to be observed between those functions.[13]

Beyond chambers and offices, there needed also to be a city. The FCAC again revisited Griffin's ideas on such matters. Beginning with a scant pre-war inheritance of roads, water and sewerage infrastructure, the committee still looked for economy. Since 1912, Griffin's critics had sought to confine the city to the south of the Molonglo River – a village nestled in the shelter of hills rather than a metropolis stretched grandly over plains. But his last plan, from 1918 – to which the FCAC was bound – still required settlement to the north. In giving shape to *their* city, however, the FCAC began by downgrading Griffin's northern commercial and residential boulevard, 'Capital Terrace' (now Constitution Avenue) and confined commercial development there under the colonnades of two modest shopping blocks, gradually built in sections after 1926 to Sulman's design. Their style – Mediterranean derived – also set a standard and scale: spare, uniform and anonymous (Sulman wanted no advertising); trade stripped of all allure; order not ornament. And isolated.[14]

A habit of dispersal also led the FCAC to create a series of discrete suburban centres: Reid, Braddon and Ainslie to the north; Kingston, Manuka and Barton in the south. Some modest housing was built, to meet pressing needs, but the FCAC's first priority was to lay down subdivisions on the model of 'a garden town...simple, pleasing but unpretentious'. Griffin's dense housing precincts and 'neighbourhood units' faced towards 'internal reserves', to encourage communally based 'social relationships'. The FCAC turned houses outwards, arguing that areas not open to public scrutiny would become 'untidy'. It favoured detached, single-storey cottages with sizeable private backyards and a focus on the family. The quality of these subdivisions was undeniable: generous set-backs; all garages, electricity, water and sewer lines to the rear; no front fences to fragment the streetscape, or hide untidiness. The philosophy they projected was equally distinctive.[15]

More fragmented 'garden groups' than integrated 'suburbs', Freestone suggests, these subdivisions reflected core elements of the FCAC's social as well as physical engineering, and they were backed by other planning mechanisms. A 1921 ordinance introduced the leasehold system that was fundamental to the capital. Business and residential leases of 90 years (99 years after 1924) were to be offered, with rents set at 5 per cent of unimproved value, and strict conditions requiring the commencement of building within a year, completion within two, and continued maintenance to an acceptable standard. 'Covenants' also determined a minimum cost for the home to be built and decreed the materials of its construction. The size of blocks in turn corresponded to these limits. Taken together, these terms set the scene for the next performance of rank on the Limestone Plains.[16]

Ainslie, for example, was to be a workers' suburb: building costs for houses were set at £700, all-timber construction was permitted, and the standard Australian quarter-acre (0.1 hectare) block prevailed. Closer in, at Reid, values began at £1000 for homes intended for skilled workers and middle-level public servants. Here, and in Braddon, brick prevailed and traces of Griffin's more angular planning remained. South of the river, covenants rose to a minimum of £1500 for blocks at Blandfordia, and £3500 for blocks at 'Mugga Heights', which could exceed 3 acres (1.2 hectares), were intended for senior officials, and would spread on an indulgent scheme of crescents showing the FCAC's own stamp. Such provision acknowledged, and perpetuated, social and economic differentials among an anticipated population.[17]

The FCAC knew what it wanted, but while it planned three years ahead it was able to secure from parliament only annual budgets, which were routinely around half of what it requested. Approval for larger projects had to be won from the Parliamentary Public Works Committee, two members of which avowedly opposed the whole Canberra venture. And despite Hughes' undertaking that 'private enterprise' would be brought into 'early co-operation', there was uncertainty about how to accommodate the entrepreneurial spirit in this public experiment, and no great enthusiasm on the part of private investors to take a risk in a government-dominated project. Relative isolation would long keep the costs of labour and materials – of everything – up to 30 per cent higher than for other Australian cities. Competition over resources threatened to make matters worse. No effective market existed in the territory even to set the value of leases. In 1923, the majority on the FCAC determined that £30 was a fair valuation for an average residential block, but one member – Colonel J.T. Goodwin, Commonwealth Surveyor-General and officer-in-charge of Federal Capital Territory administration – estimated £100, conceding this or any figure to be 'arbitrary'. Wrestling with these issues, Sulman argued for delay in that crucial move: the first release of land.[18]

Despite these constraints, there was undeniable progress: 1 162 942 trees were planted under the FCAC's regime, showing the continuation of T.G. Weston's reafforestation program; many miles of road were gravelled if not sealed; and the provision of water, sewerage and services often anticipated demand in residential areas. But the FCAC had little power, and Bruce, as the new Prime Minister, grew restless. Late in 1924, he replaced it with a

Figure 8: Thomas Weston, far left, and Mrs Richard Gipps, Secretary of the English Speaking Union, Victorian Branch, at a tree planting ceremony, around 1926. (Reproduced with permission of the Canberra and District Historical Society)

new body, the Federal Capital Commission (FCC), declaring that 'money must be made available so that [Canberra's development] will be a continuous job'. The FCC was given the capacity to raise funds in its own right (underwritten by the Treasury) and to implement its own decisions – if still under budget scrutiny for major ventures. The Commission built on the work of the FCAC, but with a fresh spirit embodied in its full-time chairman. John Butters, a 39-year-old engineer, was recruited from Tasmania where he had driven hard the development of hydroelectricity. Like Bruce, he was committed to a view that good government had much to learn from efficient business practice. His two part-time fellow commissioners, Sir John Harrison and Clarence Gorman, had careers in building and real estate. Enterprise was the word.[19]

'Big, bronzed and direct of speech', Butters began by declaring any system of government control over a project such as Canberra 'hopelessly inadequate'. Paid more than Bruce, he had authority and used it. Taking over the 109 administrative, clerical, professional and general offices already employed by departments and the FCAC in Canberra, he also recruited extensively: 39 architects joined in the FCC's first year, together with a doubling of the number of engineers to 84. Also highly paid, the more senior of them were provided with houses in the 'leafy and genteel administrative precinct' maturing at Acton, and centred around the imposing administrator's residence Butters now occupied. All this suggested consolidation, underpinned by money. In 1924–25 government expenditure in the Federal Capital Territory was £678 050; and in 1926–27 it increased to £1 911 693. The FCC was not completely unfettered: in 1925 Griffin's plan was 'gazetted', meaning that notice had to be given for any alteration, with parliament having the power of disallowance. But as with the FCAC, questions of emphasis could have as much influence as those of alteration.[20]

One element of this process was the first auction of land, held on 12 December 1924. Butters shared Sulman's unease with the imbalance that might follow the premature introduction of private enterprise into Canberra. But over the border, near Queanbeyan, the flamboyant land developer Henry Halloran was already tempting speculators to take their chances on the economic boon a national capital might be, and suggesting that the discipline of the market might be no bad thing in determining sustainable costs and prices. The December auction attracted around 300 people and considerable press coverage – despite the *Argus*' snide remark that 'a strong imagination' was required of anyone attempting to envisage their futures on 'grassy slopes'. The 289 residential and 104 commercial units offered were spread across the city, although interest was greatest on the south side, where development seemed most assured. On the day, 147 leases were sold at prices confirming a healthy imagination – even if the first purchaser of a business allotment, for £2050 at Kingston, conceded reservations about the dream that kept him in the bidding for a block with a reserve of £650. By mid-1925, a total of 153 residential and all business leases had been sold. While the next auction in May 1926 was also successful, it confirmed that for the foreseeable future the market could not be relied upon to deliver balanced development in itself. The FCC would need to take responsibility to build and rent a good deal of housing on its own behalf, given a reluctance – including among banks – to invest in homes that disbarred potential occupants from ultimate security and the Australian dream: outright ownership.[21]

Balance also had to come from an assured and manageable commitment to the fundamentals of the capital: the transfer of the seat of government. Soon after taking office, Butters declared that the FCAC's 1926 timetable for even the limited 'secretariat' model of public service transfer of public servants was unrealistic and the project as a whole under-funded. But when, in November 1925, it was determined that a 'nucleus' of at least 1100 officials must be in place by June 1927, a date now locked in by a royal visit to open the new parliament in May, the pressure increased – and so did Butters' capacity to demand resources. Such was the kind of contract in which he thrived, and to which Canberra would always be captive.

'MAKE THE BEST OF EVERYTHING'

The population of the Federal Capital Territory was 4927 at the end of 1925; it was 7700 by mid-1928, and approaching 9000 at the end of the decade. The FCC began with a construction site, employing around 1340 tradesmen and labourers. Its 'community' often had in excess of 110 men for every 100 women (the national average was then just over 102 per 100), and during one swell of construction in 1926 the preponderance of 'blue collar' workers approached 5000. Canberra was emphatically a worker's town – manual, male and rather awkwardly poised, as a locally produced promotional magazine, in its first (and only) issue for Christmas 1925 put it, to 'stimulate' Australia 'to definite homogeneity and robust maturity'.[22]

Most obviously, the capital remained a series of settlements, and most established was Eastlake – although Griffin's plan for a lake itself had been indefinitely postponed. Starkly white FCAC-built homes were soon clustered there, some for workers involved in the still limited generation of electricity from the Kingston power station (street lights, for example, were turned off at 1 a.m.; water was pumped to reservoirs from the Cotter River only in the early morning – although its steam whistle served all day and night as the public clock). Around it spread an assemblage of associated workshops,

Figure 9: The first group of 12 cottages built on Ainslie Avenue, circa 1921. (Reproduced with permission of the Canberra and District Historical Society)

yards and a railway line for coal, all by the late 1920s supporting the first suburban shopping block at Kingston. Blacksmiths worked alongside engineers, electricians, joiners, storemen and, after 1926, the mechanics of the adjoining bus depot. This clustering seemed, to men coming in from the country, 'a big show', which could offer new skills or the recognition of old, regular work rather than the customary round of seasonal rural work, and security after the tailing out of mining at nearby Captains Flat or Araluen. There were still clear hierarchies around Kingston, from those whose jobs allowed them to wear a 'hat and waistcoat' down to those just keen for 'a new start'. But there was also the sense of a common endeavour. By 1925, an Eastlake Progress Association reflected sufficient common interest, and the coming of women and families, to petition the FCC for a permanent amusement hall, a children's playground (a maypole and swings), a recreation ground for adults (mainly for cricket), a speed limit for motor vehicles, and a resident police officer to enforce it.[23]

A document of Australian immaturity 75

Figure 10: Workmen, assembled for the day's tasks, at a quarry on Capital Hill, circa 1928. (Reproduced with permission of the Canberra and District Historical Society)

Much less was available to those living under canvas, or in humpies or cubicles in the workers' camps that marked points of intensive construction, such as of the sewer mains near Westlake, or of transience, as labour moved between projects. Morning musters were still held for menial jobs on the larger projects, such as quarries or Parliament House. In 1926, around 3000 workmen were living in more than 20 such camps, including 750 in the 'family tenements' and 'Tradesmen's Mess' recycled from the short-lived wartime internment camp on the Molonglo flats. An outbreak of scarlet fever in those huts in 1925 highlighted their insanitary conditions, as did typhoid and other outbreaks elsewhere. Recalled as 'wild and woolly' places where single men predominated, the camps also developed solidarity, and their own committees to lobby for amenities. At Westlake in 1923, 62 timber cottages were provided for married tradesmen working on Parliament House, to keep them at the job. Unlined, four-roomed, but with electricity and sewerage, these

Figure 11: Working men's married quarters at Westlake, circa 1928. (Reproduced with permission of the Canberra and District Historical Society)

homes were basic and ostensibly temporary – but still an improvement on the dirt floors and hessian walls endured elsewhere. They encouraged families to put down roots. So did 120 prefabricated timber cottages built on a narrow street grid at the Causeway in 1925. While the FCC undertook to 'eliminate' all 'roughly constructed hutments and camps', and experimented with portable cottages to be moved as work schedules required, a mix of such settlements remained for years to come. The 'Mess' built for 60 single men at the Causeway was still taking boarders (if increasingly pensioners) into the 1960s, and Westlake housed successive phases of labour, including 'displaced persons' from Europe, long after World War II.[24]

And then there were the hostels, several of which were planned or under construction by the mid-1920s in the run-up to the transfer of public servants and the coming of politicians. Yarralumla homestead, resumed in 1911, hosted the first convening of cabinet at Canberra in 1924 – but, as the *Argus* chirped, electric light had to be installed in its rooms some time 'between breakfast and luncheon'. Opened in 1924, Hostel 1, soon dignified as Hotel Canberra, would become the preferred refuge for senior and especially non-Labor parliamentarians. The FCC assured clientele that it provided the first point of 'rendezvous' for those (it euphemistically noted) who did not 'desire to live in houses'. Arranged in their own hierarchies of status, tariff and services, and often sex-segregated (unless accommodating a fortunate few families, for a maximum of three years), Canberra's hostels, hotels or 'quarters' acquired a reputation for being managed by 'fierce martinets who frowned on levity'. Their relative austerity, even with generous FCC subsidies, was compounded while prohibition ruled, as it had since 1911, and until a referendum-initiated relaxation at Christmas 1928 allowed patrons to consume alcohol, at first only while seated in FCC regulated cafes. Until then, 'dry' hostel rooms and lounges, the weekend rush across the border to pubs in Queanbeyan, the clink of sugar bags brought back, or the subtle provocation of gardens edged with beer bottles near the Powerhouse or at Westlake, all reinforced Latham's point about the 'awful things' that had to be endured in place of a 'normal life' in Canberra.[25]

As they developed, Canberra's few, 'better' suburbs made a nearer approach to normality. Even if they could afford the covenants, the FCC did not allow workers to occupy the larger houses it began to build for senior public servants, sampling Tudor, Arts and Crafts, Georgian Revival and Italian styles. In 1925, Canberra's residents were already being cautioned against becoming a 'city of snobs' given the demarcations the provision of housing made all too evident. Still, a forward scout for the Commonwealth Public Service Board doubted that any 'self-respecting' Melbourne officer could live in even the better FCC offerings, given, for example, that some lacked reception halls. The houses, however, were solid. True to Sulman's emphases, they were blessed with ample yards behind (if desired) front hedges which were planted and kept carefully trimmed by the FCC itself. Their several types were alternated through the better suburbs (less so further down the scale) to avoid a sense of regimentation. The most senior officials – including (Sir) Robert Garran (Solicitor-General) and (Sir) George Knowles (his successor in 1932) – had much larger, individual homes built for or by them, often commanding Canberra's pre-eminent street, Mugga Way. The Knowles home, with tennis and croquet courts and a

Figure 12: The Prime Minister's Lodge, circa 1930.
(Postcard: F.G. Strangman, 1930)

billiard table, pioneered central heating in the city. In comparison, the Prime Minister's Lodge, built (as a temporary residence) in 1926, could seem more modest, among wandering sheep.[26]

As if to compensate for, or affirm, these segregations, the FCC added overt ideology to its fields of engineering. A priority for Butters was to forge what he termed a Canberra 'tradition' among its assembling citizens. Like many progressive-minded industrialists, business leaders and politicians in the aftermath of World War I, he believed social unrest could only be avoided through building shared responsibility for progress and welfare between employer and employee. This task had added importance, and opportunities, in an entirely new social project. 'Cooperation' was the ideal, and came with a clear image of what the Canberra citizen should be, and should not be. The second issue of the FCC's monthly *Canberra Community News* (*CNN*), launched in 1925, argued that the 'herd instinct' of cities, the easy access there to 'cheap amusement', even 'the kaleidoscopic movement of metropolitan populations', all had allure, but did little to ennoble an individual. The ethic at Canberra was 'work' towards a common goal: a city 'the like of which has never sprung up on virgin soil', in an environment that was healthy for the body, restorative to the mind, and affirming of character. If not quite to the extent envisaged in 1927 by the German geographer Karl Haushofer, who saw in the siting and development of Canberra a prospect that Australia might at last redeem its promise for a racially unified 'organic state', this ethic was comprehensively preached.[27]

Canberra's claims, as *CCN* advised in 1927, to be 'the world's biggest experiment in the systematisation of the happiness of humanity' were conditional on people behaving properly. In its first issue, the *CCN* even connected a humble civic morality to what would become the perennial Canberra topic of tomato growing and the demonstrated virtues of domestic gardening. 'Not the least of the pleasures of gardening', wrote 'C.W.' (presumably Charles Weston) 'is the comparison of results with one's fellows':

One may experience a jolt upon finding one's 18 ounce tomato floored, so to speak, by a 20-ounce specimen grown by a neighbour, but the comparison should, and does, only fix one's determination to improve... It should be remembered that while the amateur or professional may often feel disappointed, he or she should never despair.

A major sign of 'Canberritis' was diagnosed in 1925 as 'the wife who speaks of monotony monotonously': who could not see that the privations she endured were for the sake of the nation. And while Butters took pride in his capacity to negotiate with workers through an Industrial Board, established in 1922 to adjust wages and conditions to meet the circumstances of the city, he resented the 'intrusions' of organised trade unionism in campaigns over public transport or amenities, just as he derided as 'an embarrassment' a Melbourne-based public service committee's advocacy for the interests of officers shortly to move to the city. Instead of such griping, the FCC encouraged the formation of Social Service Committees in each settlement, to guide 'the promotion of culture and the provision of recreation and enjoyment'. These committees oversaw projects including the construction of playgrounds, tennis courts, cricket pitches and pavilions – the most notable being a recreation hall to serve the workers' settlement at the Causeway. Raised like an Amish barn over several weekends in 1925 by voluntary labour, matched in value by the FCC with the donation of materials, this hall – the first such facility in Canberra – testified to a community willing to pitch in for the benefit of all, almost despite official high-mindedness. Functions held there included 'smoke socials' and boxing matches ('a feed and a fight in five minutes') as well as concerts by the newly formed Philharmonic Society.[28]

All this activity was premised on the transfer of the 'seat of government' – it seemed formless and arbitrary without it. Finally, on 9 May 1927, Parliament House was opened by the Duke of York – the younger brother of the now King Edward – in a ceremony lacking some of the anticipation surrounding the inauguration of the capital in 1913. Most of those who gathered – a good many fewer than the 30 000 anticipated – were kept so far from proceedings that Dame Nellie Melba's rendering of the national anthem was inaudible and, in any case, her performance and the address by the Duke, mastering for a moment his crippling stutter, coincided with the noisy fly-over of planes from the Royal Australian Air Force, one of which tragically crashed nearby. Reaching for authenticity, the program featured 21 local 'pioneers' and reiterated the enduring debt the nation owed to its soldiers. Kept at a distance, some spectators wryly noted that even further on the margins of pageantry were two Aboriginal men – a Wiradjuri elder, Jimmy Clements, and a companion, John Noble, who travelled country shows offering boomerang demonstrations and had come to observe proceedings. As cultural historian Maryrose Casey recounts, the crowd insisted the men 'do as they pleased' when a policeman tried to move them on. For one local resident, these were 'the first Aboriginals I had seen'. A clergyman among the crowd declared they 'had a better right than any man present' to a place that day.[29]

The doors of the provisional parliament that the Duke opened that day led into light-filled chambers and galleries which, for the next 60 years, would foster much less formality among their denizens than had prevailed during the time they bided in Melbourne. That, at least, would be one consequence of the move. But now, many of the 36 senators and 76 members of the House of Representatives faced that trek not only across the nation to another city for sittings but also to the comparative isolation of which Latham (Attorney-General since 1925) despaired. As much as it was a sign of permanency, the coming of politicians (there were 62 sitting days in 1928, 52 in 1929) accentuated the transitory elements of the capital, adding little to the regard in which it was held. The best view of Canberra, the secretary of the Prime Minister's Department remarked, was 'from the back of the departing train' – an observation all the more caustic given that rail travel to and from the city had to be transacted at inconvenient times and often with many changes on the long haul back home. Even the guide prepared to mark 1927 was ambivalent in its message. The capital represented 'the will of the Commonwealth as whole', but 'if, in the course of time, it proves a failure, there will at least be a gleam of consolation in the fact that those who did the job – the manhood of young Australia – builded well'.[30]

Major newspapers hedged their bets, calculating that a parliament meeting in Canberra would generate less news – or simply less public interest – than the same body meeting in Melbourne, and dispatched fewer correspondents to endure hardship there. But this small, competitive and collegial press gallery soon developed its own Canberra culture, 'expansive [and] mildly raffish', and became an evolving factor in the political life of the nation.[31]

From 1926, weekly from 1928, a local paper, the *Canberra Times*, hammered away at another point the transfer raised: why did a city that hosted parliament have no representation in it of its own? That question gained currency with the more enduring infusion that began as the first 645 public service 'martyrs' arrived in mid-1927, some with families, with many more to come. They included 128 staff to support the parliament; 154 to run its printing office; and the central administrative staff of Trade and Customs (81), Treasury (60), the Prime Minister's Department (54), Home and Territories (46), the relatively new Markets and Migration (38), the Attorney-General's (20), the Crown Solicitor's Office (13) and sundry others. Here was an early instalment of what the devoted Canberra political correspondent Warren Denning would evoke in 1938 as 'the greatest planned movement of population in the history of Australia' – 'a steady but querulous, impatient and dissatisfied stream'. What were their rights? What were their expectations?[32]

With this influx, the first suburbs began filling out. Barton – separated from the Kingston workers' precinct by a band of parkland –

was, as local historian Nick Swain shows, always intended for middle-level officers (covenants were around £1200), and it safely secured that caste. Even among them, however, there was evidence of that reservation of which the FCC despaired: 80 per cent preferred to remain on leases and not commit to ownership. Those lessees included journalists, parliamentary staff, officers who would carve out distinguished public service careers, professionals and skilled workers, and for a time the first Federal Capital Territory police and the Commonwealth Investigation Branch. They largely did their duty, at work and at home, contributing to an active community life, laying the foundations for church groups, scout groups, tennis clubs, pipe bands and so on.[33]

But even with special allowances offered to sweeten the move (and compensate for high prices), and with exemption from state taxes, Canberra still challenged many who left behind established homes, relatives, friends, schools, city amenities and suburban comforts. Beatrice Sharwood (later Holt), a young doctor, came in 1927 with her parents – her father was Crown Solicitor – seizing the opportunity to establish her own medical practice. She recalled the arrival of many 'miserable and apprehensive people', for whom professionals like herself became especially valued members of a small community. Trying to be solicitous, Butters advised transferees: 'don't grumble more than is humanly possible, make up your mind to make the best of everything'. He sponsored demonstrations in Melbourne to convince those used to gas that Canberra's electricity could also brown meat; he suggested officers should not choose houses next door to those they worked with, to avoid 'cliques' or over-familiarity. Among the many dimensions to the experiment, the Public Service Board envisaged an improvement to the capacities of officers, not only bringing them to 'healthy surroundings' but also encouraging 'the development of an even higher degree of efficiency and a keener desire to render valuable service than was hitherto practical'. The invocations never ceased, but seemed scarcely to connect to the strains of resettlement or the aspirations it fostered.[34]

Increasingly the 'new pioneers' showed little tolerance for the feudalisms endured by the old, and asserted themselves as a relatively highly educated, affluent community with aspirations of its own. Butters' goading of Canberra's women to 'display more activity' was soon met by the initiative of the Women and Children's Committee in responding to the needs of arriving families. Led by Holt, the group developed an expansive 'mothercraft' concept, adopting innovative approaches to child and maternal welfare with a determination to break through Canberra's social or economic barriers in providing access to services. The transfer of the Commonwealth Department of Health to the capital in 1928, with its interests in preventative public health and nutrition, offered further opportunities for this group to 'be a model to the rest of Australia' with – as a visiting Melbourne expert advised – 'no mistakes to rectify and no vested interests to compensate'. If free of the old, Canberrans also grew restless with the new, especially as the FCC's vigilance, including covert surveillance to ensure that community activities matched its moral imperatives, eroded good will. Even politicians were reprimanded when overheard criticising FCC practices in private conversation, and attempts to ease discontent by introducing an elected member to the commission (on a rate-paying franchise) did little to solve the problem of its overweening power. 'The atmosphere of Canberra is insidious', observed the *Sydney Morning Herald* in 1929. The Bruce government was increasingly troubled by controversies relating to the FCC as its agent; the Labor opposition vowed consistently to abolish it.[35]

Discontent accelerated with the lull in construction following the completion of Parliament House, and the question resounded: 'what next?' Expenditure in the Federal Capital Territory of £1.9 m in 1926–27 dropped to £1.2 in the next year and nearly a third of that for 1928–29. 'The clang of hammers, the swing of shovels, the roar of motors' subsided as Canberra, so dependent on government investment, offered an early warning of wider economic uncertainty. Prices soared at the third land auction, in April 1927: a service station site reached nearly six times its reserve price of £2000. Within a year this remained the only one of 71 leases sold that day which had not been handed back, undeveloped. Empowered to raise its own loans, the FCC found them increasingly hard to come by. It closed its labour registers, only allocating work to those already employed, with preference to married men and returned servicemen. Butters did not spare cuts to his own staff, shedding architects and their expertise. Land acquisitions and housing construction stopped, as did large projects, including the national war memorial, the monumental design of which had been agreed in 1927, with a budget even larger than that allocated to Parliament House. That project, so central to images of national honour and duty, would eventually be revived, but the construction of a rail line, running through the city and connecting back into the major route from Sydney to Melbourne, would not. Soon after it opened, Parliament House saw the first of several demonstrations by the unemployed – those who had stayed in the territory. Many, facing insecurity, simply left a city to which they found, in adversity, no real attachment.[36]

Amid accumulating intimations of depression, and clear evidence that the Bruce government's project was stumbling, the federal election of October 1929 brought about Canberra's first change in government – two days before the New York stock market crashed. Labor soon acted on its promise to disband the FCC, returning the territory to a division of responsibilities between four departments – Home Affairs, Works, Public Health and Attorney-General's – all of which had many other tasks. In taking office, James Scullin vacated the Prime Minister's Lodge to share with his wife a suite of rooms at the Hotel Canberra. But such a 'spartan' gesture did not compensate for what seemed the widening distance between a government in its enclave and the challenges endured by the nation. Perennial calls for the abandonment of the city rallied – but now there was also graphic evidence that a truly national government was needed. With their new proximity to parliament's inner sanctums, journalists watched Scullin's party implode over how to meet demands for 'sound finance', the burden of mass unemployment, and the options for recovery. Labor's inexperience was part of the problem, but to Warren Denning, so was Canberra itself: it needed to be 'brought into a more definite and more intimate contact with the people'.[37]

How isolated was Canberra from the impact of the Great Depression? Public service salaries were reduced by 20 per cent in 1930 but Commonwealth officers, with the relative seniority of many transferees, neither faced nor feared retrenchment. Their business went on amid the challenge of managing the crisis and, for a time at least, the prevailing 'departmental view' was that the nation had no alternative but to tough it out. An unemployment rate of 9–14 per cent for the Federal Capital Territory in 1930–31 was low for the nation, and concentrated in workers' camps rather than suburbs. Relief schemes rostered local unemployed to tend gardens, roads and ovals, dig the city's first public swimming pool, or to plant trees on barren hills to the west. From harder hit districts men continued to gravitate to Canberra, hoping there at least work might be found. They were allowed a fortnight in the camps, where they were fed, but then moved on. Overall, expectations of, and in, the city, foundered. The Royal Military College was closed in 1930 as an economy measure, its men transferred to Victoria Barracks in Sydney, and with them went the jobs of some 165 locals who kept Duntroon running. Canberra's depression was far from representative, and its suffering was probably more readily pushed out of sight than elsewhere. What was undeniable was that, in future, the capital would have to improve its functions.[38]

'CANBERRA MIGHT BE NOBLE; IT DEFINITELY WAS NOT SMART'

'Canberra is a document of Australian immaturity', declared historian W.K. Hancock in 1930, diagnosing Australia's general preparedness to settle for 'the middling standard'. At least the city seemed to him already a 'story worth telling at length', if only as a testament to the decline of the nation's – and perhaps, Hancock wondered, inevitably democracy's – 'generous...enthusiasms'. He would have several, more substantial engagements with the course of the city's maturation over coming decades, but in 1930 he posed the question of whether Canberra's 'chaos of prettiness' in trees, gardens and insular circles could be transcended for its own and Australia's good.[39]

In 1933, the census recorded the city's population as 7325; that of the territory overall, 8947, recovering from a fall of more than 700 the previous year. Unsurprisingly, given the arrival of the public service, relative to the rest of Australia, a markedly higher percentage of residents (22 to 5 per cent nationally) were concentrated in the highest income scale on the census form. More significant, perhaps, were the finer grains of that profile. The men were twice as likely to be returned servicemen; they were also more likely to be wage and salary earners, to be aged between 20 and 45, to be married, and Catholic (23 per cent in the Federal Capital Territory in contrast to 20 per cent nationally). The biggest increase in the local proportions of religious affiliation, however, was among Baptists, Methodists, Presbyterians and members of the Salvation Army, who were 16 per cent of the population in 1921 and 21 per cent in 1933. These were hints of the attractiveness of a career in government – the opportunities it offered, the ethic it imparted: of security, advancement, or self-improvement. These four Protestant congregations were quicker to build halls and churches in Canberra than either the Church of England or the Catholics, although the latter – having refused to accept second placing in the protocol for the opening of Parliament House – nonetheless commenced a series of annual pilgrimages to the capital in 1927, attracting thousands, led by eminent prelates, and making the point that they would not be left out of the power or the symbolism the city represented.

Also fleshing out a sense of community was a branch of the Young Women's Christian Association, established in 1929 to attend to the 'welfare' of single women in the hours between their work and their hostel beds. From 1928, the Rotary Club similarly tackled 'the social division' between public servants and commercial interests, the latter hit hard by the stagnation of the city's progress and needing reassurance of their future role in it. That those heading these initiatives were the most senior officials or their wives might be expected: there was a ready congruence between ideas of civic leadership and their professional, and spatially inscribed, status. Since his arrival, the imposing Robert Garran, together with his wife, (Lady) Hilda, had exercised from the heights of Mugga Way unstinting commitment to the cultural and intellectual progress of the city. Elected inaugural president of a Society of Arts and Literature in 1927, Garran led the campaign to establish a university in the city, seeking a national research program as well as undergraduate teaching. Such eminence, however, was not without challenge. In 1932, the academic caste of Garran's literary society fomented a split, a breakaway repertory society offering lighter, more inclusive fare. Prominent in the latter was the flamboyant Lewis Nott, who came as a parliamentarian in 1927, settled as a medical practitioner, and ran a Causeway 'soup-and-sandwich kitchen' during the Depression. An untiring champion of causes, from the poor state of diet in the community to Rugby League, Nott was another exemplar of progressive enthusiasm in the community.[40]

Nott also repeatedly contested (and held in 1935–49) a seat on the seven-member Advisory Council, established in 1930 to offer recommendations on the management of the city, albeit with no powers to do more than 'advise'. The majority on the Council were *ex officio* department heads, but the three elected positions went to a more diverse group, ranging (in 1931, for example) from members of a 'Citizens Party' based in the Acton Bachelors' Quarters to Elsie Gerrard, who stood for the specific needs of women. Those elected through the 1930s were staunchly 'independent' leaders in Freemasonry (Thomas Shakespeare, owner of the *Canberra Times*), of returned serviceman, seasoned veterans of the FCAC and FCC, and Albert Gardiner, a stalwart candidate for the local branch of the ALP, which formed in 1929 and finally celebrated his election in 1939. Despite their lack of executive authority, these figures were familiar personalities, and spoke for the factions of community leadership in Canberra. They rose above the none-too-subtle official discouragement of any kind of political activity among public servants, and provided evidence of a pronounced aversion to the party polarities so often associated with the city.[41]

Schools also drew together communities centred on little more than transplanted families. Telopea Park School, opened in 1923, was one of the earliest public buildings undertaken by the FCAC and the first school completed by the Commonwealth. Enrolments grew rapidly, from 58 to 128 pupils in its first year. By 1925 there were 400, as Telopea began replacing smaller, less resourced schools in dispersed settlements. Expanding from primary level, by 1929 it was an Intermediate High School, moving into the domain of secondary education still regarded as mostly the province of private schools. Telopea reflected Canberra's diversity, even as an Anglican girls' (1926), an Anglican boys' (1929) and a Catholic school (1928) began a slower growth. The former served a more select enrolment and reflected – it seemed to some – an 'over-zealous' traditionalism by way of compensation for Canberra's rawness; the latter provoking, at least in after-school taunts, the codes of sectarianism so familiar in Australian society at the time, but with their own elements given Canberra's special composition. Size also brought Telopea a broadening curriculum, extending into technical, trades and adult education classes given the lack of other educational facilities. The quality of Telopea's teachers impressed early students, including Gough Whitlam, the son of the Commonwealth Crown Solicitor. As Prime Minister, Whitlam recalled this schooling as one element of a Canberra childhood that strengthened 'my convictions about the role of the national Government in the nation's affairs'.[42]

Leisure opportunities also expanded. The Capitol Theatre in Manuka was built by private enterprise in 1927, bringing cinema to Canberra at the time of its soaring popularity in Australia, but also boosting a struggling shopping area and providing a stage for school and other small concerts. The following year the FCC built the Albert Hall, near the Hotel Canberra. With its importunate name, it was proclaimed by Bruce at its opening as destined to be the 'official headquarters of music in the Commonwealth' – although it had been carefully budgeted to come in below the threshold of parliamentary scrutiny. It had, however, a dignity, floor and acoustics good enough to serve as a venue for ceremonies, regular dances and performances that gathered Canberrans together with few overt demarcations between 'social sets', and put the city onto the circuit of the more intrepid national and international artists. Both venues became part of a regular social calendar, the Capitol having permanently reserved seats for some families and dignitaries. A commercial radio station, broadcasting from 1931, also provided a local voice, relying on considerable ingenuity and improvisation in filling its programs.[43]

And around these developments settled a landscape that, more than any other element, defined the capital. By 1935, more than three million trees had been planted across the city in schemes that built on Weston's decorative patterned associations and softened suburban hierarchies. Whatever the strains of politics, Canberra promoted itself as 'a city of flowers', of a 'million blossoms', and this landscape anchored new residents in its undoubted pleasures.

While the wildlife that once abounded on the plains – emu, koalas, wombats – never returned, birds were present in profusion, and readily became part of suburbanised rhythms and seasons. The Molonglo ('it idles, it is not very pretty') had a few deep swimming holes that featured in children's summers and promised good fishing – at least until a tailings dam upstream at Captain's Flat broke and poisoned the water. Its floods, in 1916, 1922 and especially 1925, were dramatic, sweeping away bridges and crossings, inundating playing fields, racecourses and golf courses, but their course served to intimate the lake scheme that would one day fill the empty heart of the city more than to discomfort residents. That empty heart, and the dispersal of the city around it, meant that bus services were notoriously poor. So Canberrans walked a lot; bicycles were everywhere – 'around the back' of homes and offices but also 'around the track' as racing clubs formed, promoting themselves in half-time events at football matches and offering leisure and adventure. But it was the family car, for those that could afford it, that quickly became a defining feature of life in the city and the landscape beyond it.[44]

Not only did Canberra soon boast high levels of private car ownership (one car for every 10 people by 1927) but, predictably, it pioneered aspects of traffic regulation, even with its relative lack of congestion. The train route remained indirect, but from 1931 the Federal Highway shortened distances to Sydney – local entrepreneurs even envisaging a speedway along its route, on the then dry bed of Lake George, to entice motorists towards the capital. Cars meant escape from suburban privation for picnics at nearby rivers, or – especially with public-service leave entitlements – for extended holidays. The New South Wales south coast was a favoured destination: the roads there were rough, but the beach was a national birth right not to be denied.

The transformation of the city was much less evident in the country around it. Portions of large estates acquired after the proclamation of the Federal Capital Territory were leased after World War I as soldier settlement blocks, or subdivided to take advantage of rising land values and redress 'dilapidation' following the loss of a rural labour force. Among a rural population of 1441 in 1933 were many who entered the lottery of such schemes. Soldiers' blocks tended to be larger in the Federal Capital Territory than elsewhere but posed the same challenges for those seeking a living from what remained at best 'medium' rather than 'superfine' wool country, requiring new skills in adapting to fluctuating markets, superphosphates, stock sizes and breeding opportunities. Solidarity was evident in the formation of a Rural Lessees' Association in 1927, to protest to a territory administration setting higher rates and standards of 'improvement'. But it was revealing that, when the artist Eirene Mort offered a book of her drawings to the FCC to mark the celebrations of 1927, she evoked an agrarian landscape of nostalgic decline, as if to set it against the coming city, and to confer its own legitimacy on the growing city.[45]

Still, there was diversification in land uses. In the 1920s, leases for commercial vegetable growing were made available downstream from Oak's Estate, opposite Duntroon. The produce was sold from trucks that delivered direct to homes. A small number of Italian labourers who had come in the 1920s and established local orchards and a greengrocery by the 1930s (16 Italians – the largest segment of non-British European-born – were counted in 1933) were prominent in such services. Still, the garden city largely kept such production in the background, just as the 'boys' making those deliveries recall meeting an unspoken contempt on their rounds. Even less visible were the increasing number of people identified as 'half-caste' in the Federal Capital Territory's rural districts (69, in contrast to 33 in 1921: 'full blood Aboriginals' were not counted). Most were at Wreck Bay, a small fishing village caught in the annexation of Jervis Bay, where relative isolation at least preserved the integrity of the community. A school had been established there in 1924, and later came visits from the Mothercraft Society. But around Canberra itself, Aboriginal people were more than ever absent. Well into the 1930s small groups of Ngunawal descendants, such as Don Bell's family, gathered residual bush food in open spaces near Westlake. But their country extended north-west to Yass and Boorowa, where a new iteration of policy removed people from their camps to reserves on the barren margins of pastoral land.[46]

Land use change at such local scales contrasted with more ambitious ways in which Canberra became associated with transforming the Australian landscape. Two divisions of the Council for Scientific and Industrial Research, founded in 1926, were based at the foot of Black Mountain, near Acton, after 1927: Economic Entomology and Economic Botany (Plant Industry from 1929). Entomology was led by Dr Robin Tillyard, Cambridge- and Sydney-educated, recruited from New Zealand, whose team included French and Scottish experts on parasitic insects. In what sour public servants already dubbed 'blow-fly-city', this was one aspect of unprecedented state-funded science, directed to boosting Australian, and imperial, pastoral and agricultural productivity. Across the Molonglo, the Australian Forestry School at Yarralumla took its first students in 1927. Its founding principal, Charles Lane-Poole – French-educated, experienced in Africa and Papua – was determined to build Australian forestry as a conservation science, not just a short-term industry. Like Tillyard, Lane-Poole wrestled with tensions between adventurous research and the pressures for results-driven work to be applied across the nation. The wives of the two men, Patricia Tillyard (a Cambridge-educated feminist) and Ruth Lane-Poole, related to the Yeats family and an interior decorator, brought their own expertise and commitments to Canberra, and helped redefine it.[47]

While more idiosyncratic in retrospect, a third new institution, the Institute of Anatomy, established in 1931, reflected the ideal of Melbourne-based surgeon Colin MacKenzie, to study and promote a synthesis of human physical, cultural and psychological development. Canberra's most distinctive building until the 1950s, with art deco motifs of Australian fauna and flora, the Institute acquired artefacts and 'anatomical material' relating to Australian Aboriginal people while also building partnerships with the Commonwealth Department of Health, and connections with the practices of the Mothercraft Society on public hygiene. While for decades its galleries transfixed many a school child with 'wet specimens', including the heart of the record-breaking racehorse, Phar Lap, the Institute's wider research purpose was equally a document of its time and place.[48]

Science, then, had remarkably firm and early foundations in these inter-war visions of the capital – including the solar and atmospheric observations that continued at Mount Stromlo. Translating such expertise into the business of government posed other problems. A strike greeted the appointment in 1932 of the 29-year-old Roland Wilson as the first specifically university-educated and designated 'economist' (with two doctorates) to the Commonwealth Bureau of Census and Statistics, which had transferred to the capital in 1928. Officers resisted this violation of codes of seniority, won through on-the-job experience. Still, Wilson's elevation reflected an unassailable argument that 'the extension of the functions of government and the continually increasing complexity of the social structure' required new skills in framing and evaluating policy. The pace of graduate recruitment to the public service remained grudging: 11 graduates were appointed out of an intake of 173 to the third (clerical and administrative) division in 1934; 56 out of 345 by the end of the decade. But these appointments were concentrated in Canberra, and largely associated with it. Initiatives such as the establishment of Canberra University College in 1930, as an outpost of the University of Melbourne, further recognised the need for the capital to serve an educational market of its own. Even if the College's provision was largely a matter of part-time public-service staff teaching part-time public-service students, with high failure rates among the latter, it contributed steadily to the maturation, and cohesion, of a new community.[49]

Reflecting the conversations that began to characterise these admittedly small, reflective circles, in 1937 Robin Tillyard and senior political journalist W. Farmer Whyte launched *Australian National Review* (*ANR*) a Canberra-based journal of ideas. Its first editorial centred on the challenge of saving 'democratic freedom' at a time when 'the tremendous impact of Science' was overwhelming 'a more-or-less static civilisation'. Over 32 issues to 1939 the *ANR* published many prominent local figures. Lane-Poole wrote of the 'licensed butchery' still occurring in Australia's forests; Charles Bean – the official war historian, working with his team out at Tuggeranong homestead – argued for a 'vigorous cosmopolitan outlook' in Australian literature; the new Anglican Bishop of Canberra-Goulburn, E.H. Burgmann, relished in the city a 'conspicuous pool of talent' for advancing liberal causes. Equally, a 'Young Australian' offered the view that, for a rising generation, Canberra was remote from all that defined the modern world: from law, education, industry and the arts. It must become more inclusive. And a sage regular 'Letter from a Machine-Age Politician to his Son' recorded disillusionment that the prevailing 'science' of politics consisted only of capturing 'the swing' in political mood rather than advancing policy. But, like the modernist houses – many designed by Malcolm Moir and Heather Sutherland – that began to be commissioned by private clients in the later 1930s, the journal made clear connections to a contemporary world of change. And when a National Capital Planning and Development Committee was appointed by parliament in 1938, there was similarly a sign of the need to revive the capital's momentum. Architects were prominent on the Committee membership as it proceeded to debate a more systematic approach to planning – to the location of schools, a full university, shopping areas, and the form of subdivisions in new areas such as Deakin, North Ainslie and Griffith.[50]

Parliamentarians might have questioned the 'machine-age' attribution. Before 1935, they could not fly into the city by a regular air service, and once there loneliness could grind them down, and expose them to more scrutiny than they might like. Close quarters at the Hotel Canberra did little, for example, to moderate his colleagues' impressions of the arrogant young Robert Menzies – who could at least return to Melbourne for weekends. Such a return to Perth was impossible for John Curtin, who lived for months at the austere Kurrajong Hotel and turned to carefully chosen friendships to break 'Canberra's claustrophobic political circle'. Enid and Joe Lyons regained at least an element of normality in their marriage, when he became Prime Minister in 1932 and she moved from Tasmania into the Lodge, with the four youngest of their 10 children, another being born there. Still, Canberra seemed to Enid 'a strange place in a strange setting', filling her with 'foreboding' about the gossip and intrigue its insularity fostered, and which she watched corroding her husband. If, for most members, the problem of travel was avoided by the fact that parliament was tending to assemble less frequently in the later 1930s (the House sat for only 29 days in 1937, the Senate for 27), another emerged. The press gallery grew restless with the 'pervasive parliamentary torpor' of the 1930s, as Lyons' government attempted to play it safe, avoiding controversy, making a virtue of economy, but falling into stalemate. An Unlawful Assemblies Ordinance, passed in 1937 to prohibit protests in the vicinity of Parliament House by the still significant numbers of unemployed in Canberra, was unprecedented, and served only to stimulate further disquiet: what was government worried about? Where was power drifting in the national capital?[51]

With a population edging past 10 000 by 1939 – still smaller than the nearby regional centre Goulburn – Canberra remained hard to define. Its local sporting teams, perhaps unsurprisingly, lost resoundingly to the English cricket side in 1937, and the All Blacks' rugby team in 1938 – but at least those international competitors had travelled to the capital to play. With sneering condescension, the first diplomatic representative to be established in the capital, Britain's E.T. Crutchley, accepted that he would have to endure its narrow circles of 'ladies doing good works', especially once Sir Isaac Isaacs, appointed the first Australian-born Governor-General in 1931, chose the quiet simplicities of Yarralumla over Melbourne as a vice-regal home. The first novel to be set in Canberra, M. Barnard Eldershaw's *Plaque with Laurel* (1937), captured this uneasy mix of national capital and local village. Centring on a conference of the Australian Writers' Guild, held at the Hotel Australasia (*aka* Canberra), the novel followed delegates as they debated questions of purpose, alienation, integrity and honour. In the background, the city was a series of juxtapositions: of comfort and unease; of closed circles and empty space; of shops that had none of the style such sophisticated visitors might expect. 'Canberra might be noble', one judgement ran: 'it definitely was not smart'.[52]

But the renaming in 1938, of the Australian, rather than the Federal, Capital Territory, suggested changing views of the city and its role, as a national centre rather than a federal meeting place. Increasingly, actual conferences – of academics, doctors, planners and administrators – recognised this in their choice of the city as a venue. In January 1939, the jubilee symposium of the Australian and New Zealand Association for the Advancement of Science joined this retinue. The guest speaker, H.G. Wells – eminent British science-fiction author and social commentator – arrived hot and flustered: Canberra, and most of south-east Australia, was in the midst of an extreme heat wave, exceeding 42°C. Wells' theme was the alarming prevalence of 'instinct and violence' in world affairs, and, he argued to a sweltering audience in Albert Hall, the solution lay in 'the rapid and zealous intellectual expansion of organisation among the English speaking peoples'. Other speakers raised the more specific challenges of soil erosion, the failure of the political system to deliver scientifically informed policy, and the need for closer attention to public health. These speeches were shadowed by the pall drifting over the city from bushfires moving in from the west. Volunteer brigades, formed in rural areas in the 1920s, rallied to action, their determination undimmed by the funding cuts they had endured since the Depression. Over 500 men and women from the city also left their jobs and headed to the front. Conference delegates followed as the threat increased. Wells found a vantage point from which to watch the crisis, observing that 'a bush fire is not an orderly invader, but a guerrilla'. Canberra's fires were far less severe than those that ravaged Victoria a few days earlier, killing 71, but they still destroyed forest, farms and stock. The city became, the *Canberra Times* argued, once again a 'vast laboratory' with lessons to teach about management and responsiveness to what were truly national issues. Wells was 'exhilarated' by the spectacle. Lindsay Pryor, a graduate of Lane-Poole's school and effectively Weston's successor in shaping Canberra's landscape, was angered. It was 'self-destructive', he protested, to continue to leave so much country so poorly managed, so essentially 'unproductive', and so vulnerable. Here was one further, graphic indication of the need to change the ways in which Canberra was understood. It could not remain so undernourished, not only in its environment, but also in its community and its role in government.[53]

4

Unreal city

AN ALERT COMMUNITY

In April 1945, in the last stages of World War II, the *Sydney Morning Herald* unkindly quipped that:

> If V-2s had completely obliterated London, surviving Londoners could have built elsewhere a city that in tradition and spirit would again be London. If similar disaster overcame Canberra, surviving Canberrans would emerge as a flock of homeless people without real ties of common interest other than nationality and community in distress.

The slap was hard, but even that comparison – of London and Canberra – made a grudging point: the Australian capital had at least attained visibility, and bonds of its own. A year earlier, in a more generous account, Warren Denning, the 'guru' of the national press gallery during the tumultuous years since the Great Depression, argued that the demands of war had 'hastened [Canberra's] rise into national and international prestige'. It was a capital now 'recognised as such by world powers and, in one sense more significantly, by our own people'. That recognition was due primarily to the fact that a global-scale conflict, and the mobilisation needed to meet it, had for the first time concentrated authority in Australia's central government, and made the affairs of the federal parliament of dominating interest for many Australians. The first hurdle of national acceptance overcome, there remained the question of what further common interest could unify the city in itself.[1]

Figure 13: The heart of the nation: Parliament House from Mount Pleasant, on the eve of World War II. (Reproduced with permission of the Canberra and District Historical Society)

In 1939, on the eve of war, Canberra's population had passed 12 000. That alone was an achievement. Already it exceeded the estimates with which officials in 1913 had beaten down Walter Burley Griffin's dreams. But growth had been stumbling. Whereas the city had doubled in size in the second half of the 1920s – with an average annual increase of nearly 17 per cent through that decade (the national figure was less than an eighth of that) – it had gained little more than 2000 people throughout the 1930s. But by the time the *Herald* envisaged its 'obliteration', there were nearly 15 000 potentially homeless souls in and around Canberra; by 1947 their number passed 17 000, and 19 000 in 1949. By then, its annual increase was triple the Australian average of 3 per cent. This was consolidation – of a kind.

Against it should be set associated strains. Throughout the 1940s there had been nothing like the bold increase in investment that characterised the best years of the Federal Capital Commission (FCC) (1925–29). The stringency of the Depression led into the austerities of war, the city remaining a lean youth, nourished not as an ideal community but as necessity demanded, and without balance. In 1933, 12 per cent of its workforce was in 'public administration'; the equivalent figure in 1947 was 22 per cent, and a feeling of impermanence if not homelessness prevailed. 'A town made by Pinocchio', despaired novelist Katharine Susannah Prichard, visiting her son, Ric Throssell, who in 1943 became part of that sudden infusion of public servants. For him, it was a place of incongruities, slit trenches under open, peaceful skies and an infusion of urgent people among whom 'the Canberra-born resident was a celebrity'. And as the imperatives of war gave place to schemes for national post-war reconstruction, there remained uncertainty about where provision for the capital itself fell in those priorities. What Canberra gained in functions during the war would need to be managed carefully in the years following, through a change in political mood and resentment of its new authority. Finding such a balance was to be the essence of its history through the 1940s, and beyond.[2]

Through the 1940s, as historian Tim Rowse observes, 'the culture of the senior Commonwealth public service changed': old patterns of giving preference in recruitment to returned servicemen and precedent-bound paperwork were edged out by the recognition of higher education and training, both of a 'specialist' and a 'generalist' nature, and for a more active debate over policy development. Canberra exemplified and distilled the change, and not only in the still largely makeshift corridors of bureaucracy but also in the terms in which the development of the city, and the character of its community, were discussed. The patrician style of the inter-war years, ushered in by the FCC's 'experiment in the systematisation of the happiness of humanity', was superseded by outlooks associated with this new culture of government, and a language of welfare, security, intervention and distribution. Commentators in the early 1940s lamented that Australia had been forced to cobble together an 'all in' war effort in 'the absence of an effective Federal seat of government' due to the long-term 'passive resistance' of many interests to Canberra's authority. Towards the decade's end they argued instead that improvements in the capacity and quality of Australian government 'may be expected as [it]...becomes more diversified [and] firmly rooted in an alert Canberra community'. That change in emphasis, while far from smooth, was decisive in shaping the identity and significance of the city.[3]

FASCINATED BY THE PLACE

Australia's military and industrial unpreparedness for the outbreak of war in September 1939 set in train a concerted national program of development – an urgent attempt to 'catch up'. There were, however, serious doubts as to whether the infrastructure at Canberra was sufficient for that effort. In August there was already concern that the 4000 square metres of office space required for war planning could not be found in the city. Over the following months, 13 new Commonwealth agencies, created to meet rapidly expanding needs, were located in rented premises in Melbourne and Sydney. Among them were the core elements of government for the next six years, including separate departments of Army, Navy and Air, and those of Defence Coordination, Munitions, Labour and National Service, Transport, War Organisation and Industry, Information, Social Services and Aircraft Production. A new Department of Home Security alone joined Treasury, Attorney-General's and External Affairs in Canberra – although in time a Department of Post-War Reconstruction (1942) and Immigration (1945) would follow, in themselves testament to the widening reach of central government. From the start, Melbourne's Victoria Barracks was the centre of military planning, and in 1942 – after a hasty visit to

Canberra – General Douglas MacArthur established his headquarters as Supreme Commander of Allied Forces, South-West Pacific Area, in the Menzies Hotel, on Bourke Street, shortly moving on to Brisbane. As late as 1945, a new Department of Works and Housing, which inherited responsibility for the construction of the national capital itself, also went south, given the lack of space in Canberra.[4]

The capital's constraints went much further than office space. In 1939, its total stock of around 1660 government-owned and 400 private houses was already inadequate, especially when sittings of parliament brought in 111 members and many additional support staff and public servants. And there was that basic fact of isolation from commercial and industrial sectors crucial to the intricate management of a wartime economy, and wartime production. Canberra might have remained the *de jure* capital, but the war meant Melbourne regained – it was rather smugly observed at the time – *de facto* status.[5]

The actual division was not so simple. To a large extent the business of government had to be transacted in a triangulation between three cities, and – given the technology and communications of the day – this meant incessant travel for those involved. 'In the first 18 months of the war', Paul Hasluck noted, as official historian of the wartime government, Cabinet held 64 meetings in Canberra, 20 in Sydney and 34 in Melbourne. In the same period, the War Cabinet – first tasked 'with detailed prosecution of the war', but soon reaching into wider fields of 'general policy' – met in Canberra 36 times, 14 in Sydney, 73 in Melbourne and once in Brisbane. The demands of such travel were graphically underscored when, in August 1940, a plane carrying three ministers of the War Cabinet and the Chief of the General Staff stalled and crashed on approach to Canberra's airport, killing all on board. The prime minister had only avoided being among them because of his adherence to the particular routine with which he managed the demands of commuting. A necessity for most, rail was Menzies' preference, so for him, travelling to Canberra still meant catching 'The Spirit of Progress' overnight service from Melbourne to the New South Wales border, where a break in gauges required an early-morning change to the less comfortable 'Sydney Express' and another transfer at Yass (by car) or Goulburn (for the train from Sydney) for the capital.

This 'eternal peregrination' inevitably had its effects, not only in weariness but also on the character of work. Train carriages became like a second home to many, fostering an informality in the business of government that could seem an extension of the hallways and hostels of Canberra itself. These conditions might have been bitterly resented, but became part of the reality – the conduct and the spirit – of national government. If only by default, Canberra was its centre and rationale.[6]

Some detected the reassertion of 'a strong Melbourne character' over the Commonwealth Public Service in the departments created or moved back there after 1939: Melbourne was due process; a Canberra 'outlook and practice' was of necessity more open to innovation. As early as 1929, the prominent economist and adviser to governments during the Depression, L.F. Giblin, observed that Australia might have 'gone further than most countries in extending government activities', but it had also 'gone faster than the quality of our Public Service would justify'. The solution seemed clear, and, as the previous chapter discussed, amendments to the Public Service Act in 1933 allowed the direct recruitment of university graduates, with a particular impact on Canberra. Early challengers to the entrenched anti-elitism in the public service, such as (Sir) Roland Wilson (after 1951 Australia's longest-serving Secretary of the Treasury) were – he recalled – 'supposed to be disguised' as they made their entrance. War dispensed with subterfuge, but not necessarily with the resentment. At its outbreak, there were 49 graduates in total in the Commonwealth Public Service, far too few to meet immediate needs. As Hasluck observed, when government first scanned its ranks for 'young, experienced and capable men for responsible wartime tasks, it looked in vain'.[7]

Moving to Canberra to chair the government's overarching Financial and Economic Advisory Council, Giblin was supported by D.B. Copland, his professorial colleague in Economics at the University of Melbourne, who had been seconded to the city as prices commissioner in late 1939 and in 1941 appointed the prime minister's economic consultant. The common factor of training in economics was hardly coincidental. H.C. Coombs, with a doctorate from the London School of Economics, who joined the Treasury in Canberra 1939, reflected on the 'Keynesian Crusade' energising his peers. They were committed to the government's role in overriding unstable markets and delivering measures of control or stimulus as required for social as well as economic objectives. Canberra needed them; they aspired to what Canberra might achieve.[8]

Such Keynesian ideals had to adjust to the inevitable distortions war itself brought, and the demands it made on finance. Acts of mentorship saw Giblin, Copland, and less overtly Wilson and Coombs, recruit trusted, known men (primarily) to meet these needs. Some, such as the welfare economist Ron Mendelsohn, were 'brought back' from active service; some came from state bureaucracies or banks, sustaining networks too often obscured by an overemphasis on the rise of Commonwealth power. Several women came to take positions that would usually be barred to them as married women but which demanded their expertise. Mary Willmott Phillips worked with the Housing Commission, created in 1943 (her husband, Jock, in rationing). Flora Eldershaw, transferring to Post-War Reconstruction, contributed to discussions about women's rights that were a good deal more focused than the conference proceedings she had described in her fictional collaboration with Marjorie Barnard, evoking the Canberra of the 1930s. According to Wilson, Giblin secured his appointment as Secretary of the Department of Labour and National Service in 1940 by loudly praising his ability within earshot of its newly appointed minister during one long haul on the 'Spirit of Progress'. And rather than join the department in Melbourne, Wilson was soon so busy that he moved his office into Parliament House, to be close to his minister and in touch with the proliferating agencies of the time.[9]

Canberra might always have had the air of the *ad hoc*, but – with a 'flood' of National Security regulations soon controlling areas from labour to profits, from production to marketing, from censorship to welfare benefits and taxation, and after 1942 with a National Economic Plan extending the reach of direct control – it came to have unprecedented power. Such growth was not necessarily smooth. (Sir) Alan Watt, later Secretary of the Department of External Affairs, had accepted one of those pre-war graduate places 'with great hesitation', given the pervasive image of 'red tape' tedium in Canberra. At least initially, working 'in a large room with a lot of other people', and living in a house in which he and his wife 'had never before felt so cold', he barely endured the challenge. For (Sir) Frederick Wheeler – later a successor to Wilson as Secretary of the Treasury and known to Copland as a Commerce student – the professor's call to Canberra lifted him from 'somewhat limited horizons' as a bank clerk: the capital had appeared a 'wasteland' when he visited it as a schoolboy, but when he came to work there, he arrived in a city not much changed in appearance, but certainly in its claims. Like many of his peers, after slogging through part-time university study in the hope of finding a way past the uncertainty haunting his parents, he came with a sense of gratitude for opportunity and curiosity for the tasks ahead.[10]

Still, 'government' was an ambivalent prospect. If it promised – so school masters advised – a 'steady' job, once in Canberra, orders had to be taken from a stern old guard, 'martinets' used to hierarchy and routine. Many newcomers were greeted with sullen hostility: (Sir) Allen Brown, a graduate in Law, and later Secretary of the Prime Minister's Department, was first consigned to changing blotting paper in the Cabinet room. Copland advised Wheeler that, in the capital, 'you must always remember that the glittering prizes seem remote at first, and are in fact remote'. But steadily connections grew, as did determination to make the best of opportunities. From the start, (Sir) Keith ('Mick') Shann – who became one of Australia's leading diplomats – was 'fascinated by the place', even if the only accommodation available for him was a room in the Church of England Boys' Grammar School, with no food or hot water outside term.[11]

This was not the infusion of 'experts' associated with earlier visions of the ideal city. The times called for a more general, adaptable competence, as much skilled in the compromises of meeting pressing demands as in envisaging outcomes that would have to wait for peace and, maybe, prosperity. The pool from which wartime Canberra drew extended to business and industry leaders, men such as Sir Ernest Fisk or Essington Lewis, although there was always the challenge of integrating men of Capital into the processes of the capital. Canberra itself cultivated a different kind of authority. F.R.E. Mauldon, an Economics professor, called to offer his skills in 1939, advised a meeting of devoted enthusiasts for the Canberra

University College that the 'university man' would bring to 'administration' the vital qualities of 'flexibility' and 'poise' arising from a mix of 'assurance and humility' – cautioning only against the 'forced gregariousness' the city might encourage. But even Mauldon, Wilson recalled, was 'a bit of a plodder' when it came to proffering urgently needed advice. A good deal of sifting and shuffling was involved in finding, or making, the right Canberra temperament.[12]

In 1942, political scientist F.A. Bland observed that 'administration has taken over the legislative functions of parliament', concentrating authority in the hands of those 'whose work is seriously interrupted when Parliament is sitting'. This was a stark reversal of roles. In time, Bland was far from alone in his discomfort with what planning from Canberra meant. But in the early 1940s, these assumptions were unchallenged. (Sir) Kenneth Bailey, before leaving his professorship in law in Melbourne to join the Attorney-General's Department in the capital, declared 'the classical age of parliamentary legislation is over'. This was the age of the administrator.[13]

'Competitive collegiate' is the phrase Rowse gives to the culture that grew around this cohort. Whatever personal ambition they carried, they shared an acceptance that there was a basic need for cooperation among them for the job to hand. This was as true of the work they did, extending late into nights and past statutory Saturday morning shifts, as it was in their lives outside the office, with their families or in shared accommodation, making the most of whatever was available by way of entertainment, and in escaping whenever possible. Around them the Commonwealth service nearly doubled in size, and Canberra clearly showed the impact of that growth in hostels, boarding houses and flats. But at the time almost all of these young 'planners' understood that they had come to the city only because of the war, as an alternative to military service, and with no guarantees once its demands passed. Many were employed on temporary bases; Canberra was a form of demonstration project for whatever lives they might find at war's end. In this, too, they were emblematic of the city.[14]

This awareness of impermanency also existed because Canberra's dominance brought with it measures that would, at some point, be re-examined and possibly repealed. After 1942, when the

Commonwealth gained the power the collect all income taxation, it might have been clear that 'for all practical purposes, Australia has become in war a unitary State'. But it was far from certain what level of federal power would remain with peace. Canberra's new 'prestige' was not completely protected from the life of the nation around it.[15]

Federal Parliament had been 'unusually troubled' since 1937, with the governing conservative parties passing through a series of ministries, reflecting tensions in their coalition and leadership. Canberra's increasingly seasoned press gallery not only reported this turbulence but took a part in fomenting it. The forced proximities between politicians and journalists at Parliament House often extended to fraternity over drinks, meals, even riverside picnics and fishing trips. These conditions developed early a fetish for gossip. By the late 1930s, journalists such as Alan Reid, badged as 'special correspondent' in Canberra, followed leadership tension and party intrigue. Part of the flair of Reid's reporting was that it also began evoking the city in ways that ranged beyond parliamentary 'mystery' to feed a growing fascination for the 'human comedy' of the capital's intersecting communities: men in suits, typists seeking marriage, young people at a loose end. As Reid's biographers recount, he joined a small, devoted group of columnists who built careers around 'the tense, nerve-strained drama of men fighting for power' that came to define Canberra into the 1940s.[16]

Gaining the prize of prime ministership after Joseph Lyons' death in April 1939, but soon plunged into war, an embattled Menzies adopted the tactic of 'seeing as little of parliament as possible'. Sitting days for the House of Representatives recovered a little from the trough of 29 in 1937, but five months passed with empty chambers in 1939; there were only 43 days in 1940, 50 in 1941, then 45 and 48 to 1943. This was 'the Executive's war', but if the concept implied a necessary realignment of power, it was also true that no other comparable country so markedly limited its parliamentary engagement. And when it met, the House, and especially the Senate, did 'what it was told' in pushing through legislation, observing the higher imperatives of war. 'Honourable members' who, as Labor's Maurice Blackburn remarked in 1941, 'assemble here unwillingly and leave gladly', were perhaps relieved by this apparent downgrading of their need to attend. Equally, however, the absence of opportunities to speak for their constituents scarcely reflected Canberra's increasing impact on communities throughout Australia, or the interest those communities took in its business.[17]

Deepening divisions between the federal parties over policies, especially in relation to wartime finance, and within them over leadership, explained John Curtin's refusal to take Labor into a national government with the UAP and the Country Party. When arrangements keeping the coalition in minority government collapsed in October 1941, Curtin vowed as Prime Minister to reverse the *de facto* drift to Melbourne. 'Canberra', he asserted, 'was the seat of Australia's government, and government would operate from Canberra'. In part this emphasis reflected his need to escape 'importuning individuals' and 'special interests' for the sake of a single-minded war effort: Canberra's isolation was, in this sense, to be made a virtue, or at least a way of coping. But this ethos also enhanced awareness of the city's business. In contrast to the 'abrasive' Menzies, Curtin cultivated a loyal press 'circus', who enabled a seemingly unlikely, reserved man to become a respected wartime leader. The tense vigils he was known to keep in solitary walks around the Prime Minister's Lodge or further afield were not reported in the news, but from 1942 he and his government were present to the population each day in the regular radio broadcasts that were relayed across the nation from an expanded ABC office in Parliament House.[18]

THE URGENCY OF EVERYTHING

Canberra's political eminence, however, had little to anchor it. Construction of houses ground down as labour and materials were required elsewhere: 24 were completed in 1942–43; none at all in 1943–44. A hostel designated for 'low-wage public servants' was finished in 1941 – and then nothing. The completion of the Patents Office that year marked a similar break in administrative construction. Canberra was gaining international visibility through reporting of the war, and a diplomatic corps, established in 1936 with the appointment of the United Kingdom's High Commissioner, expanded with representatives from Canada (1937) and the United States (1939). Only the first, however, had permanent accommodation until 1943, when the US built its Georgian-style embassy. Japan's ambassador, appointed in March 1941, lived in Melbourne until his brief internment following his country's declaration of war. With a certain irony, the only major project to be completed through these years was the Australian War Memorial. The building of a shrine to soldiers of the Great War had begun in 1929, was suspended during the Depression, recommenced in 1934, proceeding slowly amid delays and wrestling over the design. On Armistice Day, 1941, it took ingenuity to find enough chairs for all the guests invited to the opening ceremony. In his nationally broadcast speech that day, the Governor-General, Lord Gowrie, determinedly set aside old clichés of ANZAC pioneering and sacrifice, declaring instead that Canberra's first monumental building represented the 'universal destruction, desolation and distress' any war bestowed, anywhere.[19]

His message hung heavy in the clear air. The current conflict might have been far away, but its threat was palpable. On that day in November 1941, as the first of many generations of school groups stood fixated by the memorial's graphic dioramas of fighting at Gallipoli, Palestine, Pozières, Bullecort and Ypres in the 1914–18 war, the *Canberra Times* recorded that 750 Canberra men, 'equal to six per cent of the local population', had already enlisted for military service, a number not including members of the militia joining from camps in Sydney. The paper was already featuring regular notices for local men killed in campaigns in North Africa and Europe. Twenty-six days after the War Memorial opened, Japanese aeroplanes bombed the American fleet in Pearl Harbor. A little over two months later the British stronghold of Singapore surrendered to the Japanese army. The 3rd Australian Infantry Battalion, a militia force recruited from an area of southern New South Wales centred on Canberra, moved to Port Moresby in May 1942; by September, barely trained for the ordeal, they were desperately fighting on the Kokoda Track.[20]

In late 1941, Canberra's press gallery had savoured among themselves stories of a reception held at the Hotel Canberra by the Japanese Ambassador, at which too much was drunk, leading one parliamentarian to offer the Ambassador assurance that Australia wasn't 'going to fight him', add compliments 'on the beauty of his wife' – it was really his daughter – but express curiosity that she should be 'wearing a parachute', which was in fact traditional dress. Levity turned to near panic by the end of the year, as the capital was suddenly overwhelmed by the demands made of it. The mishandling of evacuations from New Guinea, for example, suggested to Paul Hasluck 'the most charitable view, namely that Canberra was out of touch...a criticism only less damning than the alternative view that Canberra did know but did not care enough'. The city seemed more preoccupied with its own vulnerability. 'Typists were rattling away in the Government departments, copying important documents' in case the government needed to suddenly move, relocate, or cope with air raids. However unlikely such a threat appears in retrospect, it underscored perceptions of a ramshackle community at the head of an unprepared nation.[21]

A guard – at first an armed farmer, then the military – was set to defend the water supply in the Cotter Dam. The local Voluntary Defence Corps practised evacuating populations or ambushing invasions from the coast. The prospect that Canberra would be bombed featured in protests from the Advisory Council that the trenches being scored around public buildings, and the makeshift shelters constructed behind private homes, were inadequate protection. The white lines painted on the pavements between Parliament House and nearby hotels, so that politicians would not injure themselves while finding their way in blackouts, were another symbol of the incongruity of war coming to a bush capital. That a land line had to be installed to 'an official radio set' in Alan Watt's home, so that the computing machines in the statisticians' office neighbouring his in West Block would not disturb his monitoring of enemy broadcasts, was at least a sign of initiative. So was the reassignment of technicians at the Commonwealth Solar Observatory at Mount Stromlo from grinding lenses for telescopes to making artillery sights – a process assisted by the recruitment in 1941 of skilled European Jews who had been detained as 'enemy aliens' in Britain, then consigned to Australia. To have fled Austria and then arrive in Canberra under 'a radiant blue sky', even if with a police escort, was for one of those refugees a moment of joy. The life of the city grew with these adaptations.[22]

'Canberra people were well-insulated from the war', recalled those who travelled among the state capitals, where regimes of rationing and industrial and military mobilisation were more marked. In the garden town, at least, ample backyard vegetable plots and poultry runs meant food was rarely scarce. But many goods reached Canberra's small market only sporadically: shoelaces were often scarce; so were envelopes. Common privations took on a character of their own. Petrol rationing meant that the cars that had been prominent in the 1930s largely disappeared from a city already predicated on them and in which public transport was rudimentary. Already ubiquitous bicycles brought a more humble dimension to the navigation of rough roads and timber bridges. Years later, watching swarms of bicyclists in Indian streets, (Sir) Peter Lawler – later a leading diplomat and public servant – was instantly taken back to his first impressions of Canberra when he arrived as a graduate from Sydney in 1942 to work in government. The 'manpower' directives that elsewhere sapped manufacturing districts in Canberra threatened the availability of men and vans to deliver milk. But in a city where shops were still distant from homes, such mundane impacts cast into relief the privileges and dependencies on which life in the city was based.[23]

Community effort in rising above such inconvenience was, as elsewhere in Australia, soon evident. Camouflage nets were knotted at schools, and any number of events – dances, stalls, knitting groups – raised funds and made 'comforts' for the war effort. Leading citizens – women especially, already prominent in bodies such as the Victoria League or the Red Cross – often initiated such programs, finding a ready patron in Lady Gowrie, the wife of the Governor-General, whose son was killed in action in 1942. Local farmers pledged a portion of their wool clip to pay for the purchase of aircraft, and in 1942 instituted the annual National Sheep Dog Trials, held at Manuka Oval, to raise funds for war widows. Other morale-boosting activities included a visit by the revue *Battle for Australia*, staged by members of 'Moral Rearmament', first in Parliament House then at the Albert Hall in February 1943, with its resounding message: 'More sweat in the factory, less blood on the battlefield'. Casualty lists nonetheless brought bloodshed closer. In late 1942, reports arrived of the death in New Guinea of May Hayman, who had been a nurse at the Canberra Hospital and then a missionary: executed by the Japanese, she would be remembered in a stained-glass window in St John's Church, Reid. The community also comprehended as best it could the deaths in action or prison camp of the three sons of Walter and Marion Eddison, who had taken up a soldier settlement block in Woden in 1920. Following a 'stirring address' by the resident Chinese minister on ' this gigantic struggle', the 1942 annual convention of the local Returned Services League resolved 'that all internees should be employed under similar conditions to the Allied internees in enemy countries'. But a small local Italian community endured no persecution and Italian and German 'aliens', including some prisoners-of-war, brought in to work the pine plantations around the city, scarcely caused alarm.[24]

Many women, including married women, gained paid work in the absence of men, or joined the forces themselves: in the auxiliary services, including as telegraphists at the Royal Australian Navy Wireless Station (HMAS *Harman*), established at Canberra in 1939 and active from 1943; or further afield in the Australian Women's Army Service. In 1938, Gorman House – built in 1925 – was declared a women-only hostel and built its own community among new arrivals.

A local doctor expressed concern at the 'tension' he observed among the 'spirited' women public servants, living in hostels, with few opportunities to leave the city given travel restrictions, and denied 'the congenial surroundings of home life'. A sympathetic correspondence followed in the *Canberra Times*, reflecting just one aspect of parallel lives in the city. Jean Salisbury travelled to the capital frequently as a typist for the War Cabinet, but 'the urgency of everything' meant that those in her position 'didn't mix much with people who lived in Canberra unless we worked with them'. From 1929, the YWCA provided rooms to safeguard the welfare of single women coming to the city, but a very different concern promoted the founding of a local YMCA in 1943. This initiative reflected a shocked awareness that boys in a small city, dominated by the 'authoritarian influence' of 'bureaucrats', now lacking the guidance of men who had left to fight, and often still living in marginalised temporary workers' settlements, were growing up as 'tough' as, if not more so than, their peers in the most disadvantaged areas of

Unreal city 111

Figure 14: A new infusion – women workers having lunch in the sun during World War II. (Reproduced with permission of the Canberra and District Historical Society)

Melbourne. Canberra's divisions of class and rank had not disappeared: the children of 'good' suburbs were still 'not allowed to play' with 'kids' from camps, for all the change around them.[25]

Re-established in Canberra from Sydney with the easing of the Depression in 1937, the Royal Military College, Duntroon, ramped up its training of officers; Royal Australian Air Force squadrons were stationed at Canberra's airport, considerably improving facilities shared with a base named after James Fairbairn, the Minister for Air who died in the 1940 crash. They were joined in tasks of coastal surveillance by Dutch pilots, evacuated from the East Indies, accommodated in a commandeered Queanbeyan hotel, and conspicuous around the district and above it, flying low and fast in their Mitchell B25s. A small retinue of Indonesian infantry came 'in service' of the Dutch, but were given only tents. Even Canberra's inadequate hospital services were rejuvenated in a new building which was first requisitioned by the Australian Army in 1942, then allocated to the United States Armed Forces to treat wounded personnel from the Pacific. The American staff participated enthusiastically, if experimentally, in local Rugby competitions while they awaited patients. Dutch doctors and dentists joined their complement. Again, however, a certain unreality surrounded these cosmopolitan elements: American and Dutch medical staff soon moved north with the war, never having treated a patient of their own in the capital.[26]

Canberra, then, could show the fickle expedients of wartime, but also its demands. It had, for example, brought in Coombs in 1939, sent him to Melbourne in 1942 to introduce rationing, and brought him back in 1943 to head the new Department of Post-War Reconstruction. With such personal upheaval, the city could be a 'grim' and 'ghastly town' for wives. Elsie Curtin, moving from Perth to the Lodge for at least a third of each year, found it 'lonely'. Rather than endure it, Lallie Coombs established a family home in Sydney, to which – for much of his professional life – her husband was often just an 'occasional visitor'. The wives and families who came and stayed, supported by better salaries, or thankful for the prospect of gaining their first home, made the best of summer heat, winter cold, distance and labour (7 tons of wood, for example, was on average consumed by each house in winter; the essential household axe was often wielded by women in the absence of men) and the relative freedoms of the place itself. As Patricia Clarke writes, 'society' in Canberra remained – or had perhaps become more intensively – hierarchical and gendered during the war years, or at least more characterised by circles of like-minded people, recreating as best they could the games, dances, conversations, hobbies and interests that had defined them elsewhere.[27]

'Family' becomes a recurrent, if often surrogate image in Canberra during these years. Among senior officials, as Coombs himself put it, the dynamics of the time 'made convivial colleagues a family'. An 'official family', L.F. Crisp notes – drawing on his own experience of working under Coombs – developed especially around Ben Chifley, first as Treasurer and, after Curtin's death in 1945, Prime Minister. Patterns of consultation, 'formal or informal', became 'an ingrained habit' that was then 'institutionalised' among a group of 'ministerial, top-official and "off-sider"' level men who conceived, debated, framed and implemented a program that ranged across domestic and international policy into the late 1940s. Such work brought great satisfaction, but could also lay foundations for rivalries and sheer ambition. Gerald Firth, an English-born economist, grew wary of the 'radicalism' he and others embraced in Coombs' Department of Post-War Reconstruction, as much an expression of personal loyalty as ideological conviction. Escaping briefly to the United States in 1945, Copland found himself reflecting on the 'corrupting influences' of Canberra – its intense proximities, its egos, and its insularity.[28]

Still, it offered work that could 'revolutionise' skills and perspectives. The Treasury, Hasluck noted, once an 'unimaginative and conservative' bastion at the heart of Canberra's inter-war practice of government, was impelled to develop 'rapidly and naturally a lively interest in higher policy and the organisation of the war effort'. 'The adaptability of the Australian public servant', he adds, was 'shown in few more striking examples than in the way officers who had hesitated over thousands were soon expediting the approval of millions'. Such power extended and consolidated, in a small community, into patterns of sociability and reputation among the 'boys' who gathered when they could at the Royal Canberra Golf Club, or in the non-members' bar at Parliament House, or at the Hotel Canberra or Wellington. Canberra's tired, driven officials – men who had shaken the hold of old-fashioned seniority with the claims of merit and expertise – became the new face of the city, but they lived in a disconnect between managing the nation in the aggregate and abstract, and the society that would ultimately have to endorse the powers they sought. Already, in 1942, building a new constituency, Menzies was rallying 'the forgotten people' to reclaim the citizen's responsibility from the government's regulation, restore power to parliament from the executive, and to bring to 'our rulers ... the cold wind of public opinion'.[29]

Throughout the war, Eilean Giblin – a feminist, born into a wealthy London family – made the best of her time while her husband steered the highest levels of government policy. Often alone, she drew on the resourcefulness that had seen her work as a shearers' cook, live in the New Australia settlement in Paraguay, and find purpose as a potter. She struggled at Canberra's dinners and parties to contribute to conversations among senior officials but still grew frustrated with the inefficiencies she heard these men had to endure. 'In a dictatorship', she confided to her diary, 'incompetent people would be given the book in double quick time'. 'Canberra is full of silence', she recorded – noting the contrast to 'the noise and strain and worry' of Melbourne. On one of her many walks she noted the strange character of the city around her. Parliament House, for example, 'seen through White Poplars and Pin Oaks looked unreal, artificial'. She came across a workers' camp – which had remained since the 1920s, whether accommodating labourers or the unemployed – 'with broken windows stuffed with bags; but families live here'. Their address, she noted, was Capital Hill, 'the centre of Canberra, and what in future will probably be the heart of Australia'. The paradox stayed in her mind.[30]

PARVENUS AND UPSTARTS

The passing emergency of war urged Curtin's and then Chifley's government to act on the 'social contract' that had so far infused their morale-raising campaigns. This task centred on the Department of Post-War Reconstruction, established in Canberra, its senior appointments having an average age of 36, and most of them already envisaging a future in the city and for it. In 1945, the department's Regional Planning Division produced a vision for the Australian Capital Territory as part of its recasting of Australia's social and economic map. The combined resources of the south coast, the Southern Tablelands and the Monaro, boosted by further irrigation and hydroelectricity, could enable Canberra 'to become a modern city completely adapted to and integrated with the region of which it is a centre'. Another ambition was a new national university to be established in the city, with a research-only mandate, defining fields vital to national development. Institutes of 'government' or 'social sciences', 'social health' or 'medicine', 'Pacific and Asiatic Studies', and 'physics' with an emphasis on nuclear energy, were canvassed in 1946–47. Town planning was another field in which such a university might specialise – not least because of its location. As another dimension of its national vision, the venture was in part premised on a small group of Australian 'refugee professors' who – it was hoped – could be enticed back from overseas if Canberra was made sufficiently attractive.[31]

A similar move for the future saw the creation of a Department of Immigration. Recruiting heavily from ex-servicemen, and said to favour Catholics in a public service still with sectarian strains, Immigration began small and highly centralised in Canberra. But by 1949, it had a staff of 210 in the capital, and its officers began heading overseas again in suits not uniforms and like 'angels or arrogant gods' to select from queues and camps in Europe those who might be given a chance in Australia. These tasks were bold, but still in Canberra a transitory atmosphere surrounded them. Post-War Reconstruction was accommodated in the old hospital buildings at Acton; Immigration was allocated space alongside other departments moving back to the city in timber-framed, fibro-cement clad 'wool-shed' buildings erected as temporary offices in 1947 – and still there 30 years later.[32]

As incoming Chairman of the Public Service Board, (Sir) William Dunk advised Chifley that in staff and resources his charge was generally 'run down and out of date'. In its revival, no measure was more urgent than improving the capacity of Canberra to attract and hold officers capable of acting out his mantra: 'Civilisation is management'. Dunk would prove among the city's strongest advocates, lamenting the 'psychological as well as practical problems' of recruiting staff when Canberra could offer young people and single women especially so little in terms of 'a normal social and community life'. In another symbol of the time, when moves were made to resume the construction of the permanent Administration Building, suspended during the 1930s and proposed to accommodate 3000 public servants, its foundations were found to be shoddy. That project, too, would need to start afresh.[33]

So did aspects of the parliament sitting in Canberra. In October 1944, Menzies chose the capital as the venue for a conference of 15 organisations drawn from around Australia, all 'opposed to Socialism with its bureaucratic administration and restriction of personal freedom'. That conference, as political historian Ian Hancock notes, determined to form a new party from 'the untidy and unhappy remnants of non-Labor politics'. Contesting its first election in 1946, Liberal party members entered a federal parliament which now sat for longer, saw all members granted secretarial assistance to cope with their representational work, and campaigned for a substantial expansion in its size to meet post-war demands. The introduction of live national radio broadcasts of parliamentary sittings that year offered those who cared to tune in across the nation a direct connection with its business and routines. In this post-war world, L.F. Crisp noted in a pioneering textbook on Australian government that constituents seemed more likely to value their 'man in Canberra' as a figure 'who can do something for them in their increasingly numerous contacts with Departments, Authorities and Boards'. Closer judicial review of the functions of central government accompanied the vote in referenda which curtailed Labor's ambitions in areas from social services to economic regulation. Not just signs of political reaction, these were traces of a new kind of political contract in which the power and symbolism of Canberra would figure: a return to the tussles of federalism; an urgency given to questions about the role of government; and a modernisation in the styles through which it would be conducted.[34]

The census of 1947 captured the extent to which the city still stood apart from the Australian average, and to which it was changing within itself. The population of the Australian Capital Territory remained, for example, more 'masculine' than any other part of the country, apart from the Northern Territory. It was also significantly younger, with a birth rate nearly twice that of the nation, and death and infant mortality figures nearly half the norm. If the community had become less typical, it had also become more distinctive. The marked expansion in the city's residents contrasted to a relative decline in the population of local rural districts. The strains of Depression and war had seen the end of several struggling soldier-settler properties in the territory. Rural occupations for Aboriginal peoples may have similarly declined, but at least the resumption of building offered options for work, bringing some people back to country long lost to their families.[35]

There was much building to do. Not only offices but also houses and the services to support a growing community were required. Parks and clubs, Dunk and others urged, were vital if Canberra was to be attractive to people who could always choose work elsewhere. Progress from nothing began slowly – Canberra being only one, and still a relatively small and isolated, area in which chronic shortages of labour and materials prevailed well into the 1950s. In 1948 – a year in which around 250 houses were 'delivered' to the Department of the Interior – 2700 people were on the waiting list for a home. Even with an often-controversial series of 'priorities' influencing progress up that list, it was calculated that a married public servant would wait three years for his turn. Those not on the government payroll scarcely had a chance at all. Private builders might be engaged if they could be found, but their costs were high and they still had to negotiate delays and continuing restrictions. It fell to the government to build up to 80 per cent of the housing stock, and to rent it at rates that seemed high in contrast to elsewhere in Australia but reflected local costs and pressures. And to those pressures, as local lawyer Frank Brennan observed, was added the fact that 'those who came to Canberra in the post-war years did so with a completely different outlook than the earlier generation of pioneers': increasingly they came not only *en masse*, with an intention to stay and build careers, but with expectations of what a 'modern city' should provide to keep them.[36]

Expedients were employed to meet these demands. The National Capital Planning and Development Committee backtracked on ideals of the garden city and proposed halving the size of suburban blocks. A city which, in the 1920s, had marked rank by the timber or brick construction of homes, began experimenting in the construction of flats and various forms of cheap and efficient prefabrication: 'econo-steel', monocrete and so on. These 'homes for workers' – small in size and in the allocation of rooms – were placed in subdivisions, such as that marked out at Narrabundah in 1946 for over 350 'units', which were meagre and severe departures from anything Griffin or Sulman might have envisaged. The streets were numbered, not named. An older guard of officials grudgingly accepted such aberrations – and screened them, as local historian Alan Foskett notes, by 'the mass planting of quick-growing trees'. Yet those who began moving into these subdivisions in the late 1940s – mostly tradesmen and their families – exemplified that demographic profile of 1947: young, with children, keen 'for a stable place to call home', if as 'a stepping stone to a better life'.[37]

Many new arrivals bided their time in hostels, still enduring strict rules (dinner at 6:00 p.m. sharp; no alcohol; often strict 'artificialities' of sex segregation). This experience could also be inclusive as 'people from all over the place and many different social-economic groups came together' in this first stage of settling in. But alongside these arrivals were schemes that negotiated a parallel desire to 'improve' the stock on which government could draw, such as the careful selection of diplomatic cadets, to boost the capacity of the Department of External Affairs. Donald Horne, just out of uniform, recalled among his own cohort of cadets a prevailing, self-conscious ethic of 'modernising Australia', a deference to 'people with degrees', and a reverence for 'the departments' that would guide the esoteric tasks of nation-building. Horne, amid a circle of similarly displaced souls, 'loathed Canberra': it showed as much about the unravelling of the politics and provincialism of an Australia he wanted gone as it did about the nation to come.[38]

Another series of hostels, recycled from defence facilities, provided less salubrious accommodation for a different infusion of labour. In late 1947, the immigration program delivered the 'first party' of 'Baltic immigrants' to arrive in Canberra. A typist still working long hours at the Department of Immigration, Meryl Hunter recalled her first sighting of 'New Australians' in Canberra as 'objects of derision as they carried all their wordly possessions in bulky briefcases wherever they went'. Accommodated at Mulwala Hostel, these 'Balts' were 'single girls and war widows', the *Canberra Times* noted, selected as 'housemaids or domestics'. At Mulwala they joined a group of English women, imported as typists, who were peeved at being derided as 'pommies' if they complained, and not impressed with this new company. 'There is something lacking in the place', a Londoner observed: 'nearly everybody seems to be living in a world of their own' – of disparate, disrupted worlds. Eastlake and Riverside hostels were synthesised in Tom Hungerford's novel *Riverslake*, and held nearly 900 tradesmen in 1949, most from Central Europe, each hostel a microcosm of the leap Australia was attempting to make in reconciling its need for labour with the cultural, industrial, class related and personal strains of sudden change.[39]

New suburbs for higher ranks – Griffith, Deakin, Turner, North Ainslie – were, as before the war, laid out as dispersed, hierarchical enclaves, but now with some provision for corner shops, neighbourhood schools and sporting fields, showing the influence of a more family-oriented planning. A Griffith Parents' Group pressed for the more systematic provision of services for children, mothers and families. A local nursery school was established in Manuka in 1944, a play centre in 1945, and a conference convened to address children's reading and speech, and the seeds of delinquency. Led by (Sir) Arthur Tange (from Post-War Reconstruction, later Secretary of the Departments of External Affairs and of Defence) as president, Mrs Frederick (Peggy) Wheeler as secretary, and advised by Betty Minter, the wife of an American diplomat and a trained preschool teacher, the group had the skills to lobby government and the standing to gain support. The stern civic duty espoused in the inter-war decades was replaced by an insistence that 'local people must have the services to which they are entitled' – services that ranged from public transport to accommodation for a surprising number of aging people still living in neglect in workers' camps. Even the sporting groups that began to regain strength with the return of settled patterns of leisure reflected a more communal than athletic approach to their pursuits.[40]

Inevitably the question of Canberrans' own political representation re-emerged. A spur was the prosecution of a tireless campaigner for the city's development, Ulrich Ellis, for breaching the regulations that prohibited him, as a public servant, from 'commenting publicly on any administrative action': Ellis had questioned manipulation of the waiting list for government housing. The disjunction between a city with no say and a capital with plenty was sharpened in 1948, when both chambers of the Commonwealth parliament were nearly doubled, but with the one seat created in the House to represent the Australian Capital Territory confined to the right to vote on issues directly affecting the territory. Four local candidates ran in the December 1949 federal election: Mrs J.W. Ashton, an Independent, prominent in welfare and cultural groups; Malcolm Moir, architect and president of the Chamber of Commerce, running for the Liberal Party; Sid Rhodes, of the Trades and Labour Council, for Labor; and

Dr Lewis Nott, another Independent, a prominent medical practitioner with a long association with the territory's Advisory Council. The campaign was keenly contested, the poll recording remarkably few informal votes. Rhodes led the primary count, reflecting strong local Labor organisation (despite blue collar/white collar tensions in his preselection). Nott won on preferences, declaring his victory an endorsement for community-focused rather than party-driven politics, and finding irrelevance in a chamber dominated by the latter.

Far more significant, however, was the overall result of the 1949 poll. Labor was defeated. Menzies' incoming Liberal Party marked a dramatic ideological and generational change, with profound consequences for the capital. Yet while the elements of that change took shape, it was clear the city itself was reflecting on a tumultuous decade. According to the *Canberra Times*, locals had grown restless with 'the parvenus and upstarts' in the bureaucracy – especially Post-War Reconstruction – 'who are accepted very largely on their own valuation and who lack tradition, experience and balance'. Such self-importance was matched by regret that dances at the Albert Hall or the Lady Gowrie Services Club were no longer attended by decent couples or 'servicemen with respect for their uniform' but by men in 'open-necked sports shirts and plum coloured trousers' who ogled the 'shop girls, typists [and] receptionists'. Nostalgia had never been possible for Canberra before, and seems forced here. But what was the next move? In its 1949 report, the Public Service Board documented decline rather than improvement in all the indicators that might mark Canberra's 'stature as a national capital', from waiting lists for housing to the continuing 'burdens' imposed on efficient government by the dispersal of its departments, many of which – or large components of which – continued to be based in Melbourne (including the Defence departments, Supply and the bulk of Health) or Sydney (Repatriation, Social Services, Supply, and the bulk of Works and Housing). Were the 'ties of common interest' likely to strengthen unity under such circumstances? Perhaps not yet, but the city was settling a little deeper into its site. Its carefully tended trees, Denning noted in 1947, might seem 'unreal' at first, 'until they impress their personality on you'. Hungerford wrote of

> those long golden evenings of summer bronze...when the bleached white of the higher paddocks merged so gently with the violet shadows of the gullies, when the hard bright green of the pines on Stromlo was touched with scarlet and the faint, sharp tang of sheep drifted past your nose at road-crossings, and magpies and currawongs and pewits and gang-gangs carolled...their neighbourhood gossip onto the dusty air.

There were many such reveries in the late 1940s, and in these sentiments of place, if nothing else, Canberra was acquiring a reality on which to build in the years to come.[41]

5

Moving up, and moving in

A QUIET REVOLUTION

Beginning in 1950, annually until 1966, and then biennially until 1970, Canberra hosted the 'Citizenship Conventions' that marked the evolution of Australia's post-war immigration program. The change of government in December 1949 did not disrupt final planning for the first gathering, held over a week in January, but it was the Liberal Party's R.G. Menzies rather than J.B. Chifley who, as Prime Minister, spoke to over 200 delegates. Assembled in the Albert Hall, not far from Parliament House, they represented 100 community, religious, industry, union and other interest groups from around Australia. While Canberra in the past had provided the venue for many conferences seeking the status of national representation, none had been as inclusive in participation or theme, or so supported by the imperatives of government policy. None would provide such regular signposts for the evolving nation over which the city presided.

All attending that first meeting were encouraged to work towards the 'rapid assimilation' of those who were arriving with 'developing momentum'. (Over 38 000 assisted British residents and 75 000 European 'displaced persons' were among the 147 000 people who came to Australia in 1949; 1950 would see a peak of 149 000 not exceeded until the 1980s.) Bipartisanship prevailed. Menzies expressed 'the deep gratitude' owed to the Labor Party for initiating this ambitious policy, and urged delegates to strive at overcoming the 'active or passive resistance' meeting immigrants. Australians must go 'to no end of trouble to make every migrant feel at home'. More pointedly, they must recognise that 'in an unpeaceful world', there was no alternative but to welcome those who would add to the stock of 'the King's men and the King's women'. Subsequent conventions expanded on these themes with increasing sophistication. By 1960, over 250 delegates considered the challenge of maintaining a pace of economic development sufficient not only to support population growth but also to embrace new sectors of production, welfare and services in which all citizens must feel 'at home'.[1]

Canberra provided the necessary stage for these performances. The conventions reflected changing tasks in government in the post-war decades, as the virtues of 'good neighbourliness' edged into arguments for integrated planning. They also offered parallels to what Canberra was becoming in composition and character. Through the course of the 1950s and into the 1960s the city began to promise what historian and social theorist Hugh Stretton declared in 1970 to be 'a quiet revolution' in the quality of Australian life: it pointed past the 'gross injustice' that had often diminished inclusiveness and equity elsewhere in Australia. This chapter will deal with that revolution, as Canberra transformed from the 'unique little monstrosity' described by a visiting American in 1954, to representing, by the mid-1960s, a more integrated Australian community.[2]

With an urban population of just under 20 000 in 1950, but accelerating to 30 000 by 1955 and double that by the end of the decade, Canberra seemed to be entering a 'take-off' phase of self-sustaining growth much earlier than its planners anticipated. In 1950, however, its gait was still clumsy. In the week of that first convention, the *Canberra Times* – balancing its own mix of small town news and a capital city brief – offered accounts of an intensifying global Cold War alongside the announcement that the eastern lake basin was to be 'abandoned' from the gazetted Griffin plan in another economy-driven revision of the 'ideal city'. It featured 18 young women competing in the second annual Legacy Bathing Beauty Contest, to be judged before an eager crowd of 6000 on the

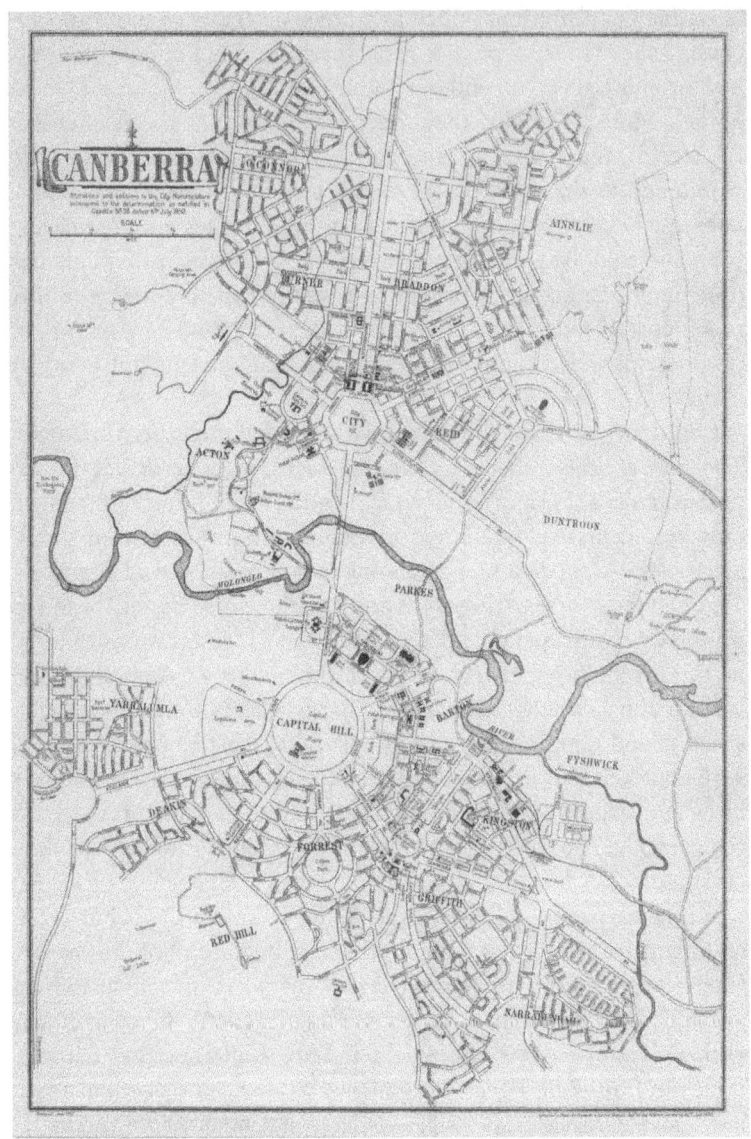

Map 2: Canberra in 1950 – a 'monstrosity'? (Reproduced with permission of the National Library of Australia)

banks of the Cotter River. And as delegates mingled, the paper ran appeals from other recent arrivals who took care to vouch that they were '*British* migrants', desperate to escape hostels where the King's English shared very mixed company.[3]

Amid such news, the convention added a 'carnival air' to the capital. Canberra hosted a range of associated activities, including an 'arts and crafts' exhibition representing 'the best of the homelands' that 'New Australians' had left behind. Among those judged by the *Canberra Times* to show a 'painstaking detail rarely seen in Australia' was Werners Linde, who had once designed Latvia's currency and postage stamps but had then fled Soviet persecution. In 1949, he arrived on the first of the International Refugee Organisation's ships to Fremantle, finding work as a cook in a Perth girls' school. He travelled east with his son to prepare the painting he offered for the convention. Displayed above the portal of Canberra University College (CUC), his expansive, rather disconcerting canvas (see page 126) vividly depicted young men in rural labour, with industry in the distance, and centred on two bare-chested figures heaving the Australian flag to triumph. In its own way the painting was an earnest testimony to assimilation – and intended perhaps as an emblem of the capital, which Linde found 'so wonderfully quiet' after the turmoil of his recent life. It found a permanent (if spit-ball spattered) home looming over bemused students at the nearby Telopea Park School. As the week drew to a close, an audience of 1100 overflowed the Albert Hall for a concert featuring a Ukrainian pianist, a former professor of violin at Riga Conservatorium, and a Bulgarian baritone. Canberra provided a fitting stage for these disrupted, talented lives to reclaim expertise, and vouch for their dedication to a new home.[4]

Several musicians that night were members of a touring 'New Australian Opera Company', recently formed at Bathurst's Immigration Camp. But not all performers had travelled to Canberra. The Greek, Polish and Estonian dancers were locals – and they reflected another distinctly Canberra dimension to the week's proceedings. In 1947, the census listed 33 Greek-born residents in the ACT; there were 84 by 1954. The figures for those years for Polish-born were seven and 558 respectively; and for Estonians, two and 100. In 1947, 11 per cent of people in the territory were overseas born,

Figure 15: Werners Linde's painting for the 1950 National Citizenship Convention. (Telopea Park High School, Canberra; reproduced with permission of Dr Werner Linde)

8 per cent of whom came from Continental Europe. In 1954, the figure was 21 per cent (55 per cent European) at a time when the Australian average was 12 per cent, of whom 42 per cent were European. Population growth in the Australian Capital Territory in this period was not only more than double the national average, but remarkably more diverse in composition. Alongside the convention's high-minded proceedings, Canberra was entering its second act as a labouring city, and those Western, Eastern and Northern Europeans were prominent among its construction and building workers. To that extent, Linde's painting had its truth – even if the convention preferred to represent its proceedings with an image of two local children, a Scottish boy and a Ukrainian girl, running hand-in-hand in traditional dress in front of Parliament House. In 1950, Canberra was finally becoming the flag bearer of Australia's identity. And it would – more than any time in its history, and in its own ways – need to work through significant issues for the nation at large.

CHEATED OF ITS DESTINY

In 1950 it was already clear that the government's 1947 plan for the transfer of over 7000 public servants to Canberra in the coming decade was in trouble. By then the lingering austerities of war were exacerbated across Australia by the building pressures of post-war inflation and full employment. In Canberra the challenges were particularly daunting: the city still lacked basic infrastructure to attract and hold labour, to ensure a steady supply of materials for construction, and to keep down costs already magnified by distance. Several million bricks might have been stockpiled at Yarralumla when the city entered its first phase of concerted building in the 1920s, but there were few to be had in 1950. Attempts to meet such shortfalls, including continued experimentation with prefabricated housing, only contributed to a pervading sense of the provisional if not second-rate in the city.

As Chairman of the Public Service Board, Bill Dunk continued his 'dogged' campaign for the capital's consolidation: the quality and capacity of national government, he insisted, depended on it. But whatever inter-departmental cooperation he had secured in the late 1940s ebbed away with the lack of an overarching coordinating authority and a certain pervading scepticism about what Canberra had become under Labor. Menzies' new ministry was said to have begun 'extremely worried at the general tone of the advice' they received from officials in central agencies who they suspected retained sympathy for the previous government's plans. They sought the upper hand. There was no cull of senior ranks – the Prime Minister at least had a high regard for the seasoned advice of men such as H.C. Coombs, Allen Brown and Roland Wilson. But departments retreated to their specific functions, their permanent heads playing for influence with the ministry rather than power over it, and forming among themselves, especially in the select company of the Commonwealth Club after 1955, protocols of 'attitude, behaviour and standards' to keep them safe. Even the press gallery seemed cowed by a government that did not need them to sell the big story of reform, and was prepared to discipline journalists who strayed too far onto its carefully guarded 'privileges'.[5]

With 'a lordly wave of the hand', Dunk recalled, Menzies instructed him to 'Carry on, Sergeant Major' – an allusion to military-style direction and menial rank that was perhaps double-edged. That encouragement was undercut in June 1951 when the Prime Minister called for a report from the Board on 'ways and means' of cutting 5 per cent, or 10 000 employees, in the cause of 'economic balance'. Retrenchments were confined to the ranks of 'temporary' officers left over from the 1940s, but the taunt of control remained: a nerve had been exposed that critics of a bloated bureaucracy over the coming years needed to touch only lightly for effect. Equally, within a service so much in flux through the previous decades, hierarchies became firmer among those who watched closely the affairs (and pay scales) of court.[6]

As 'stop-go' fears settled into 'steady as she goes' under Menzies, the public service lost some of its allure as a 'safe' career. Dunk's

DEPARTMENT OF THE TREASURY. 431

Number	Name	Date of Birth	Date of First Appointment	Office	Division	Scale of Salary
	CENTRAL STAFF.					
1	Wilson, R.	7. 4.04	9.12.32	Secretary	I	4000
2	Vacant (Watt)			Deputy Secretary	II	2296-2606
3	Henderson, J.M.	5.11.06	14. 9.21	Senior Finance Officer (a)	III	1274-1428
	General Financial and Economic Policy Branch.					
4	Wheeler, F.H.	9. 1.14	18.12.39	First Assistant Secretary	II	2296-2544
5	Randall, R.J.	13.10.06	16.12.46	Chief Finance Officer, Grade 2	III	1614-1800
6	Nimmo, J.F.	11. 1.12	3. 1.39	" " " " 1	"	1490-1676
7	Woodrow, H.R.	28. 5.11	19. 7.34	" " " " 1	"	"
8	Bury, L.H.E.	25. 2.13	10. 5.46	Senior Finance Officer, Grade 3	"	1366-1552
9	Pryor, F.C.	11.11.19	8. 4.41	" " " " 2	"	1274-1428
10	Fleming, B.E.	21. 6.15	5. 4.48	" " " " 2	"	"
11	Reynolds, E.A.	13.11.10	18. 2.48	Senior Research Officer, Grade 2	"	1154-1244
12	Vacant (Fleming)			" " " " 2	"	"
13	Moore, A.G.	27. 1.21	1. 7.46	Senior Research Officer -	"	956-1124
14	Conron, C.W.	17.11.23	4. 3.40	" " "	"	"
15	Whitelaw, R.J.	16.11.21	9. 5.47	" " "	"	"
16	Vacant (Reynolds)			" " "	"	"
17	Hurley, B.F.	16. 4.25	23. 3.42	Research Officer, Grade 2	"	908-1004
18	Moore, B.F.	10.12.24	23. 2.42	" " " 2	"	"
19	Gray, R.L.	7. 6.24	9. 2.48	" " " 2	"	"
20	Davey, N.W.	2. 2.21	2. 9.35	" " " 1	"	764-908
21	Daniel, R.	16. 2.26	6. 2.50	" " " 1	"	"
22	Reid, D.F.N.	14. 8.22	6. 2.50	" " " 1	"	"
23	Vacant (Moore)			" " " 1	"	"
24	Vacant (New Office)			" " " 1	"	"
25	Visbord, E.M.W.	21. 9.28	1. 4.51	Clerk	"	232-620
26	Campbell, R.G.	13. 3.28	22. 2.51	"	"	"
	Budget and Accounting Branch.					
27	Vacant (Brophy)			First Assistant Secretary	II	2296-2544
28	Parker, G.R.	22. 8.94	1.11.12	Chief Finance Officer, Grade 2	III	1614-1800
	(Budget and Estimates Section).					
29	Cox, F.H.	6. 3.96	25. 8.13	Chief Finance Officer, Grade 1	III	1490-1676
30	Israel, J.R.	17. 1.16	9. 4.34	Senior Finance Officer, Grade 1	"	1214-1304
31	Fyfe, R.C.	25. 7.19	18. 2.35	Clerk	"	1004-1124
32	Jobson, N.	25. 5.16	22.12.32	"	"	956-1064
33	Maunder, J.I.	21. 4.21	15. 2.40	"	"	812-908
34	Selleck, A.J.	23. 5.26	8. 4.43	"	"	764-860
35	Vacant (Reid)			"	"	232-620

Figure 16: The Stud Book – an excerpt from the 1951 *List of Permanent Officers of the Commonwealth Public Service*, making Canberra's government hierarchies clear. (National Library of Australia)

Board prepared to establish a training centre in Canberra in 1954, to recognise the new demands made on 'management' at higher levels by an expanding economy. The service, however, generally failed to fill all vacancies as job seekers found better options elsewhere. Amid these pressures, Dunk railed against the simple intransigence of those – including increasingly militant staff associations, which did not want their members pushed around – who refused to commit to the city. As he lamented throughout the 1950s, 'the public service's Melbourne fixation is cheating Canberra of its destiny'.[7]

Destiny aside, certain aspects of the Canberra project ground ahead as a matter of inevitability. Reflecting simply the expanding role and reach of post-war government, departments already based in Canberra expanded in staff from, at Treasury, 398 in 1939 to 8515 in 1952; 398 to 1255 at the Department of Prime Minister; and 30 to 715 at External Affairs. And whatever reservations the new government had about the orientation of Labor's Australian National University (ANU) as an agent in national development, its pioneering staff had already begun to occupy temporary 'shed-like' facilities at Acton and construction had commenced for buildings to serve many other researchers on the payroll but necessarily at work elsewhere. The ANU, in several ways, exemplified the transitions under way in Canberra, from the expertise it assembled to the style it projected.[8]

An ideal of policy engagement at the new university was giving way to one of academic integrity, but spurred a remarkable intellectual and cultural consolidation nonetheless. University House was to set standards in providing accommodation and a social hub for academics and graduate students otherwise lacking in the city. Its elegance was one product of the brief, unhappy tenure of Brian Lewis, the architect charged to give coherence to the campus overall, but defeated by contending ambitions and interests. Its furnishings showed the more enduring influence of Frederick Ward, employed as the ANU's design consultant, who merged fine craftsmanship with new techniques and materials emerging from wartime innovation. Lewis' bold gesture faltered; Ward built through Canberra's deepening networks of taste, affluence and a sense of discrete mission the capacity to gain recognition for areas such as industrial design in Australia. Taking shape nearby, University House was the ANU's Research School of Physical Sciences, including a wing for a particle accelerator that would, its Professor, Marcus Oliphant, pledged, forge Australia's path into a future of peaceful nuclear energy. This vision enticed Oliphant back from the University of Birmingham – but the ANU's other three founding 'advisers' on research fields in social science, the Pacific and medicine, declined to return. The university's 'opportunities in abundance' were still emerging from a dusty landscape.[9]

Such apparently lavish investment in the university could be contrasted to progress elsewhere in the capital. In 1949–50, 410 houses were completed at Canberra and 545 in 1950–51, dropping to 489 in 1953–54. This was far from enough. It was estimated that around 1000 people were forced to cross the border each day from Queanbeyan's 'dormitories' for work. In 1952, the waiting lists for government-employed and non-government applicants were amalgamated to address discontent arising from preferences accorded to the former – but the tally only lengthened. By 1954, 2600 applicants faced more than two years to edge to the top, and up to four if they required a three-bedroom house. The demand for land saw auctions reintroduced in 1951 (leases could simply be acquired over the counter throughout the leaner 1940s), but the surging tide of 'key money' premiums threatened distortions the system was supposed to avoid. Those renting larger pre-war homes, or able to afford higher covenants, were paying proportionately less than those in the scramble for newer, smaller houses. Various attempts to correct such 'abnormalities' stumbled amid increasing suspicions that the government was engineering scarcity to raise revenue and rein in uncoordinated growth.[10]

While they waited, new arrivals took what they were offered or could find. The government 'guest house' at Kingtson had three beds to a room; there were four rooms to a 'cottage' and six cottages to the block. Higher-ranking public servants could take advantage of accommodation in the next tranche of hostels, such as Lawler and Havelock Houses, opened in 1949 and 1951, which retained codes of dress and demeanour long ago deemed appropriate for 'superior level accommodation' but now provoking protests from more relaxed, younger residents. Only two of 80 rooms were available for married couples at Narellan House; Gorman House – no longer only for women – had more double rooms, but in 1957 they were still furnished with single beds. Families at higher grades were accommodated at Hotel Acton, but the limit there was two children, requiring those with more to send Dad on alone, or leave the eldest children with grandparents or at boarding schools. What might have passed as improving stoicism between the wars seemed increasingly bizarre for a city supposedly setting the parameters for an Australian 'way of life'.[11]

The relief of gaining a house was often tinged with the wry observation that in the model capital, the streets in new subdivisions remained unpaved and the homes themselves lacked the electrical appliances to which people were growing accustomed elsewhere. Weighed in the balance might be the routine delivery of groceries and ice, and the still overarching benevolence of the Department of the Interior – known simply as 'the Department' – extending from the clipping of hedges (at 80 cm) to the provision of shrubs and trees (including cut pines at Christmas). Like the special allowances offered as an inducement to move, such benefits could seem an indulgence to those looking on with an eye for economy. By 1953, Wilfred Kent Hughes, the minister for both Interior and for Works and Housing – Canberra his self-proclaimed 'kingdom' – identified its 'privileges' as high on the list of 'squandermania' infecting government programs. But for many Canberrans free firewood was modest compensation for isolation from metropolitan life, public-transport accessible shops, friends and family.[12]

These circumstances bred frustration, but also fostered forms of sociability that were less formal than those that had characterised Canberra in the past. Between 1948 and the early 1950s, 134 houses were relocated from Tocumwal Airfield, in the New South Wales Riverina, or perhaps more accurately they became houses in transit, having left as 'shells designed as a form of camouflage, to give the appearance of a township rather than a military barracks', and arriving to be divided into relatively spacious three and four bedroom homes. In the bare northern suburb of O'Connor they were arranged in a neat, generous subdivision, with parkland space and cul-de-sac streets. Moving in as a wave, residents came from a diversity of occupations and backgrounds. Two recently arrived CUC professors – the economist Heinz Arndt and the historian Manning Clark – lived there alongside carpenters, bricklayers and public

Figure 17: Civic Centre in 1958: cars already an issue in unresolved space; the 'Swedish Style' flats in the distance. (Reproduced with permission of the Canberra and District Historical Society)

servants. But it was the dynamic among wives and children that soon established a genuine conviviality, bolstered in 1953 by the provision of a preschool. Many moved out as better options became available, but here was an early intimation of the 'neighbourhood planning' which, as Stretton noted, would cautiously ease aside the prevailing 'scandalous' segregation of Canberra's inter-war suburbs.[13]

Pressures on housing encouraged other forms of innovation, including the construction of blocks of medium density and four-storey flats adjoining the city centre after 1954 (seven-storey blocks were added in 1959). Derided by some as a further decline from the bungalow ideal, to others they showed responsiveness to 'Swedish style' architecture, and were prized – and commanded high rentals – as such. These modern flats were one of the ventures urged by Trevor Gibson, in 1949 the first qualified town planner appointed to the Department of Works, although soon transferred to the more welcoming ranks of Interior. They reflected his determination that Canberra attend to post-war priorities rather than continue deferring to Griffin's 'paper' schemes. An 'economical distribution of population', he argued at the first Federal Congress on Regional and Town Planning, held auspiciously in the Albert Hall in 1951, must take 'precedence over...ornamental pattern' and address the 'sociological imbalance' already evident in a resource-starved community. Gibson's manifesto (delivered to an audience wearing pyjamas under their suits against the cold) marked a fresh departure, but joined Griffin's in waiting for action. A housing target of 1000 units dropped to 320 competitions in 1954–55. While a sustained program of building infant and primary schools, and even an Olympic-sized swimming pool, often in themselves prize-winning exemplars of clean, modern design, sought to woo transferees, more basic needs often remained unmet. Even the central Administration building, in its style a leaden leftover from the 1930s, remained only 'about 55 per cent complete' at the midpoint of the 1950s, and over a third of the public service remained resolutely in Melbourne.[14]

In these straitened conditions, every initiative was likely to produce another problem. And the combination of muddle with parsimony was getting worse. Going the way of the east basin, lost from Canberra's lake scheme in 1950, the west basin was deleted in 1953 by Works with little explanation beyond the preservation of existing land uses (including the Royal Canberra Golf Club, a bastion for several senior public servants: their likely influence over this decision was widely resented). Then it was announced that a four-lane bridge would be driven across the middle of the remaining central basin, violating the geometry fundamental to Griffin's plan, and likely to do little to ease the 'rather amazing' (as Gibson noted) traffic congestion already evident on Canberra's sharp corners and spindly links. The community rallied against such arbitrary proposals, and ultimately they were rejected. But in the process they added to the litany of complaints that kept Canberra's member of parliament since 1951, Labor's Jim Fraser, consumed by a burden of representational and advocacy work unmatched by those holding seats with at least some level of local or municipal self-government. 'More mistakes in planning had been made in the past two years',

Fraser argued in 1954, than in Canberra's whole history: he dedicated himself tirelessly to his constituency's woes. With his general point the eminent architectural critic, Robin Boyd, agreed: the city had 'reached its nadir'.[15]

The depths seemed plumbed when a subdivision of prefabricated timber houses, shed roofed with front doors under the eaves of carports on narrow street frontages, was built at 'Narrabundah Heights', again without inter-departmental consultation. Dubbed the 'hen houses', they offended on every score, not least in being sited so that 'people are looking into other people's windows'. Residents on 'heights' should not endure such indignity. Boyd, at least, defended the scheme for its absence of 'featurism': a 'social triumph' in coordinated building mixed with artistic 'control'. Most revealing in this controversy was the contrast drawn in outraged debate in the Advisory Council between the modest 'demountables' built down in Narrabundah in the late 1940s, which 'were good living houses' on grid streets for lower-income groups, and this development, where land suitable for those on higher incomes, and presiding over a residual, graceful Griffin crescent, had been 'wasted'.[16]

Such fine distinctions scarcely concealed the extent to which the city depended on those that built rather than occupied such housing. In 1954, 2360 men – nearly 8 per cent of the population – were directly engaged in manual construction, as employees of the Department of Works, contractors or day labour. It was estimated that at least another 1000 workers were required to meet current schedules. 'Blue' collars contributed proportionately more than 'white' to a masculinity ratio in the Australian Capital Territory that was still 12 per cent above the Australian average. The Trades and Labour Council was a prominent local institution, with plenty of industrial and broader social issues to advance – and it proudly assumed these broad roles in the absence of intermediary forms of government. In 1952, the Canberra Branch of the moderate Australian Workers' Union had around 1200 members; 1100 were signed up to the more radical Building Workers' Industrial Union (BWIU). The latter was especially attentive to the living conditions of its members in Canberra's lesser hostels: by 1954 there were over 1307 men in workers' hostels: more than twice the number in 'government' facilities. And then there were those forced to carry their '"issue" cups and cutlery' between 'board in private rooms, backyard sheds, caravans and shacks' at a time when several government hostels were been converted for better-paying residents.[17]

And it was among these workers that the reality behind the Citizenship Convention's polite invocations had a particular resonance. In 1955, a visiting *Sun-Herald* journalist observed that the capital was 'a polyglot city now, with a touch of King's Cross in its make-up. Parliament and the Public Service speak English, but among the migrant workers who have done so much of the new building there is a babel of tongues'. That sense of incongruity reflected a marked characteristic of Canberra in the 1950s: its ethnic diversity, and the multiple stories it contained.[18]

By the early 1960s the Italian-born community was the largest non-Australian or British-born group in Canberra, but its development in the early 1950s was not encouraged as such. Immigration officials were even concerned that the pursuit of family or 'chain' sponsorship by early post-war arrivals might result in an 'influx' of 'Southern Italians' to Canberra, given that 'these people as a class are not very highly regarded'. Undeterred, or unaware, Pasquale Damiano, a hairdresser from Mirabella Eclano, Campania, who arrived as a labourer in 1951, lodged over 200 nominations, many for people from his own village, and built links among them once they arrived. He was part of the third generation to leave Mirabella, but unlike his predecessors, who went to America, he did not return. Despite such efforts, by 1954 the ratio of male (260) to female (68) Italian-born residents remained one of the most exaggerated disproportions among the larger migrant groups in the Australian Capital Territory. Unlike other Australian cities, Canberra offered no established 'Italian suburb' to receive new arrivals; nor did construction work encourage the networks fostered by agricultural or industrial concentrations elsewhere. Dispersed across suburbs, as Domenic Mico recalls of his childhood in Canberra, Italian children might be teased in school yards as the 'cowards' of World War II and plead with parents not to plant vegetables in their front gardens – a sure sign of being 'wogs', made more conspicuous by the uniformity characterising the capital's emerging neighbourhoods. But steadily connections grew. Italians traded among themselves: milk was exchanged for ricotta or decent bread; fruit was shared in glut.

An Italo-Australian Society was established in 1953. The first Italian priest arrived in the district in 1955. By 1957, Canberra supported its own Italian language newspaper, *La Campana*. Its message was pious and strict: Italians must resist corrupting Australian influences on matters of faith, values and behaviour. Despite this, Mico detected a distinct type of 'Canberra Italian', their ties cherished in family homes, in family businesses and in niches of hairdressing, building supplies and joinery.[19]

Other immigrant groups found comparable pathways. A group of Maltese workers were first consigned to huts at Fairbairn, considered to be the 'bleakest part' of the city and unsuitable, it was judged, for men whose English was good and skills valued. In 1948, the construction firm A.V. Jennings, catching the wave of post-war housing demand, signed a contact with the Department of Works to build 1850 homes in Canberra over five years. By 1951, stalled in delivering the project, Jennings negotiated instead to import 150 unmarried German builders to provide the craftmanship that couldn't be enticed to Canberra by other means. The men, only 15 of whom spoke English, came on two-year contracts, their fares deducted from their pay. Many were disillusioned on arrival by their rough accommodation in wooden huts or at the Capital Hill hostel – the latter built in 1948 to house 500 single male workers and recalled as 'worse, considerably worse' than any displacement camp or army barracks endured by anyone elsewhere. All left such lodgings as soon as they could, some before, breaking contracts and simply disappearing. Some experienced social 'ostracism', even though the BWIU at least assured members that these 'brothers' were neither 'wogs' nor Nazis. Industrial solidarity prompted the union to include a German as well as an Italian and Polish language page in their local newsletter, and took up their case in a dispute with Jennings over whether their contracts included a return fare. There were 13 Germans in the territory in 1947, but by 1954 numbers had swelled to 538. This consolidating German community soon achieved a more even gender balance among themselves than the Italians, and were more 'highly regarded' and favoured in the hierarchies of assimilation.[20]

The families of public servants, moving into their homes, noticed that the work parties planting or trimming hedges usually included recent immigrants working under Australian overseers. Established in 1951, the local Good Neighbour Council became one of the most active of Canberra's many voluntary organisations, its activities ranging from alleviating the isolation of immigrant men accommodated out of necessity in tents by the Cotter River by organising concerts, dances, picnics or films every Saturday. A blind eye was turned to the buses of prostitutes arriving from Sydney on pay nights to tour workers' hostels. High regard instead was accorded those who rose above the ranks to prove the 'painstaking' skills the nation craved, and which the capital sought to showcase.[21]

Prominent among the rising stars was Karl Schreiner, a civil engineer and architect, who fled Austria in 1939 but was interned following his arrival in Australia. In 1945, he came to Canberra to work in the Patents Office. Denied permanency, despite being a naturalised citizen, he and his wife Alice – also an Austrian-born engineer – built their own construction company, graduating from footpath contracts to completing 200 houses a year by 1957. Private clients included Frank Fenner, a leading ANU scientist – a pioneer in virology – whose sleek Robin Boyd-designed house challenged what its architect derided as a 'kaleidoscope' of derivative styles then prevailing in Canberra. Schreiner was a colourful figure, wearing traditional Austrian dress, establishing his own workshops and timber yard, and speculating on the capital's rising tourist industry until bankruptcy ate away his ambition. He had found a niche serving those sections of a Canberra society for whom, as an *Australian Home Beautiful* feature on the city noted in 1955, taste was marked by patronage of 'New Australian' craftsmen, who offered good prices and the authenticity of 'small groups working in almost primitive conditions'.[22]

With determination, immigrant communities navigated assumptions about who they were and how they were to fit it. Linde's bare-chested labourers were more likely to be, as architectural historian Milton Cameron argued, 'European master-craftsmen and cabinet makers who arrived in Australia via the Snowy Mountains Scheme'. And 'New Australian' was a label sometimes worn askew. A small Jewish population was divided between those who organised as a visible community group in 1951, actively advancing their interests,

Figure 18: Two men in front of the Russian Orthodox Church, Kingston, mid-1950s. (Reproduced with permission of the Canberra and District Historical Society)

and those who preferred to remain apart and inconspicuous. Greek immigrants established a small Orthodox chapel in a hostel building but soon began planning for a cathedral. One face of such diversity was evident when, in 1957, the *Australian Women's Weekly* judged Canberra as finally shrugging off the 'fair average' with a 'salami-pumpernickel' touch. But the delicatessens catering to the 'continental' tastes of a sophisticated clientele had their counterpart in the largely hidden and 'temporary' camps, such as Westlake, where successive waves of immigrants, mostly refugees, established gardens, with ducks, geese, hens, pigeons and rabbits and goats or cows for milk. The suburbs discouraged such husbandry, but offered other opportunities. By 1961, the 'Jennings Germans' led in building a social club in Narrabundah – one of the many such clubs formed across the city. Latvians established a basketball competition, but it was soccer that really took off. The 1950s saw a succession of

Italian teams – Torine, Roma, Napoli – pitched against Dutch, Greek, Czechoslovakian, Maltese, Hungarian and Croatian teams, with a competitive fervour soon prompting the recently formed ACT Soccer Association to require clubs to 'drop their national names'. Alex Jesaulenko, who arrived with his family from Austria in 1949, played soccer first, and Rugby when he went to St Christopher's School, but took up Australian Rules at Eastlake Football Club when it looked as if he might have a chance at high-level competition – these, too, were tracks of assimilation, although 'wog, wop and dago' followed him throughout.[23]

When the Italian community built their own Italo-Australian Club with voluntary labour in 1962, another sign of local adaptation was evident. It was designed by Enrico Taglietti, a Milanese architect who first came to the capital in 1955, after attending an Art and Trade Show in Sydney. Deciding to settle in what excited him as a still 'invisible city', full of opportunity, he built a practice creating interiors for new boutiques and gained prominence designing hotels serving a higher-end tourist trade, and an office building with a rakish underground cinema. His angular, sculptural approach was a marked departure from Canberra's established style, but it became desired in public and private commissions at a time of transition in so many aspects of the city. Taglietti redeemed the heavy horizontals of a city kept low and modest with a flair that was both ostentatious and cosmopolitan. Linde's peasants of 1950 contrasted markedly to the work of this urbane professional of the 1960s, whose 'calligraphy' of organic forms harked back to Burley Griffin but with the stamp of post-war modernism, and the lure of pleasure and consumption.[24]

GOVERNMENT IS CHOICE

The social dynamics of the 1950s did not diminish the inherent peculiarity of a city in which three-quarters of the population were in either the public service or construction. Nor did they address the fundamental lack of a stimulus to that polarisation. Since 1949, the Menzies government had gone through rocky years of economic and political consolidation, managing turmoil within its own ranks and beyond, a central aspect of which involved debates over the appropriate role of central government, whether in public works and investment, in law and liberties, or in generally taking the wheel of national development. Towards the middle of the decade Menzies sought to regain initiative, one means he used being a demand for more 'direct and continuous contact' between ministers and departments to ensure closer attention to advice on complex policy. The virtues of proximity were evident in the work of several Canberra-based portfolios; inefficiencies in others were aggravated by some senior cabinet members running their ministerial offices in Sydney while their departments remained in Melbourne. Younger, rising ministers, such as Paul Hasluck, were noted as accepting that Canberra was the place in which they needed to spend 'a good deal' of time, not least to check for the tendency of departments to assume that they could manage their minister rather than the minister manage them. Menzies would later confide that the hardships endured by his daughter as a young mother, and as the wife of an External Affairs officer, sharpened his awareness of conditions in Canberra. But his frustrations with governing from it came first. A rebalancing was necessary, both in accountability and in symbolism, in representing a national government that must rise above the interests of the states.[25]

That symbolism was strengthened during the four-day visit to Canberra by Queen Elizabeth II (the first visit to Australia by a reigning monarch) and her husband, Prince Philip, Duke of Edinburgh, as part of their 1954 Royal Tour. The scale of ceremonies in the capital – a parade of 4300 troops, a ball for 1000 and a State Dinner for 700 – won fulsome praise, even if 'the cutlets à la Canberra (veal, tongue and giant asparagus spears covered in aspic in the shape of a turtle)' prepared for the dinner by leading chefs failed to win gastronomic longevity. The tour brought unprecedented attention to the city, including 30 000 visitors. Residents noted a burst of 'hyper-activity' as 'the Department' ensured that houses on the royal route 'were prettied up in pastel pinks and greens and creams and whites'. Special arrangements were made to keep the streetlights on for another hour during the royal couple's stay, but a glow still endured after their departure. Mervyn Jones, a local entrepreneur, enhanced the facade of his Civic Theatre with a display of Aboriginal motifs. The Duke of Edinburgh declared open the

ANU's University House and the Queen 'unveiled' a 70-metre aluminium column in memory of United States–Australian collaboration in World War II. These were baptisms of a kind for Canberra – as a centre of learning and as an international player, a stylised American eagle atop a column presiding over all else.[26]

The month after the Queen left, prominence of another kind came with the defection from the Soviet Union of Vladimir Petrov and his wife Evdokia, who were both on the staff of the Russian Embassy. The capital was suddenly central to the assertion of Australia's place in the consuming politics of the Cold War. At the time its diplomatic community was growing (18 missions; eight others were based in Sydney), but it was still likely to be regarded as a hardship post. Its rounds were insular and, by force of circumstance, less exclusive than those in more established capitals. As Hal Myers, a press gallery journalist, recalled, 'you could almost have survived' in Canberra on the food available in an endless stream of cocktail parties in which the same faces (from ambassadors to local businessmen) appeared – although, Myers added, emerging uncompromised from 'long and dangerous' dinners was a more exacting skill. Petrov was already conspicuous in this world. Ostensibly the Third Secretary, he arrived in 1951 as an agent of the Soviet Ministry of Internal Affairs, tasked with recruiting spies and keeping watch on Russian émigrés and refugees. From the start this jovial, outgoing man, with an elegant wife and a dog loved by neighbourhood children, was uncomfortable with the embassy staff, which he found 'to a unique degree...a microcosm' of Stalinist repression. In the capital, the Soviet diplomats fitted well with Cold War stereotypes: their heavy, black cars sped furtively through and out of the city; the occasional gleam of stainless steel dentistry in their few smiles represented an incomprehensibly alien word. Petrov was soon identified by agents of the Australian Security Intelligence Organisation (ASIO) as somebody who might be lured to adopt 'the Australian way of living', and to defend it by sharing whatever secrets came with him.[27]

Canberra's ASIO branch had been mainly concerned with assessing the security clearances of public servants while also, as the *Canberra Times* reported in 1952, targeting 25 active local members of the Communist Party of Australia (CPA) for close observation and keeping more than a 100 'sympathisers' or 'bad security risks' under 'unobtrusive' if remarkably intrusive investigation. The activities of the latter group were not especially clandestine: their meetings, held in venues across Canberra, from Ainslie to Manuka and the Causeway, were sometimes disrupted by jeering members of the public. The business of the CPA was much harder to crack. Since the late 1940s the government had been made aware by American and British intelligence services of the leaking of information to the Soviet embassy primarily from External Affairs officers in Canberra – leaks which in themselves forced Labor to establish ASIO in 1949. First from a flat in Braddon, then from a house in Turner, and coordindated first by Doris Beeby, daughter of a judge and a union organiser, and then by Frederick Rose, an anthropologist working in several government departments, this flow of classified material reflected the 'study' and cultivation of a range of contacts or more-or-less unwitting sources among Canberra's overlapping circles of bureaucrats, political staff and journalists. When R.G. Casey, as Minister for External Affairs, declared in 1952 that a 'nest of traitors' was active in Canberra's public service, questions intensified about 'laxity' in a capital seeking to be dealt into the world of high security.[28]

Canberra was not an easy town for 'unobtrusive' surveillance. It was hard not to be seen in its open spaces. The agency briefly contemplated leavening the city's lack of nightlife by sponsoring a cafe to which diplomats might be encouraged to 'resort' for 'relaxed' conversation. Petrov, however, was not so difficult to track. Not the most professional of agents, he drove to Queanbeyan or Cooma for transactions, hid parcels under a rural railway bridge, took to the Brindabella ranges, or was lured to Sydney for pleasure. His eventual defection, the documents he brought with him confirming espionage, and the resultant Royal Commission, which reached deep into reputations and networks – including the office of the leader of the Opposition – anchored Canberra in Cold War politics and changed its political landscape for over a decade. Arriving in 1959, seasoned by harder left-wing politics in Melbourne, Amirah Inglis still described as 'scorched' the mood among many of the more left-leaning 'inhabitants of a small public service town, close to embassies and politicians' and with a proletariat nowhere in sight.[29]

Petrov and Queen Elizabeth supplied contrasting symbols of the capital as interesting and consequential. But such ornate fragments of politics and culture hung awkwardly off Canberra's spare frame. Journalists might cover such big events, but still noted as 'depressing, even frightening, the virtual abandonment of the principles' that were supposed to guide the city's progress. Citizens were said to be increasingly coming to Canberra to meet with their representatives, or to see them at work, but there was not much else there to greet them. Reflecting this disquiet, in September 1954, Liberal Senator John McCallum urged his colleagues not to skimp on a new building to rescue the collection of the National Library from inadequate storage in damp, dispersed locations. He then rallied to a larger theme. 'Government is choice', he said. But what kind of choice was reflected in the 'segregation' still marking Canberra's suburbs, the 'haphazard' implementation of its plan, and the 'curious uniformity' of its public buildings? A quiet and scholarly man, McCallum carried principles that were not always compatible with rough-and-tumble politics. But when, in November, he called for the creation of a Select Committee to 'arrest any vicious tendencies that have crept into the creation' of the national capital, he had picked the right time and found full bipartisan support.[30]

McCallum's measured terms in calling for the committee gave way in its report, tabled in October 1955, to trenchant critique. The seven members declared that the Commonwealth Parliament must either 'assert its position' over the city or – in a formulation borrowed from Dunk – 'surrender it'. The 'dawdling, doddering manner', which had prevailed since 1913, must end. The public service transfers proposed in 1948 must go ahead – and so should a relocation of national institutions, beginning with the High Court, the Federal Arbitration Court, the Commonwealth Bank and the Australian Broadcasting Commission. All ministers should make their homes in Canberra. Many of the committee's recommendations touched on perennial themes: inflated costs would prevail until construction was managed as an integrated project in which the needs of workers received systematic attention; 'expedient' building and miserable standards for them would offer no long-term efficiency. But most of its discussion focused on the capital's future role, weighing Griffin's formality against the need for a sense of 'scale' and 'balance' more appropriate to post-war values, and in accord (as McCallum noted) with the taste of 'the ordinary man – and it is he who has sent us here'.[31]

Taking evidence from 83 witnesses, McCallum's committee listened carefully as University of Sydney town planner Peter Harrison argued that Griffin had arranged one of 'the greatest civic compositions the world has seen', albeit one with 'extravagance' in some of its details. They applauded the work of Lindsay Pryor, as Superintendent of Parks and Gardens, in laying down a long-term vision of the city in planting that had yet to be matched in building. They took careful note of arguments for 'closer settlement' and encouraged experimentation in housing, but ultimately their enthusiasm for Canberra's 'pastoral atmosphere' suggested a clear preference for maintaining its dispersed suburbs. McCallum's 76 recommendations left few matters to chance or evasion, and gained coherence from a core proposition. A single authority, established as a corporation, with planning, construction and development powers, guaranteed long-term finance – a structure recognising distinct areas of professionalism and free from ministerial meddling – must take charge of the city. Canberra, McCallum insisted, must become more than a graveyard 'where departed spirits await a resurrection of national pride'.[32]

Vindicated, the *Canberra Times* called for 'immediate' action on past mistakes. Major metropolitan dailies were more wary of the 'grandeur' McCallum seemed to propose. However, the report gained backing from the top. Kent-Hughes had wrestled with the minutiae of Works and Interior, railed against 'masses of red tape' and shown little sympathy with bold schemes. In 1956, Menzies dropped him from the ministry. Allen Fairhall, a young backbencher, replaced him, soon receiving a letter from the Prime Minister tasking him to 'straighten out' Canberra in areas ranging from its 'villainous little cottages' to 'the prevalence of the squat, flat-topped building which needs only a few bales of hay and a goat on the roof to be painfully reminiscent of Suez or Port Said'. Prime Ministerial pride was clearly engaged. 'Proposals for Canberra expenditure', Menzies added, would receive 'a very cold eye' until 'I am satisfied that the business is being attended to in an...effective way'.[33]

Fairhall set to work, establishing in March 1957 a joint parliamentary committee to examine planning decisions, announcing in May that the eminent British town planner, Sir William Holford, would review progress, and introducing legislation in August for a commission based on McCallum's recommendations. Menzies kept up his own pressure. On the eve of the joint committee's first meeting, he announced that the policy-making core of the Department of Defence (some 1100 officers) would be transferred from Melbourne by 1959. His department and Cabinet repeatedly sent back to Fairhall draft legislation until it was satisfied that the proposed National Capital Development Commission (NCDC) would have genuine independence.[34]

Jostled along, Fairhall introduced five-year planning for Canberra. Progress was soon evident: 654 'dwelling units' (houses and flats) were completed in 1956–57, in contrast to 454 the previous year. Holford arrived, walked the site for two wintry weeks, garnered advice, and declared that while Canberra might be 'one of the best experimental towns in the world', it remained only 'on the verge of becoming a city' and well short of the 'quality' defining a league of 'federal capitals' including Washington, Ottawa and Pretoria, and those in prospect for Brazil, Nyasaland and the West Indies. An old design had been 'hanging over its head' for too long. The city must embrace trends in modern urban planning and the functions appropriate to 'a cultural and administrative centre'. It must become a 'tertiary city': one which would express Australia's achievements in 'surplus wealth' in its landscaping, entertainment, shopping, arts, enlightened causes and expertise in the corporate as well as public sectors.[35]

Holford envisioned a 'chain reaction' unleashed by crucial initiatives, beginning with the consolidation of the parliamentary triangle and the full realisation of Griffin's lake scheme, and addressing the void at the city's heart by siting a permanent parliament house on its southern shoreline, a hub of 'active' government. Next, a 'first-rate civic auditorium' should vouch for a city able to attract 'prestige' in performance and quality in the services available to residents and visitors. Canberra must also become a 'fully motorised town', its suburbs feeding into an 'American "freeway" system', enabling 'fast and frequent' cars to connect private lives, in 'frankly picturesque' neighbourhoods, to work and leisure. This was textbook civic modernity, over which Holford ventured to place a 'Royal Pavilion' – an Australian residence for the monarch, but more constantly a 'magnet' from which a national culture would radiate – to ensure Canberra remained observant of its fundamental loyalties and traditions. Critics have argued that Holford's vision kept the 'frame' of Griffin's vision while 'throwing away the picture' of organic urbanism. Some such reinvention, however, was inevitable, for where Canberra had once been envisaged as realising the best in its citizens, now it was judged as a kind of test of their capacities for citizenship. As Sir William departed, he regretted that he had seen in the capital 'a tendency in some areas for residents to take less care of their gardens and homes': they must learn to do better.[36]

In October 1957, while Holford completed his report in London, Menzies established McCallum's NCDC to 'undertake and carry out the planning, development and construction of the City of Canberra as the National Capital of the Commonwealth'. A statutory authority, the Commission was required only to advise its minister of its plans and policies, and had control over its own finances and freedom from the practical tasks of local administration. Land would be transferred to it, transformed by it, and then returned for management to the Department of the Interior – a relationship hardly flattering to the latter. The NCDC's first commissioner, (Sir) John Overall, brought an authority won first in military command, refined in political negotiation as the Commonwealth's chief architect, and proven when he began by staring down Menzies' attempt to insert a government representative as one of his two associate commissioners. Overall ensured that those appointed to its initially small 'task force'-based staff of 33 would develop an integrated expertise in planning, engineering and design that was new to Australia. Unsuccessful in winning from Treasury a guaranteed five-year budget, the NCDC nonetheless functioned within such a discipline, setting targets for itself and regularly assessing its performance against them. Many staff were energised by this approach, although some felt uncomfortably stretched beyond habits set in more straitened times or badgered for results (the commissioner was known as

'Haversack Jack – always on your back'). 'Pig's arse' was the retort from Bill McLaren, as Secretary of the Interior, when Overall sought his support. But it was understood that if an NCDC issue found its way to Cabinet, the Prime Minister would take its side – and Overall proved astute in cultivating that favour, ensuring that whenever possible Menzies was affirmed in a sense of Canberra being his child.[37]

The 'monstrosity' the NCDC inherited was itemised in the first of many studies it commissioned, setting a pattern of research-led planning. Around 10 per cent of Canberra's residents lived in hostels; a quarter were under 10 years of age; the number under 21 had grown by 27 per cent in two years; the incidence of traffic accidents was increasing twice as fast as population – a swathe of facts accumulated to define issues of imbalance, long exacerbated by the absence of any master plan, and needing comprehensive action. Holford provided a model, but its implementation remained to be determined. To meet the immediate pressures for housing and related utilities would require – Overall judged – 95 per cent of available resources. The remainder would be carefully targeted to other priorities. A 'continuing and stable program' of investment was developed to court private interests and public confidence: early initiatives included clearer guidelines on land use, more frequent auctions of leases, exploration of new forms of building finance, a preference for larger construction contracts and for the 'packaged' provision of all services in one operation. These systems won the confidence of a new generation of large-scale property developers such as Dick Dusseldorp of Civic and Civil and, as of 1958, Lend Lease, who gained their own prestige through association with the capital, and enabled others, such as Jennings, to complete contracts lagging by nearly 10 years. 'True designers, economisers of land and works, strictly practical experts', according to Stretton, the NCDC invested in plant and equipment to increase the efficiency (if also the wages) of labour, and tailored plans for houses and other buildings to lessen demand on trades or materials in short supply.[38]

The Commission's imprint was clearest in the suburbs designed to meet the press of population, now calculated as growing steadily at 10–12 per cent each year and to reach 100 000 by the early 1970s. The first of the Defence transfers delivered 240 families and

120 single employees in January 1959; in 1960 Canberra reached its historic peak of 14 per cent growth in one year. Suburbs designed to take this infusion – Dickson, Downer and Watson to the north, Hughes and Curtin in the south – showed an evolution of 'neighbourhood unit' principles: clear boundaries between arterial roads and internal distributions to slow traffic and ensure that no facility (preschool, school, shop or clinic) was more than a half-hour prampush from homes. These schemes also showed a 'hesitant' move, noted by Stretton, towards a 'social mix' of incomes, backgrounds and family units, and the recognition of the needs of mothers at home and the safety of children on streets. Groups of 'bachelor flats' were more integrated with suburbs; precincts of mixed occupancies in Red Hill, facing shared parkland, were another innovation; a group of five different housing types, designed by the prominent architect Sydney Ancher for Northbourne Avenue in 1962, were – as historians Tim Reeves and Alan Roberts note – a remarkable exercise in proportion, placement and massing. Establishing a Homes Advisory Service, in 1960 the Commission convened a 'Modern Homes' exhibition to promote 'open' family living.[39]

These innovations were also intended to be among several inducements to increase the (for the NCDC) alarmingly low proportion of privately built housing, which was linked to monotonous streetscapes, untended gardens, and disengaged residents. But the scale of the Defence transfers, at a time when the waiting list for public housing anywhere in the city was in excess of 4000, added to conflicting messages and objectives. The argument ran that relocation of this department was so important in building momentum that nothing should retard it – and steadily the trucks arrived, laden with each Defence family's goods, delivered direct to new homes, while others watched and waited. With these origins, Alan Foskett contends, the purpose-designed Defence suburb of Campbell, adjacent to the War Memorial, developed a 'caste' of its own, and a certain social rigidity in its transplanted military and bureaucratic hierarchies. The construction of the Defence precinct of office buildings nearby at Russell, around the American eagle, compounded this impression: another prominent, privileged military stamp on the city; another political imperative.[40]

FEW INDUSTRIES AND TOO MUCH INDUSTRY

Despite these tensions, the 'civic composition' of the city continued to evolve. McCallum regarded Canberra's 'Garden City' aspect as its 'most important feature', and the NCDC readily adapted to it. The ornamentality of the Weston inheritance was moderated in the 1950s by an informal, utilitarian approach, a general trend in Australia landscaping being applied afresh across a growing city. Using eucalypts more extensively, testing hybrid forms, Lindsay Pryor reducing his 'planting palette', aiming at 'fewer and larger open areas' and 'green belt' effects. Holford identified the combined effect as 'picturesque', and it served well the modern suburban forms NCDC planners began weaving over their sites. Perceptions and uses of Canberra's environment adapted to these scales, the pedestrian in the suburbs, the car moving between them and beyond. The 'motorised town' allowed journeys further afield for recreation that had once been improvised closer to home. Into the 1960s, for example, Thredbo's and Perisher Valley's downhill slopes began luring Canberra skiers away from their inter-war rustic runs at Mount Franklin. Spreading subdivisions by the beaches on the South Coast also attracted increasing, regular numbers of Canberrans away for weekends and holidays.[41]

In contrast to the suburbs, the population of the Australian Capital Territory's rural districts remained static through the 1950s. A soil conservation council established in 1947 offered advice on the remediation of extensive areas of degraded land, recommending pine plantations and 'wood lots' for areas past repair after nearly a century of farming. Views of extensive erosion worried politicians as they flew in and out, but lessees had protests of their own regarding the insecurity arising from the reduction of their rights in some cases to 10-year or even quarterly terms, or from facing the immediate resumption of properties with the revival of a land acquisition program that had largely lapsed between the wars. Some of the most damaged land was projected for inclusion in the 'new town' for Yarralumla Creek (Woden Valley), where keen gardeners would soon begin importing precious topsoil and setting sprinklers to lawns. Some noticed a subtle softening in the 'micro-climate' as they settled. Whatever links might once have existed between country and city were eased aside as the territory's National Parks Association, formed in 1960 among Canberra's scientists and academics, coordinated a campaign for the conservation of areas where grazing threatened 'natural heritage' or which were valued more for managed recreation. Developing its 'aesthetic', the NCDC decided that the 'existing grey-brown colour of the landscape should predominate', edging from lighter greens in the city to darker shades at its boundaries. Large areas of 'treeless grazing land', it argued, represented 'an urgent need for major landscape planning' on the city's margins. 'Aggregations of small holdings' might contribute to this process; the farms of the past were a more dubious prospect.[42]

Canberra's environment was itself becoming an expression of 'surplus value'. Not all, however, was in surplus. A drought in 1953–54 led to water restrictions and the introduction of charges for the domestic use of a resource which had once seemed abundant. By 1955, when residents were running twice as much through their taps as Sydney, Melbourne or Adelaide, it was clear that the city needed at least one more dam on the Cotter River. In the swings of Canberra's climate, the following year's flood allowed residents to envisage again the feature they would gain if ever the Molonglo became a lake. While NCDC officers, Stretton noted, 'ascribe their most outstanding achievements to the land rather than themselves', such modesty should not obscure the extent of its transformation at their hands.[43]

For all that, as an extended *Women's Weekly* feature of 1957 observed, Canberra was becoming 'home'. It was especially valued as 'a great place to have children' – and plenty were being had, leading demographers to see Canberra as 'a population of families' by 1961. The city centre might be ragged, but well-serviced neighbourhoods put a premium on casual sociability and volunteer support for many services, for sport, leisure and care. Still – as the example of Campbell suggests – suburban 'mix' could not be guaranteed, and the burdens of isolation often went unarticulated at the time. Early enquiries on the need for psychiatric services in the territory reflected distinct patterns emerging among 'a "floating" population, among whom were large numbers of junior public servants who went heavily into debt "to keep up with the Joneses", and of

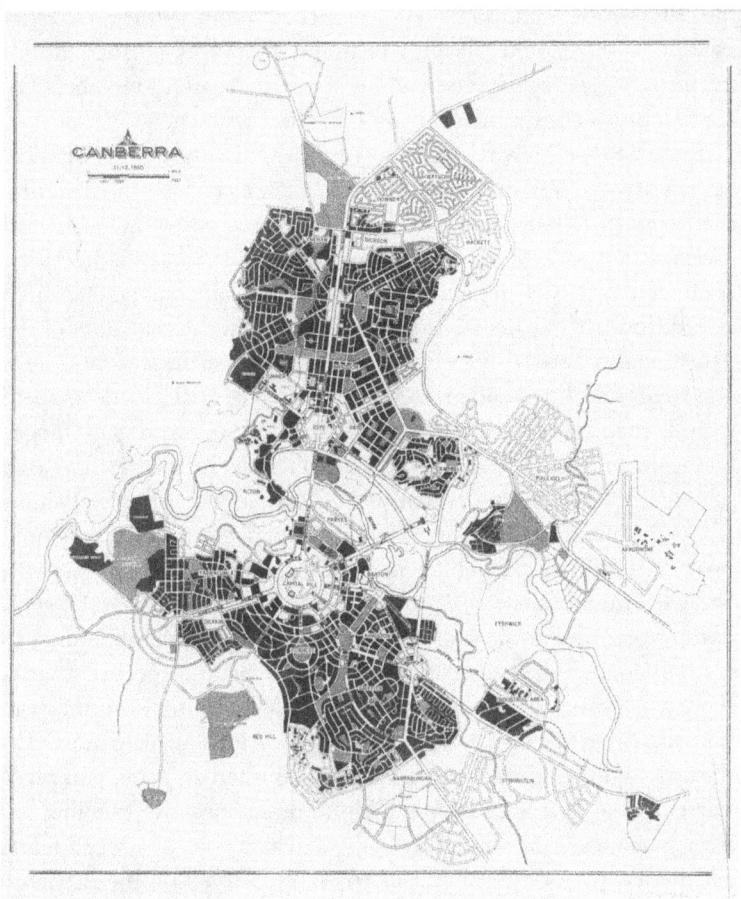

Map 3: Canberra in 1960: the NCDC's work in progress – still experimenting with urban form and growth options. (Reproduced with permission of the National Library of Australia)

young mothers deprived of extended family support'. As children grew, they became restless with a local lack of opportunities: the BWIU protested that Canberra had plenty of jobs for labourers, but few opportunities for apprentices. In 1959, the NCDC conceded the 'sociological problems' likely to arise if 'teenage groups' continued to lack opportunities for employment. By 1963, a report prepared for the Good Neighbour Council noted that a high percentage of the children of immigrants left a city they found culturally barren as soon as they could – leaving behind parents lacking such mobility. Into the 1960s a phenomenon reported as 'migrant melancholia' seemed prevalent, particularly among older women.[44]

Yet, as Hope Hewitt observed in 1961, not only did Canberra have more children and trees per head than elsewhere in Australia, there were also 'more societies' (albeit many still showing a gendered division: a men's 'association'; a women's 'auxiliary'). In 1950, a film festival was inaugurated; from 1955, an annual National Eisteddfod. An expansion of venues meant that the centrality of the Albert Hall to social life – to meetings, dances, presentation balls and so on – declined and more selective, diverse activities developed: from jazz to bush dancing and rock and roll to 'old-time'. Daughter of a pioneering Council for Scientific and Industrial Research scientist, wife of a senior Treasury official, and lecturer in English at CUC, Hewitt herself exemplified the opportunities the city could provide. Her own particular interest, Canberra Repertory Society, had been funded since 1953 to employ a full-time producer, its standards rising above 'slick drawing-room comedy' and extending to commissioning the rising composer, Peter Sculthorpe, to write a score for a satire of Canberra's fetishes. This was fun. Voluntarism was also often all there was to meet a need. Ann Dalgarno arrived as the wife of an engineer in 1948 and established an agency to place nurses in the homes of people with no other support. Tackling her own loneliness, she joined the Liberal Party, ran as its candidate for the territory's federal seat in 1958, and served on the Advisory Council after 1959. The National Council of Women – prominently public service wives – similarly organised emergency housekeeping services and clothing exchanges, lobbied against the closure of shops on Saturdays for those without access to transport during the week, and provided the NCDC with forthright advice on housing needs and design. Much was achieved by such community initiative and advocacy, including educational services and residential care for disabled children (the Koomarri organisation) and for the elderly (the Goodwin Home).[45]

Canberra by the early 1960s, then, was striking a new balance between its 'capital' and 'city' status. All indicators of progress were relished, even a 'price war' between grocery chains in 1957 which showed small-town custom challenged by modern competition. In 1960, Overall convinced Lend Lease to construct Australia's first three-storey, air-conditioned shopping mall in Civic, along with eight multi-storey office block sites – the coming of a 'business centre'. While one department store had to build its own hostel to attract experienced staff, that at least was an investment in the future it was prepared to make.[46]

Nor was it simply a question of material advance. Ecclesiastical appointments reflected a recognition of Canberra's particular claims. Eris O'Brien became the second Catholic Archbishop of Canberra and Goulburn in 1953, and by 1955 made the capital his official residence. Louvain-educated (rather than in Rome), O'Brien was a respected historian of colonial Australia, and for a short time his auxiliary was Guilford Young – at his appointment in 1948 the youngest to hold that office and of equally formidable intelligence, trenchantly applied to current affairs. Such eminence, however, also needed to accommodate the demands of what was then Australia's fastest growing archdiocese. During O'Brien's tenure to 1967, the Australian Capital Territory expanded from one to 10 parishes, and in this process the provision of education became a pressing issue. Catholics still formed a much higher percentage of Canberra's population (31 per cent) than the national average (25 per cent), and new arrivals looked to schools not only to sustain their faith but also to build community, and to secure influence. These pressures fostered self-declared 'revolutionary' initiatives, such as the establishment in 1957 of a girls' school to serve the expanding northern suburbs, which was to be staffed by nuns from four teaching orders. Such innovations served the church's swelling congregations but also pushed a difficult question firmly onto the government's agenda.[47]

In 1956, in recognition of expectations that transferred public servants would have the same choice of education for their children in Canberra as in Melbourne or Sydney, the Menzies government moved to break with the convention of keeping public funds out of private schools. Bitter sectarian debate in the past explained this convention, and still brooded around it. In the case of Canberra, it was argued – most forcibly by O'Brien – an exception could be made by the Commonwealth without infringing settled practice in the states. But as a precedent, the move aroused alarm among secularists and strict Protestants. Sectarianism always had its own instincts in a public-service town – who would gain advancement in the new careers of government? The issue of state aid forced it into the open. The controversy fell heaviest on the shoulders of O'Brien's Anglican counterpart, who faced the 'wicked dilemma' of declining funding for his own schools on a matter of principle, or opting instead to accede to the shared need to boost standards in a city strong in expectations but short of funds.[48]

Already a prominent campaigner for social welfare, Ernest Burgmann had been appointed Anglican bishop of Goulburn, a diocese including Canberra, in 1934, but – like O'Brien – gravitated towards the prospect of the national capital as a site from which to engineer a better Australia, and to circles of high-minded liberals there. In 1946, Burgmann had also relocated to Canberra; in 1950 his diocese was renamed 'Canberra and Goulburn'. Even before the uproar over state aid, Canberra's politics had become a little less congenial for him: his questioning of orthodoxies in national and international affairs, most prominently after his 1954 collaboration with ANU and CUC academics in offering an alternative view of communist insurgency in Indo-China, meant Burgmann felt the sudden temperature drop of Canberra's Cold War. State aid again tested his congregation's tolerance, and its coming might have done something for ecumenicalism and equity in Canberra but ultimately little to ease the marking out of territory. At least, in 1957, he was also able to gain the compensation of establishing St Mark's Library in 1957, as the foundation for a national theological centre, and ideally for a national theology.[49]

O'Brien and Burgmann's stature accorded with ideas of the capital, but Hector Harrison, minister to Presbyterians, arguably cut more of a figure in its community. From a Salvation Army background and ministry in Melbourne's industrial suburbs, Harrison liked the call to higher service he associated with Canberra, sharing it with the senior public servants still prominent in his congregation. He had been summoned to the deathbed of John Curtin as a trusted companion; he approved of eliminating advertising from a city which should uphold a 'sense of normal cleanliness'; and protested at any co-opting of the sacred to give solemnity to affairs of state or the military. Such uprightness earned respect in a city still seeking authenticity – even if Harrison opposed the 'Continental Sunday' which he saw spreading like paspalum into the capital's soul: the church-sanctioned dances, excursions and sporting competitions increasingly being held on the week's one day of reflection. What was Canberra coming to?[50]

'History has not been kind to the development of Canberra', the NCDC noted in 1961, but the future was looking better: the city was acquiring 'character'. The pace of public service transfers continued, and diversified. The Tariff Board moved up in 1962; the central office of the Department of Social Services was to follow. These two agencies represented much in the expanding agenda of national government. Within the ranks of the bureaucracy there were also pulses of change. An inquiry reporting in 1959 urged the creation of a senior 'administrative civil service', in which higher levels of education, 'equality of opportunity' (including lifting the marriage bar for women) and capacities for executive leadership would be recognised. These recommendations met a cool political reception – the government was not ready for an open embrace of change. But 'slowly and unspectacularly' many were implemented. Still heading the Public Service Board, Dunk was noted as driving a process which would 'bring about the elimination of his own species, the man who rises to the head of a Department without the benefit of a University education'. Canberra would, inevitably, show the influence of such a change.[51]

In the 'chain reaction' Holford envisaged, those building the city and working in its offices were being joined by those providing them services, from supermarkets to schools. In 1954, 47 per cent of the population were public servants; in 1963 – even though another 2400 officers made the move that year – their proportion was 35 per cent. The NCDC welcomed the 'intelligent, critical interest' a more diverse population was showing in the city around them. Critics could still lament 'the eerie, smug self-satisfaction of the Canberra mind', fearing that the city's spiral of 'few industries and too much industry' might only become more insular, and insulated, in this growth. But they equally noted that those spirals were including the representatives of national industry and pressure groups, commercial interests and lobbyists, who were lifting the game of politics to new levels of professionalism. A fresh generation of journalists, such as the *Financial Review*'s Maxwell Newton – a former Treasury officer – was giving an intellectual edge to the Press Gallery, engaging in a hard-headed analysis of policies. Even Canberra's social life began to play a more active part in those processes. Its circles were worked by figures such as 'Keith Newman, the brilliantly effective secretary of the Returned Services League', handsomely headquartered in Campbell, who – with his wife – missed no chance to exercise his 'inherent political nous'. The pressure of such networking meant that public servants could be heard complaining at having to rise to new demands of accountability, especially after Menzies nearly lost the election in 1961 and seemed jolted to a determination that Canberra had better catch up with the pace of national change.[52]

The ANU continued to provide a symbol of such transformations. Into the 1950s the university supported research of an unprecedented range and depth – in medical and physical sciences, economics, demography, history, anthropology and much else. But its privileges did not lift it above political scrutiny, whether of the ideological leanings of appointees or not-so-subtle messages about how to keep the 'warm eye' of the Prime Minister when it came to funding. Internal realignments were equally indicative of change. As its historians Stephen Foster and Margaret Varghese argue, the ANU's balance between the pure and applied in research, and the need to get the 'right *type* of man' (usually) became an even more demanding task as the university grew and formalities grew with it. When W.K. Hancock, an eminent Australian historian who had once before turned down association with the university because it might veer to 'mediocrities', returned in 1956 to take up the directorship of the Research School of Social Sciences, he made it clear that any overarching 'program of research' – driven by purposes beyond those of scholarship – must be rejected: academic integrity mattered more than voguish ideas of relevance. Marcus Oliphant resigned his headship of Physical Sciences in 1963 precisely because of such a lack of unity, purpose or direction.[53]

Whatever these differences over direction, the ANU had unquestionable standing, could exert influence of its own, and was an object of interest. ANU scientists led in lobbying for the founding in Canberra in 1954 of the Australian Academy of Science, with a Royal Charter, and by 1959 its space-age copper-domed headquarters, designed by Roy Grounds, was an arresting addition to the city. Ideas of 'service' offended ANU purists when their university was forced to amalgamate with the CUC in 1960, to save money, to bring an element of balance to the provision of higher education in the city, and to keep in the Prime Minister's favour. The amalgamation also provided an opportunity to lock in place a council with a significantly large proportion of government nominees, just to make sure the university behaved.[54]

Alongside this institutional realignment, the ANU was undeniably a part of Canberra's distinctive community. For R.F. Brissenden, a lecturer in English, 'the university cut through the cake, through the bureaucracy and through the various layers' that defined the city – and not only in the serial parties that compensated for isolation. As Manning Clark relaxed his first impressions of its 'provincial savagery', the capital became – as Mark McKenna observes – 'an experiment in creating a national culture' that paralleled his own work re-envisaging Australian history. Amid much else, Heinz Arndt applied himself as an economist to assessing the city's capacity to fund and govern itself, to identify areas of need among its poor and its immigrants, to stimulate a debate about a politics that could leave old ideologies behind, and for policies that would better reflect Australia's future as 'a small, rich industrial country'. Such thinking was not peculiar to Canberra, but its intensity there was striking.[55]

By 1963, much that would define Canberra – its culture and cultures – was in place. But its form remained in fragments, needing coherence. In September 1963, the valves had been closed on the dam built at Yarralumla, at the point where Griffin had proposed to form his 'lake scheme' over 50 years earlier. Long debated, this scheme was deemed by the NCDC as 'essential' to the integration of the city. It had ultimately required direct Prime Ministerial intervention to override Treasury objections to its expense. The valves shut, people waited, but the months were dry; the lake was 'painfully slow' in filling. Then it rained and the Limestone Plains disappeared. Walking across the valley to their laboratories one morning, two ANU professors, Colin Courtice and Bede Morris – world experts on the lymphatic system – noted the water level rising. Returning home in the evening, they found the river running steadily over the bridge. 'Like two schoolboys we took off our shoes and socks, rolled our trousers up and waded across, shoes in one hand and briefcases in the other', rejoicing that they would be the last people to take that route. A simple moment of reflection. With the official naming of Lake Burley Griffin in October 1964, Canberra could no longer pass as a 'monstrosity', even if its 'quiet revolution' was far from over.[56]

6

Quiet revolution

IT NEEDS BRAINS

'If you want to see the Australian ruling class', Frank Clune advises in a travelogue of 1964, 'go to Canberra' – the 'air of life there is superannuation'. Wry views of the capital were not new, but Clune hinted at a fresh attitude. The city could be teased with grudging respect, but no longer ridiculed as irrelevant. 'There is a dairying industry in Canberra', he quipped: 'milking the taxpayers. It needs brains to keep those poor cows contented'. While resentful of the 'honey-pot' of the Commonwealth Treasury, Clune was 'thunderstruck' by the 'figure-juggling juggernaut' of the new computing system at the Bureau of Census and Statistics, where trends in Australia's growth were rendered intelligible in seconds. This was useful knowledge. Donald Horne might have regarded Canberra as a place of 'exile' in *The Lucky Country*, also published in 1964: an 'administrative garrison' – but his eye was on the businessmen who were failing to make the most of prosperity. Canberra's function was different, narrower, but in that range showing signs at last of a self-perpetuating pattern. 'Nothing is vulgar here; everything is genteel', Clune jibed. But even in these attributes Canberra did not belong to its residents: 'it belongs to the nation'.[1]

By 1964, Canberra's experiment had passed from a test of viability to trialling forms of living from which all Australians might learn. The National Capital Development Commission (NCDC) judged not only that the surges and stumbles of the city's past were over, but also that a steady state of expansion at 9 per cent a year would push beyond old targets: to 250 000 people in 15 years; perhaps 500 000 by 1990. A formula of 'coherent growth' was in place, expressed in a sequence of 'new town' developments that would ensure all who were drawn into its dynamic gained what Australian cities had so far failed to deliver: simultaneous progress in the assets of urbanity and the amenity of suburbs. Beyond its claims as a capital, the NCDC's chief planner, Peter Harrison, argued that Canberra modelled the kind of regional centre Australia desperately needed – cities that drew energy from 'think industries': education, communications, services. Why, Harrison wondered, set any limit to what such growth might encompass?[2]

Planners could be expected to make this case, but Canberra received other endorsements. Bought by Sydney-based Fairfax and Sons, the *Canberra Times* rebadged itself as a 'national newspaper', to be taken seriously alongside other metropolitan dailies. Launched from Canberra in the same year, Rupert Murdoch's *Australian* – even more defiantly national in coverage – began by demanding 'greater maturity' from a country that had yet to appreciate that the great boon of full employment was not in profits but in the welfare of 'the community at large'. Drawing on contributors reflecting the 'broad outlook' of the capital, the *Australian* worked with Canberra as a symbol of these new opportunities.

Its first edition began a series of profiles of Commonwealth departments, commencing with External Affairs. The article opened with the image of smartly dressed men being dropped at their offices by wives in dressing gowns, who then sped back to the suburbs. It went on to explore other ironies in a city where an 'extraordinarily highly professionalised' corps of public servants wrestled to transform a bureaucracy still locked in inter-departmental rivalry, starved of 'men of ability', and without resources for 'long-term planning'. This, surely, must change. The paper's first architecture feature dealt with a 'solar house' built for a Canberra academic. An early science feature surveyed the Mt Stromlo observatory. Amid extensive coverage of international news – the need for a 'hard line' in South-East Asia, and for 'advancement' in Papua New Guinea – Canberra nestled as a centre of interest for discriminating journalism. As the paper observed of the public buildings taking shape around Lake

Burley Griffin, the capital was evolving into a city that looked good from any side.[3]

Returning after a decade to see what had become of the capital he had so formatively surveyed in 1957, Sir William Holford chose 'acceleration' as the word most expressing its progress, 'not only in local projects but in national policies'. By the end of the 1960s, the NCDC envisaged a city unique in its 'social and cultural innovation', its opportunities for enabling private 'choice' in the context of carefully managed 'growth and change', and its scope for public participation in those processes. That was the spirit of the times.[4]

If these were golden years, they were soon to change. Into the 1970s, these same elements – growth, sophistication, professionalism, choice – began generating their own tensions. It was not simply that national prosperity faltered as, correspondingly, did the local curve of population (tracking to 226 000 by 1980; 282 000 by 1990). The nature of Canberra's experiment also came into question, not as the extravagance of the past but as a series of assumptions about what government should do, and a community expect. The election of the Labor Party in 1972 brought into federal government ministers who spoke of using the capital as a 'laboratory' for reform. But the city that had become central to the 'contentment' of the herd also became more complex in its role as a restless mood spread. By 1975, Canberra's gentility was tested in the unprecedented political drama of the dismissal of the Whitlam government. Even its honey pot soured as Treasury brooded over the nation with a message of stern discipline. Canberra had perhaps come as close as it would to being an ideal city, but the 1970s exposed more starkly than ever the contradictions present in its desires.

FINGER-TIP CONTROL

A series of decisions made around 1963 – 50 years into Canberra's history – set a fresh course for the city, not least in the increasing confidence with which the NCDC defined its tasks. The pace of expansion still threw up challenges, including a spike in premiums paid at land auctions in 1962, leading to restrictions to assist those making their first bid for a home, but also marking a point at which private investment – whether in housing or in commercial development – at last exceeded public. The waiting list for leased housing began to fall, and some of the £14 million spent by the Commission in 1963–64 went into planning or constructing more of the trappings of a capital: an office block for Treasury; an impressive, Parthenon-like National Library by the lake, to replace decades of stingy provision for a collection that extended beyond a mandatory lodgement of everything published in Australia to encompass major historical holdings; a mint; and a theatre centre, in itself an innovative mix of large- and community-scale performance spaces. Worthy civic intent prevailed in the design of these ventures as well as their purpose – and around them the form of the capital, if still incomplete and unresolved in scale, became clearer. In 1968, the visiting American urban planner, Edmund Bacon, declared that 'Canberra confirms beyond anything else I know the dominant importance of space design'.[5]

The Commission's executives would later be irritated by their critics' view that they were, in those years, captured by the ideology of the private car, but it is hard to underestimate the extent to which functions premised on that unit – that ultimate 'symbol of modernism', as historian Graeme Davison argues – began to determine the city and its spaces. The car, Peter Harrison maintained, was just one expression of the priority the Commission placed on the convenience to which Canberrans had a claim, especially since their planners enjoyed the great advantage of 'finger-tip control' over land for the entire city area, and had won the capacity to lock down ahead of need precisely those modernist benefits: mobility, access, efficiency, and – pre-eminently – choice. But, even in those elements, the car prescribed the paradigm within which such benefits would be enjoyed and distributed. And that paradigm would prove one of the most initially attractive, but intractable, aspects of the capital.[6]

Bold projections of Canberra's growth inevitably posed the question of *how* the city should expand. The model of the 'neighbourhood unit', adopted in the late 1950s, was steadily refined with that blend of imaginative and practical expertise that, by 1970, so impressed Hugh Stretton. By now its formulas were clear: in each unit children should be able to walk from home to school in less than half an hour; viable schools would serve units of around 4000 people, with population densities recognising the overwhelming preference for detached family housing. Within each neighbourhood there should be a hierarchy of roads optimising safety for residents but connecting outwards to enable smooth access to shopping and work centres – hence those shuttling wives in dressing gowns. These neighbourhoods might generate a certain 'sameness' in house design and siting, but the sociological compensations were judged to outweigh the aesthetic. In time, the homes people made, it was hoped, would add variety to the houses they moved into. Canberra's neighbourboods, as geographer G.J.R. Linge judged at the time, were literally the nurseries of an energetic city, driven by 'expectation and aspiration'.[7]

These nurseries were already pushing at the edges of existing plans and provisions. By 1960, the Commission was designing a new town to the south-west, in the Woden Valley; within five years another, Weston Creek, was envisaged in the haste of meeting need, and not quite integrated into the road sequencing planners cherished. The task remained to achieve consistency and coherence across a sequence of such towns, each serving as a 'satellite' rather than as a competitor to Canberra's 'civic centre', and congruent with the functions of the parliamentary core which was, after all, their source of gravity.

In 1961, the NCDC commissioned the first of a series of studies which placed the concept of 'free traffic flow' as central to meeting this challenge. Turning to pioneering models of American traffic engineering, the Commission embraced 'transport corridor planning'. This model had its own transcendent modernist appeal: a compression of distance, as Davison notes, to a minimum of time, and an ethos of fluidity, speed and convenience. In it, roads determined land use, and the first report from the American consultant Alan Voorhees, delivered in 1963, proposed a system that would disperse as much as possible the points at which 'traffic uses' were 'generated' while 'absorbing' to the greatest degree the major flows between them. A second report, in 1966, proposed a system potentially serving a million people in the form of a 'Y-plan': one freeway spine stretching 19 kilometres south and two stretching north across the New South Wales border. It was an arresting concept, with a graphic power to match the Griffins', but with geometry now determined by the ease of private, mechanised movement over

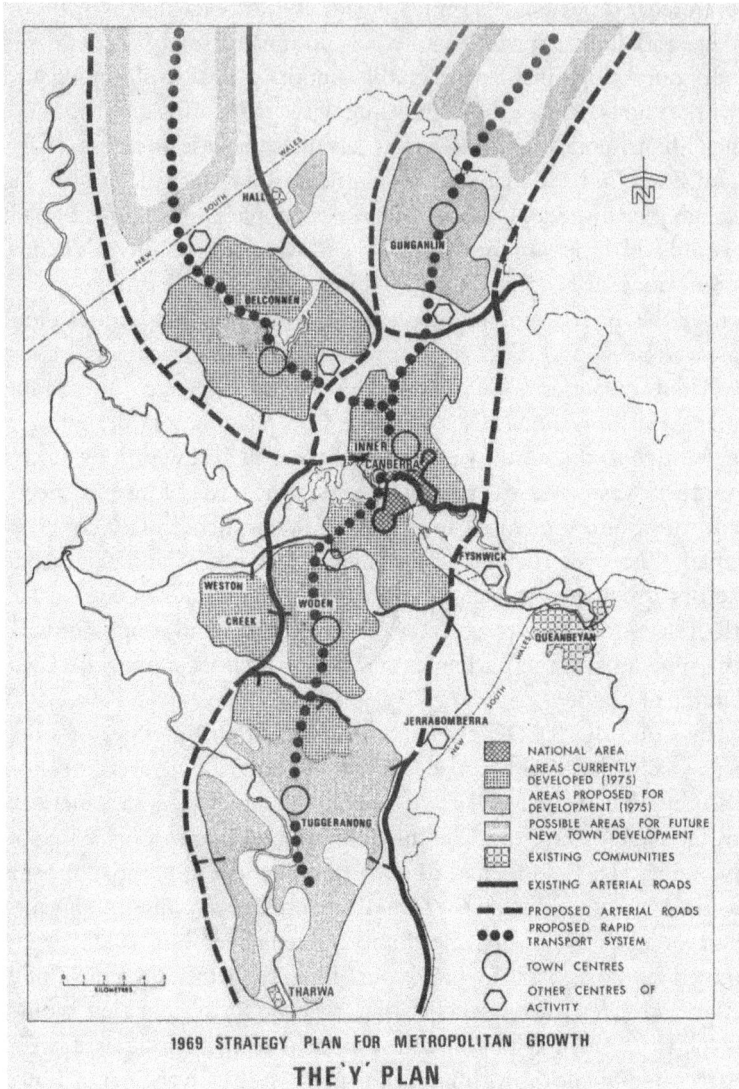

Map 4: A formulation of the 'Y-Plan'. (Reproduced courtesy of the National Capital Authority © Commonwealth Copyright. All rights reserved)

extended space rather than by the arrangement of lives within an organic ideal.

A series of towns could be arranged along these spines: each of around 100 000–120 000 people; each with substantial autonomy in their balance of 'living' and 'activity' areas; each fundamentally committed to the evolutions in the neighbourhood model while interconnected by rapid transit routes. The Y-plan, like Griffin's axes, was perfectly adapted to Canberra's alignment of valleys, and sensitive to its landscape: but it enshrined movement more than symbolism. It was also a supreme statement of the NCDC's aspiration for control over land and the ordering of lives: it was a formula, a flow, an algorithm with a logic of its own.[8]

In itself, this scheme did not exclusively privilege the private car. Among its enthusiasts, Holford urged that it presented an opportunity to seize what 'inventions' might come in a fusion of a residential collector and express bus services, graduating from neighbourhood to satellite to centre. The NCDC did not share that vision. Canberrans, Harrison argued, were set in '"car reliant" travel habits': that they owned 70 per cent more cars per capita than the rest of the nation proved the point, as did the decline in usage of existing bus services. Low-density neighbourhood units would also make it hard for public transport to gain patrons sufficient to cover costs. And in a city where so much care had gone into perfecting the suburb, why would people want to wait in streets when they could propel themselves quickly home? As Patrick Troy and Noel Butlin observed in 1971, a 'active population...on higher than average incomes' had generated a style and standard of living that effectively 'demanded' easy movement by car, and tolerated associated costs and risks. (Canberra's first traffic lights were introduced in 1965 in recognition of a remarkably high rate of accidents – unhelpfully, a fault kept them all on red at first.) Even the graphics used to promote the Commission's vision, as urban historian Karl Fischer has noted, seemed 'almost cynical' in their scattering of pedestrians and the isolation of bus lanes down the middle of purposeful dual carriageways.[9]

By 1970, in a weighty manifesto, *Tomorrow's Canberra*, the NCDC celebrated a 'dispersed, polynucleated structure' which 'would favour a younger population seeking increased space

Figure 19: Modern planning, modern citizens: Woden Town Centre, Health Centre, Library and office tower. (Reproduced with permission of the ACT Heritage Library, ACT Administration Collection. Photographer: Rae Trindal)

standards and opportunities for enlarged social responsibilities'. Since 1966, the 'new town' of Belconnen had developed rapidly on the first of spur of the northern Y; by the early 1970s planning was well advanced for Tuggeranong to the south. All aspects of the city – its shape, experiential dimensions, environmental awareness – centred on an image of a car-reliant citizen moving between these satellites. 'Canberra will be a long, thin city with the countryside everywhere at hand', *Tomorrow's Canberra* projected, although adding that in traversing those distances, transport corridors must be 'designed to give a sense of orientation and continuity to the driver' who might otherwise lack a sense of where they were, where they were going. Edmund Bacon saw it as 'proper' that a pioneering nation should have a capital no longer closed in circles but embracing 'straight connectors' reaching effortlessly over 'great sweeps of open space'. This pioneering, however, was now of a suburban frontier, and of land that seemed infinite.[10]

The first new staging post, Woden, set the scene. The town centre trialled precepts in civic design: government and commercial office space initially for 5000, ideally bringing 'jobs to people' rather than vice-versa; a mall-based shopping complex; a 'recreation precinct' of library, health and community services – all centred on a pedestrian campus. Medium-density housing adjoined the site; a services sector for motor, building and wholesaling trades was added in 1970; a nearby community hospital in 1973. The breadth of the project strained NCDC expertise, but it was constructed expeditiously, drawing on generous Commonwealth funding and private investment. Every week through 1972 workers poured a floor of a 26-storey office tower, paid for by an insurance company – both elements being a remarkable planning departure. The town centre's concentration of people led in 1968 to the introduction of an express bus service to Civic, and in 1972 an interchange to coordinate suburban bus services. But the centre still remained essentially an island amid parking areas provided for the majority who used it, and who left at close of business. It reflected the strained balance a new town had to strike.[11]

Still, Stretton argued, Woden in general exemplified 'the Canberra method' of integrated planning. A tussle over parkland zoning revealed residual class tensions over who should be encouraged into whose space; a flood, killing seven as it surged across low-lying intersections in the valley in 1971, raised questions about whether development had been too rapid. But NCDC planners rejoiced that, in general, residents coming into the valley showed 'healthy signs' of enacting a community in soon forming clubs and sporting teams. The engineering seemed to have worked.[12]

Less pleasing was 'the tombstone park' of the parliamentary triangle, where much remained unsolved. The NCDC was restless to finalise the building of a permanent Parliament House, the 'major element' around which the precinct must take shape. Assuming Holford's nomination of a lakeside site would prevail, the Commission's vision (intimated in flagpoles and plantings of gorse bush) was of an intensively built 'great theatre-in-the-round': a 'monumental plaza' (parking underneath), onto which parliament and government buildings would face. An imposing uniformity in style would be presided over on Capital Hill not by Holford's tribute to the monarchy, but by a 'National Centre', comprising a coronet of pavilions devoted to recording 'achievements' in 'the history, natural resources...economic development...native life,...and fine art'. This concept, imbued with strengthened symbols of Australian politics and culture, was also an attempt to cope with the daunting scale bequeathed by Griffin in which, as Roger Johnson, the Commission's leading architect, observed, buildings could have 'the cut-out quality of targets on a shooting range'. But such integration was upset in 1968, when Parliament rejected the lakeside focus for its chambers, opting for either Camp Hill (behind the provisional building) in the House of Representatives or Capital Hill, in the Senate, as an eminence more fitting to their function. After the Prime Minister resolved the issue in favour of the House, the Commission went back to its drawing boards, grumpily defaulting to a tradition of setting a 'very minimum of buildings' in a landscape of 'open space' – and chastened by the impression that a sizeable number of parliamentarians still doubted the urgency of proceeding with anything.[13]

There was some consolation that the NCDC could still claim pre-eminent achievement in fashioning that landscape. By the late 1960s Canberra's lake shore and Anzac Parade were the largest and 'most carefully calculated essays' in 'man-made landscape' and civic design in Australia. The latter, formalising in raw red gravel an Avenue of Remembrance rather incongruously scored in arterial traffic between suburbs, was as bold a gesture of inscribing history (again military, and solemn sacrifice) onto Canberra's landscape as the city would ever have. The former, unfolding in major engineering works and in decorous set pieces such as Commonwealth Park, offered an ambitious laboratory for the concept of 'site planning' that gelled, through the NCDC's influence, with an emerging professionalisation of landscape architecture in Australia. Both projects reinforced the continuing task of integrating a dispersed city – and to that extent they complemented the work of traffic engineers. At the time and since, critics have regretted that the dominance of 'horticulturalists', and an aesthetics of recreation rather than 'dignity', limited what was achieved in such projects. Now badged as 'a city within a landscape', Canberra into the late 1960s was certainly responsive to its times: the ornamental avenues of older suburbs became the more intimate, varied streets of the new;

changes in recreational use in new towns, from organised to social sport and leisure, redefined the requirements for open space running through them into less formal corridors. Baby-boomers and a baby-boom found in Canberra's outer suburbs an affirmation of their desire for space and ease, though it could prove strangely vacant once acheived.[14]

ACTIVISM, EVEN IF IMPOLITE, OVER APATHY

In 1966 Barbara Higgs of Watson – a suburb gazetted in 1960 – formed an Australian Capital Territory branch of the Housewives Association, determined to push beyond 'traditional' tactics in representing the discontent of territory residents with the 'scandalous' prices they endured for basic foods. That, at least, would be the first grievance to be addressed by the 'militants' gathering around her. Banner-waving was of little use, Higgs claimed, in a city attuned to more 'subtle' influence, and so habituated to 'autocracy'. It was, after all, only in that year that Canberra's long-serving representative to the Commonwealth Parliament, Labor's Jim Fraser, gained rights to vote on matters extending beyond the territory. Proposals for a municipal council had been dormant since the late 1940s. Agitation might be building for action, reflecting the basic anomaly, even 'comedy', of a community so immersed in government being so lame. But the obstacles to reform seemed great. Not only was Canberra planned for 'effect', Higgs argued, with 'no thought given to the needs of the individual', but planning had induced 'apathy'. In a campaign gaining national attention, she was an early voice in a trend: Canberra's 'genteel' citizens were more assertively asking what all their sophistication was for.[15]

Through the 1960s Canberra's politics gained several layers, its circumstances throwing the problems of growth and choice into focus. Formed in 1963, the local Council of Social Service (ACT-COSS) had no trouble in finding members among the range of voluntary organisations in the city, but developing leadership on pressing agendas – of child care, mental health or aged care – proved difficult when, it judged, many residents felt 'hindered in the exercise of their citizens' rights by restrictions imposed by their government employment'. The Council found academics and the clergy ready for comment, but 'an informed public opinion' seemed harder to harness. The demand for services such as marriage guidance counselling, also introduced in the territory in 1963, was higher in Canberra than elsewhere. Higgs' assertion that more mothers in Canberra were being forced to seek work to meet the costs of living was accurate, and brought tensions of its own. Here was a population struggling to adjust not only to a new place, but also to new patterns of life. Canberra might have exemplified the discontents of (in the *Bulletin*'s phrase) the 'patio intellectuals' of Australia in the late 1960s, but it would also test capacities to relieve them.[16]

It was not that administering institutions were unaware of these problems, but prevailing structures frustrated coordinated solutions. In 1963, as incoming Secretary of the Department of the Interior, (Sir) Richard Kingsland, understood that the capital, while only one aspect of his 'sprawling' responsibilities, was his 'biggest worry', if also the 'most interesting part of my job'. His department – if still ridiculed as the 'Inferior' rather than Interior – required, and gained, revitalisation in matching the prestige of the NCDC with the day-to-day management of the city and territory. At best 'creative tension', at worst bitter rivalry, existed between the two agencies, Kingsland encouraging the NCDC to attend to both the social needs and hidden, long-term costs sometimes set aside in the Commission's push for large-scale development: public housing that might be a 'world beater' in concept but lacked provision for garages or carports; offices under elegant copper roofs but with no air-conditioning. Resigned to losing out to the Commission's greater influence over Cabinet, Kingsland turned instead to 'administering the city by persuasion, even threat' in advancing the causes he valued, given the lack of legislative backing for many initiatives.[17]

Such influence could be put to good effect: Kingsland took pride in establishing, in 1965, the Canberra School of Music to support the cultural life of the community. The school was an 'unrepeatable' venture, according to the composer and pianist Larry Sitsky, who was reluctantly lured to it in 1966 on the cusp of the international impact of his opera 'The Fall of the House of Usher'. In Canberra, Sitsky delighted in finding zealous audiences, 'starved of music', and an ethos of 'creating rather than recreating' among colleagues similarly enticed to the capital. A moment of solidarity between Interior and the NCDC saw in 1966 the construction of the Griffin Centre to provide space in the city for the meetings and activities of a diversity of amateur societies, reflecting the city's growth: this 'red-brick beckoning building' was jointly managed by 47 member organisations by 1967, from bird and gemstone fanciers to the Alliance Française; it was a focus for a social and cultural questioning that took a more activist turn in the 1970s. A churn of ministers continued at Interior, several 'spoiling for a fight' that Kingsland welcomed in seeking to recognise the complexity of governance for a city in which an active community had to mesh with the assigned purposes of a national capital. Such issues, Australian National University (ANU) political scientist J.D.B. Miller observed in 1967, had no precedent in Australia, and had been tackled no better in any other purpose-built capital.[18]

Local political representation, such as it was, reflected similar dynamics. The Australian Capital Territory Advisory Council had expanded from five to seven elected members in 1959, but the high rate of informal returns in the compulsory voting for members of an ultimately powerless body signalled a lack of community engagement. Still, building on a rote agenda dealing with costs of living, rents, health services and rates, the Council was a forum in which issues could at least be argued to Interior, and there were signs it was sometimes listened to. An increasing proportion of Independent members (four in 1961–64; five in 1964–67) advanced causes such as the need for resources for 'youth expression', especially places where those with 'sophisticated needs' could meet, relax, dance and talk. Alan Fitzgerald, a journalist who ran for the Council on a 'do nothing' ticket in 1967, to mock its impotence, found, when elected, that there was business worth attending to. The resignation of the entire membership in 1969 also made its point: when would this frustration of democratic representation end?

In 1967, the Council's Labor Party representatives – never as beholden to union or factional influence as elsewhere – had shown a determination to move beyond the parish pump, championing four protesters arrested during the visit of the South Vietnamese President in 1967. In 1968, the push within local branches to take a stand on other issues of 'progressive' social concern brought the party into deeper controversy. Its leader on the Council, Gordon Walsh, mounted a successful preselection challenge to the long-serving, revered but community-service focused Malcolm Fraser, who had taken no stand on issues such as Vietnam. Concerned by this ruction, New South Wales' head office overturned Walsh's endorsement, but a bitter division remained between 'old' and 'new' interests and alignments in the local party. The local Liberal Party, slower in organising itself given a small business constituency, had long puzzled over Labor's electoral strength in such an affluent community. (Could it be explained by the number of Catholics – 32 per cent to the national average of 27 per cent? Or of renters?) With less at stake, it more easily accommodated a 'small-l' campaign for reform on issues including censorship, abortion and pollution, waiting for a time when the politics of this middle-class community would awake to their natural alignment.[19]

These local transitions, of course, mirrored the national politics which dominated life in the capital. The journalistic coup of 1963 – a photograph of Arthur Calwell and Gough Whitlam, as Labor's federal leader and deputy leader, loitering in the dark outside the Hotel Kingston while the '36 faceless men' of the party conference, drawn from around Australia, decided on policy inside – confirmed Whitlam's determination to professionalise his party, and more than incidentally its claim upon the capital. Leader from 1967, Whitlam proudly reflected on the ways in which he had been shaped by being, for the first time among Australian politicians, the Canberra-educated son of a senior Commonwealth public servant. Canberra, as Graham Freudenberg noted, 'furnished' Whitlam's mind: 'The Program' he set to developing, drawing on extensive policy advisory groups (several with their own foundations in Canberra, especially at the ANU), foreshadowed an unprecedented role for, and image of, government.

On the other side of politics, in the Liberals' unsettled search for a new style of leadership following Menzies' retirement in 1966, John Gorton set aside his party's patrician view of the city in which he had chosen to live early in his parliamentary career. Briefly, in 1963–64, he was the 'sleeves rolled up' Minister of the Interior that Kingsland most enjoyed working with in his contests with the NCDC. As Minister for Education he pushed hard, against Treasury, for the establishment in 1967 of the Canberra College of Advanced Education as an investment in a broader future for the community. As Prime Minister from 1968 to 1971, however, Gorton encountered the thresholds beyond which Canberra was not prepared to follow such an independent-minded leader.[20]

In 1970, seeking to win votes for a Liberal candidate in the by-election following Jim Fraser's sudden death, Gorton hoped to capitalise on local discontent with the disparities arising from recent land revaluations. Unilaterally, he declared an end to Canberra's leasehold system, replacing it with a reliance on rates for revenue. The distinction might have been arcane for many Canberrans, and rates were certainly a more familiar, and perhaps reassuring concept for those who wondered what might happen at the end of the 99-year terms by which they held their homes. But Gorton had undone the foundational premise that had defined the city from the start: that the 'unearned increment' of property values should accrue to the public rather than to the private interest. And then there was his appointment of Ainsley Gotto, a 22-year-old woman, as his private secretary; and his replacement of a long-serving departmental secretary, Sir John Bunting – who exemplified discreet consultation – with (Sir) Lenox Hewitt, who was notorious for liking 'detail and control' and was determined to push the Prime Minister's agenda, and his own. This was not the Canberra way in administration. From a political perspective, there was also mounting discontent that Gorton deferred more to the select company he assembled at the Lodge than to his Cabinet; and at his tendency to similarly treat parliament with disdain in perfunctory debate. Gorton crossed boundaries the capital still cultivated: ultimately, he would not be tolerated.[21]

It was not simply that Canberra preferred to maintain the status quo – more that its various components had a deep sense of controlling their own destiny, and resisting direction. The bureaucracy was already refining its patterns. Succeeding Dunk as Chairman of the Public Service Board from 1960, (Sir) Frederick Wheeler determined to build on the consolidation of the service in Canberra with reforms aimed at increasing its capacities in policy development and boosting its public standing. New tests and salary structures enhanced gains already attributed to the transfer program: in efficiencies within and between departments; in 'closer contacts' between departments and their ministers; and in the recognition and rewards that came to 'the professional, career public servant'. None of this diminished Canberra legends of interdepartmental rivalry, and probably accentuated them. The Department of Trade, established in the capital in 1956 (renamed Trade and Industry after 1963) famously wrestled with Treasury for influence, each department entrenching oppositional internal cultures: the Treasury elite versus Trade's practical 'operators'. As Secretary of Labour and National Service, Sir Henry Bland resolutely kept his department in Melbourne, declaring Canberra 'incestuous' and prone to making a 'song and dance' about policy when the priority was practice. But the capital was undeniably where the action was. One of Menzies' last acts might have been to disparage the recommendations of the Vernon Committee of Economic Enquiry, which called for more coordinated national economic planning: he had declared that elected governments should not be dictated to by experts. But expertise was increasing its hold *within* government, if in a 'gatekeeper' mode designed to carefully manage the pace of reform, and which still left it to Canberra's central agencies to generate the kinds of policy innovations they judged the times required.[22]

Logistical bottlenecks brought a temporary halt to the public service transfer program in 1966–67, following the move of Social Services; it resumed in 1968 with Supply. Those departments already in Canberra continued to grow in recruitment, leading to a new phenomenon. A fresh generation of officers was coming straight to the capital, often lured by more active campaigns by departments, aimed at capturing the interest of university students, offering specialised opportunities rather than the generalities of 'service'. Once in the city, the most promising found themselves actively mentored by senior figures who mapped out the full dimensions and prospects of work in policy development and delivery. For these officers, Canberra became a matrix of possibilities, and they applied themselves accordingly. They read the runes on where to move next, what meant advancement or atrophy. In departments such as Immigration – relatively low on Canberra's hierarchy – the Secretary, Peter Heydon, used Wheeler's reforms to boost his officers' ability to handle the gradual liberalisation of policy on racial restriction, his own Calvinistic sense of the high moral calling of such work still impressing young recruits. In departments higher up the league table, the message was more implicit. This rising cohort of officials was changing the character of government – especially as some chose to take their increasingly valued skills and contacts sideways into the major industry lobby groups setting up the capital, and whose traffic was turning away from ministers to working the middle ranks of departments. Astute members of the press gallery caught the change, journalists such as Bruce Juddery branching out to 'till the public service', adding further spice to Canberra-watching.[23]

This rising currency of professionalisation had many dimensions. By 1969, some 8 per cent of Canberra's population possessed tertiary qualifications (5 per cent holding university degrees, in contrast to 3 per cent in New South Wales and Victoria). Canberra cultivated the graduate, the 'university man'. It even took a certain vicarious satisfaction in the addition to the ranks of white-coated insect, animal and plant scientists at the CSIRO of the even more esoteric corps who staffed the three space tracking stations established to the south of the city in the mid-1960s – at Orroral Valley, Honeysuckle Creek and Tidbinbilla – to support NASA's satellites and moon shots. And at the ANU the research-only Institute of Advanced Studies continued to enjoy unprecedented resources while the standing of undergraduate teaching in the School of General Studies steadily increased. While the argument was made that such a university should be kept small, selective and focused, pressures to expand were mounting and inevitably the character of the place changed. Between 1968 and 1969, as teaching and research staff grew by 13 per cent to 798, the number of undergraduates increased by 9 per cent to 3731 (second only in growth to Melbourne's newer Monash University). Among those enrolments, the dominance of part-timers, once concentrated in public servants taking the Bachelor of Economics, gave way in 1970 to a majority of full-timers, owing much to the first generation of massed school leavers from the territory. Even in areas with professional alignments, such as law, new courses recognised the need for a greater breadth of academic training in preparation for public policy work. If there was discomfort that the ANU might become a regional, even local university, to which proximity as much as national prestige was the attraction, there was also recognition of the opportunities this orientation offered for innovation.[24]

In 1965 an Urban Research Unit was established, growing from an interdisciplinary conference on the 'Metropolis in Australia'. A Canberra perspective on such issues gained strength when Peter Harrison left the NCDC for the unit in 1967, and its expertise soon began feeding into one of Whitlam's policy development areas. The creation of the Strategic and Defence Studies Centre (SDSC) in 1966 built on different networks but similar trends. Its origins were in the anxiety of Canberra's international policy circles that they lacked the resources to understand the Asian region in particular and the status to be heard in the areas where information and funding for such work was controlled. Soon winning support from organisations such as the Ford Foundation, and providing a safe space for exchanges between government and academics, the Centre achieved its objectives – but not without critics. It demonstrated, the *Bulletin* alleged, 'how our foreign affairs establishment protects itself against ideas' in a cosy circle of experts – a harsh judgement, but reflecting the kind of contract many saw underpinning the ANU's progress.[25]

The university also bulked large in the membership and activities of Australia's 'learned academies', the Academy of Science being joined in the capital by an academy of the Humanities, formed with a royal charter in 1969, and of the Social Sciences, incorporated from the Social Sciences Research Council (SSRC) in 1971. As the historian of the SSRC Stuart Macintyre contends, a Canberra paradox took shape through the 1960s: an urge on the part of academics to gain influence verging on unadventurous utilitarianism, coupled to the cultivation of a safe, almost insular 'scientism' that seemed determined to avoid critical engagement with current issues. It was not that research was not valued, but that it was carefully packaged. The frisson of concern about whether the government would be 'embarrassed' at C.D. Rowley's eloquent and incisive study of Aboriginal people in Australian society, written in Canberra as a fellow of the SSRC, in itself made the point.[26]

The ANU's students disappointed the more radical among them with similar traits. In 1967, John Iremonger, a student leader, lamented that genuine 'discontent' was largely 'alien' to the ANU's cohort, given the relative comforts the university enjoyed in its 'unique relationship' to government. Gratuitous 'vandalism' and boisterous 'flag-filching' from embassies seemed the only disturbances students brought to their 'sleep-walking city'. A core of dedicated activists made the best of their proximity to politics, and some would later move into that world – such as Megan Stoyles, whose 'Make love not war' T-shirt, worn in protest at the visit of United States President Lyndon Johnson in 1966, made the cover of *Time* magazine. It was also true that Canberra's intersecting, experimental student 'scenes' were relatively untroubled by the heavier policing experienced elsewhere. When the temper of student protest rose into the early 1970s, the ANU found itself in the upper registers of Australian campus unrest. But here, at least, student demands were met by figures such as H.C. Coombs (now Chancellor) and J.G. Crawford (Vice-Chancellor) with a tolerance that reflected their sense that this university, perhaps more than any, needed to listen. Coombs, disappointed by how far his charge had strayed from the 'powerhouse of social reconstruction' he and other planners had envisaged in the 1940s, expressed his preference for 'activism, even if impolite, [over]...apathy'. L.F. Crisp, another post-war reconstructionist, now an ANU professor of political science (and a heavy player for 'old' Labor in Canberra) took a different view, disgusted at how cavalierly this university had succumbed to 'modish' radicalism. Here was a Canberra paradox, again.[27]

In the Canberra community itself, pressures for reform were also building, in that same restless coupling of capacity, influence and frustration. Revealingly, among the most prominent causes was education – the commodity in which the city traded almost as much as politics. In 1966, a parent-initiated campaign began, registering dissatisfaction with the increasingly under-resourced New South Wales school system which had run the territory's schools since its foundation. 'A Shortage of Everything' was one *Canberra Times* headline, backing a series of articles, public meetings and conferences that gathered remarkable levels of support for the establishment of an independent secondary school system, more suited to the particular community Canberra was becoming, and drawing on its expertise. The ANU economist Noel Butlin calculated that the taxation paid by the territory's residents – reflecting higher average incomes – could support their own school system. Don Anderson, head of the university's recently established Educational Research Unit, undertook an innovative survey of student experience; Richard Campbell, an ANU philosopher, chaired the committee which formulated an alternative model. The driving force, however, remained with citizens. The senior secondary college system which emerged from this lobbying reflected their participatory ideal of schools governed by boards on which parents and teachers would share influence over staffing and curriculum.[28]

Canberra, they argued, deserved an 'imaginative and experimental' approach to education, recognising the 'professionalism' of teachers and avoiding the 'conformity' imposed on them and their classes by public examinations. Tasmania had adopted a matriculation college system to build a 'critical mass' of students for university. Canberra, however, faced a different problem. Most territory students stayed until their final year, an affluent community stirring aspirations but also exerting 'greater pressure to succeed' on its children. Anderson's survey suggested that the 'discernibly hierarchical' nature of a public service town and the relatively high proportion of married women in paid work were among the factors placing a pressure of expectations on Canberra's youth unmatched elsewhere. They needed schools more attuned to the development of a sense of individual responsibility and choice if they were to cope with such demands, and fit in. Critics derided the 'privileges' the capital again assumed in this approach. But Canberra was presenting itself as a vanguard of 'post-industrial society', as the delinquency of youth with nothing to do transformed into the alienation of students from the narratives of career, status and security which underpinned their parents' ambitions.[29]

The Commonwealth responded positively to this campaign – the area was one among many where new national initiatives were sought, and Canberra could, once more, be a test case. In 1968, it assumed responsibility for education in the territory; by 1972, Malcolm Fraser, as Minister of Education, announced that a statutory authority would control Canberra's government schools from 1974. After its election in December, Labor accelerated this process: an interim Schools Authority was established in September 1973, overseeing the development of curricula and the reorganisation of schools. Translating a concept into practice exposed points of conflict. School boards clashed with teachers' unions over the selection of staff. Participatory systems left processes of decision-making uncertain as a new administration, and philosophy, sought its feet. Momentum built: the first of the territory's secondary colleges opened in 1974, the outcome of a process judged 'one of the most dramatic and important [Australian] experiments in educational administration'. Government support was extended that year to the School Without Walls, a cooperative venture built around principles of education in a 'non-stratified, non-role structured social environment', set apart from 'compulsion, authority, apathy and competition'.[30]

Here, perhaps, was the obverse of the Canberra paradox: a community with little power could safely serve as a laboratory for those testing the boundaries of change, and find in policy-from-above reforms that might have emerged more tortuously from politics. Another campaign, emerging in 1969, demonstrated similar elements. The Australian Capital Territory still laboured under a dusty dowry of laws inherited from New South Wales in 1911. In the absence of any local legislative process to reform it, this inheritance was judged 'scandalous' by the mid-1960s. The territory Law Society, academic lawyers at the ANU, the Advisory Council and a concerned public lobbied for revision of what Sir Percy Joske, serving as a judge of the territory's Supreme Court, declared to be an 'ineffectual and absurd' situation. The Commonwealth resisted these protests, but the Law Council of Australia undertook a review of the criminal code for all territories, including the Australian Capital Territory, with the prospect that this exercise might serve as an 'experiment' for national application. The result fell – by general consensus – well short of the 'progressive thinking' the Canberra community especially sought to reflect. One aspect exemplified this failure: the recommendation that offences of buggery and indecent assault be replaced with the charge of 'sexual offences against the order of nature'. This archaic formulation was a tipping point: it prompted several ANU academics to form the Homosexual Law Reform Society, which soon drew remarkable support within the city and beyond.[31]

An article by political scientist Henry Mayer in the *Australian*, urging support for the Canberra group in exposing 'how very vicious the dinky-di Aussie can be', had that effect. Its convenors soon received encouraging letters from around Australia, including requests for further information and invitations to speak. Locally, the *Canberra Times* ran interviews with a local detective, who indicated that some 20 homosexuals were 'known' to him personally from patrolling 'beats', but who estimated around 2000 more were 'active' in the city, although 'not highly organised'. The territory's Health Service's Director of Psychiatry offered assurance that homosexuality was a 'fixable problem' if the 'patient' was 'motivated'. The debate generated by coverage of several cases of 'indecency' between consenting men in and around Canberra suggested that such formulations were no map for the future in terms of the reach of the law and its impact – a point underscored by concurrent reports of victimisation and the rise of organised assaults on and intimidation of male homosexuals in the capital. There were also welcome signs of 'enlightenment' among Canberra's police and judiciary, and from the Commonwealth Attorney-General. Canberra, then, had given the issue a certain national prominence. But by 1971, Canberra's branch of the Campaign against Moral Persecution, a movement formed in Sydney earlier that year, conceded that it was a challenge to build solidarity in a community where many potential supporters were 'public servants who are afraid of losing their jobs'. Sizeable numbers might attend discreet events, but few formally registered their names. The capital could provide a stage for the coordinating stirring messages, but offered less support for living them. Four years after the South Australia government's decriminalised homosexual acts between adults in 1972, the Australian Capital Territory did the same.[32]

The women's movement negotiated these tensions more successfully, reflecting the place Canberra was becoming. Susan Ryan, later a senator representing the territory, recalls the stimulation of Canberra's 'cosmopolitanism' through the 1960s, particularly among the 'new' Labor party members growing 'mad for Whitlam' and pushing against the 'old' party just as it had over Vietnam. Branch meetings became 'explosive' in arguing issues such as equal opportunity. Other influences came from Women's Liberation (WL), the Canberra group forming in 1970, energised by engagement with an emerging international feminist literature, stimulated again by

Figure 20: Women's Electoral Lobby – ACT members holding a children's party in front of Parliament House in August 1974 to demonstrate about cuts to the child care budget. (Reproduced with permission of Chris Ronalds AM SC)

the currency of education in the city, or by the chance that brought people to a new town and its opportunities (Beryl Henderson, for example, came from an Israeli kibbutz to a job as an emergency housekeeper, then taught English to migrants and later worked in the capital's Family Planning Association's clinic, opened in 1971 after much WL lobbying). Visibility for these causes came with booklets, rallies, street theatre, T-shirts screen-printed in a suburban garage, and houses providing support and contacts. Feminism was a cause that found ready roots, or jolted consciences, in a suburban, nuclear-family oriented, relatively affluent society. Not only were discussions among Canberra women particularly 'intensive and demanding', but there was also women's own experience of the city's backdrop of alienation. As a WL newsletter observed, the question 'What can you achieve or contribute?' was pertinent in Canberra when gender divisions in marriage, child care and employment were so conspicuously entrenched and celebrated, all around.³³

Additional impetus came in WL partnership with the Women's Electoral Lobby (WEL), formed in Melbourne in early 1972, and soon with a branch in Canberra. Hosting WEL's first national conference, that branch became the centre for representations to government on issues such as divorce and abortion law reform, and paid maternity leave. Some questioned whether the Canberra group's focus on 'insider' lobbying was consistent with 'grass roots democratic structures', but its impact was undeniable in capturing the politicians that featured on WEL's 'form guide' of approval. In 1973, Elizabeth Reid, a founding local member and ANU philosophy tutor, was appointed to Whitlam's prime ministerial staff as an adviser on women and children.³⁴

Considerable exchange occurred across these movements and causes: Canberra was a focus for national as well as community protest, and a site for a sometimes awkward melding of the two. The national level had its most powerful exemplar in the creation of the Aboriginal Tent Embassy, first erected outside Parliament House on Australia Day 1972, under a beach umbrella carried down from Sydney. Beginning as a protest at the federal government's refusal to recognise land rights, the Embassy was a symbolic protest that endured through two violent demolitions by police. It gained immediate publicity in representing a dispossessed people, set in bold contrast to the 'flash surroundings' of other nations' delegations, and posing the simple question: Had Aboriginal people 'received a fair deal?' As a symbol and strategy, the embassy also drew support from many other groups, including the women who set up their own embassy for those unrepresented in the centre of representation. The Aboriginal Embassy was part of a momentum that broadened consciences, and played particularly on the context of the national capital. Pat Eatock, a Queensland Aboriginal woman, came to support the Embassy; with WEL backing, she ran as an independent candidate for the Australian Capital Territory in the 1972 federal election, determined to argue for Aboriginal, women's, workers' and children's rights from 'the centre of Australian political life'. With 'baby, nappies and disorder' in tow, she felt as a 'deserting mother' she also gave authenticity to campaigns for a women's refuge, established in 1975. Joining a group of Aboriginal women who chained themselves to the steps of Parliament House, Eatock noted the lack of black faces in the city ('I'll have to get a trip down to Wreck Bay') but stayed on to become the first non-matriculation student to complete a Bachelor of Arts at the ANU.[35]

And, as part of this wave of questioning, by 1970, the 'city within the landscape' was also generating its own, overarching environmental awareness. Arriving at the Parliamentary Research Service from New York's Model Cities Program, Peter Ellyard was central to the formation in Canberra of the Society for Social Responsibility in Science (CSSRS), which coordinated discussion of the social and ecological consequences of modern development. Two-thirds of SSRS members were professional scientists, reflecting the local concentration of such expertise in the CSIRO, the ANU and government departments. Steadily the organisation expanded to organise programs and conferences which engaged high school students – young people with 'time and energy' and the capacity to influence their parents – on issues drawing clear connections between local trends and larger consequences. Water quality in Lake Burley Griffin was one of many questions being posed about how effectively issues of urban environmental quality were being handled. Why was there such a paucity of debate over the Commonwealth's short-lived proposal to develop a nuclear power station at Jervis Bay? How did Canberra's ritual burning of autumn leaves model the dynamics of air pollution? In such a job-oriented town, how did people understand the fit between their quality of life and their work? How sustainable was Canberrans' reliance on the private car, especially when the NCDC targeted areas of bushland and lake shore for freeways? A rock musical, *Earth and Sun*, might not have drawn the anticipated crowds in 1971, but the Society's model of generating debate soon spread to Sydney, Adelaide and Brisbane, and contributed significantly to the conduct of the capital's most protracted controversy: the construction of a telecommunications tower on Black Mountain.[36]

Rising over the centre of the city, Black Mountain was a 'benign' presence. One flank was the site of the National Botanic Gardens, opened to the public in 1967 – itself a product more on the Department of the Interior's initiative than on NCDC backing – which forged a connection between the scientific collection and public appreciation of Australian native plants. The summit was topped by two thin, relatively unobtrusive television antennae. The rest was a remnant nature reserve, gazetted in 1970 and reflecting the advocacy of the territory's branch of the National Parks Association: on that steep ground, wildflowers, birds and insects still abounded. In that year, however, the NCDC also released the first plans for a 196-metre, concrete and steel tower, proposed by the Australian Post Office and the Department of Works for the top of the mountain to improve telecommunications services. While it had worried over the unsightly intrusion of private television antennae into the suburbs in 1963, the Commission seemed at first entranced by this symbol of modernity, complete with protruding drums housing equipment and a revolving restaurant. Public alarm, however, escalated, prompting the NCDC by 1972 to oppose the plan as an affront to the scale of the city and the principle of maintaining its hills in their 'natural state'. Prominent figures, including local industrial and political Labor laders, senior academics and community groups, placed the issue in the national context of environmental contestation. Yet scientific and professional evidence, picketing of the site once construction commenced in 1973, court injunctions and appeals, all failed to stop a project which, critics argued, was obsolete well before it was completed in 1980. Even the NCDC, for the first and last time, was overruled by the Executive Council on the issue. Spiking above tree-clad slopes, the tower – however gradually it settled as a landmark for the capital – proved a monument to the limitations of its community's voice, and an enduring provocation: overtly as a symbol of political imposition; subtly in terms of the disjunction between city and landscape.[37]

NOT UPTIGHT AT ALL

In 1970 Kep Enderby succeeded Jim Fraser as the Australian Capital Territory's Labor federal member. A lawyer who gained prominence in defending ANU student demonstrators in the 1960s, Enderby considered 'dramatic resignation' from his seat to highlight his 'lost dogs, blocked sewers' workload in the absence of local government. But with the election of the Whitlam government, he welcomed appointment to the new portfolio of Minister for the Capital Territory. He began with the familiar idea: the territory could become the 'social laboratory' of the nation. The incoming government endorsed this view: the NCDC was attached to the new Departments of Urban and Regional Development (DURD), reflecting Whitlam's view that it was 'the body most expert in the planning of [the] new decentralised cities' that were integral to his vision of enhanced, more equal access to social services and amenity. DURD's minister, Tom Uren, had deep faith in the Commission's 'know-how'.[38]

The combination of Enderby as Canberra's local member and relevant minister, and the expanded role of the NCDC within DURD, seemed auspicious. ACTCOSS, embracing the theme of 'social action', applauded the 'new thinking taking place in Canberra' after the change of government. The local branch of the National Council of Women had always appreciated the extent of its influence, whether in gaining (belatedly) jury service for women in 1968, or establishing, in 1969, its own environment sub-committee. But in 1973 its president, Edna Watson, rallied her members: 'Never has there been more need for the voice of the community – the ordinary man and woman, the family, the consumer, the general public – to be heard. And never, to be fair, has there been a greater willingness on the part of those who make the decisions which affect our lives, to listen to that voice'.[39]

Clearly, the Canberra experiment was entering a new phase. The NCDC's neighbourhood 'production line' continued, land-servicing proceeding well in advance of demand. A steadily increasing majority of housing was being privately built (including by innovative construction companies, such as Pettit and Sevitt, and local designers, such as Gary Willemsen) and (after 1971) owned. Large innovative construction projects included schools, major office complexes, road works and utilities, consolidating satellite centres and the suburbs around them. Built from 1970 for 3600 workers, the award-winning Cameron Offices in Belconnen adopted the architectural style of 'new brutalism' that was becoming a set-piece in Canberra, with the ironic objective of creating a 'memorable image' of what progressive government could mean, monumental yet overtly emphasising economy and functionalism (the verdict came 30 years later with the demolition of all but two of the complex's nine pavilions). For a while, at least, DURD persuaded the NCDC to give concerted attention to the provision of public transport as a statement of access and efficiency.

Innovation in housing proved more enduring, as the Commission developed a program for medium-density development in projects such as Woden's Swinger Hill (named after an early surveyor, not the residents), applauded by Robin Boyd as a 'challenge to Australian suburbs' in its mix of terrace and courtyard units. 'Urban change' was also recommended for older, inner suburbs as Canberra entered the most marked generational turnover in its history: Kingston, for example, in its aging demography and lower household occupancy, was targeted to support 'downtown' activities ('antique shops, inexpensive restaurants, second-hand bookshops'). Quick compulsory public acquisition was the aim in these areas, to forestall private speculation but also seemingly to bulldoze residents reluctant to move. The first hints of metropolitan inner-city diversity also disappeared in this process: run-down Kingston was developing Canberra's first area of student squats, supporting bands with names such as The Roaring Wombats, a geodesic dome in a backyard, a vegetable garden dug into the middle of the street, and a derelict aeroplane hoisted onto the roof of a cottage in which 'many a person took wonderful voyages across the universe'.[40]

The NCDC juggernaut had its obstacles, however. In the late 1960s inter-governmental intransigence, and some basic concerns about zoning and development impacts, defeated its ambitions to follow the engineering and demographic logic of the Y-plan push across the New South Wales border. This impasse was one of several that turned the Commission inwards, seeking to find a new consensus. It began 'greatly expanding' the resources allocated to community consultation within the city and beyond. With regard to the latter, a concept of the Canberra's 'region' developed, defined by the reach of the city's services and opportunities to surrounding districts: what could not be gained in new territory might at least be cultivated in sentiment. For the former, in 'think-ins' and 'search conferences' the Commission began bringing together small groups to canvass what the city would look like if it took account of trends from 'nuclear isolation' to 'communal living', to fewer hours devoted to more flexible work, and to a frequently expressed desire for a clearer separation between the functions of the national capital and its residential communities.⁴¹

Responses to citizen lobbying led to the establishment of an open-air, fresh produce market in Fyshwick. Planning for the Belconnen Town Centre – to serve 120 000 people – proceeded with the guidance of a specifically appointed non-profit statutory authority, which commissioned surveys showing residents' preference for 'social life' over 'open space', and avoidance of the 'sterility' of Woden, with its moat of car parks, at all costs. Going against a Canberra orthodoxy stretching back to the 1920s, people wanted a 'one-stop', 24-hour 'main street' feel, complete with 'dives', 'weirdos' and markets. Planning for Tuggeranong – projected at its inauguration in 1973 to take 170 000 in the fastest development so far – followed similar consultations that gave precedence to 'environmental design' rather than the seemingly dated neighbourhood unit. Suburbs were to fit the 'natural boundaries' of Canberra's most beautiful valley, ranging from 10 000 to 30 000 people but based around 'local activity areas', each with a licensed 'corner store' or cafe – even a public health centre. This 'territorial unit' approach would later be judged to have produced an 'amorphous' result, and the Commission also began quietly registering the costs and delays that came with soliciting such public input and then being faced with the demands of responding to it – particularly as it anticipated increases in Canberra's annual growth from 9 to 12 per cent by 1975. But that was the spirit of the times.⁴²

It was, after all, the 1970s: it was time for change. It was impossible not to be carried on the surge of the new government. Whitlam's commitment to 'reform and renovation' saw, in 1973, a record of 253 bills introduced into the Commonwealth parliament, and 203 passed. Members clocked up the greatest number of sitting days in 50 years. The press gallery rose to the pace. So did the bureaucracy. Within weeks of Labor's election, six departments were abolished and 18 created, taking the total from 27 to 37. Transfers to Canberra might have been postponed in 1973–74 and 1974–75, to be (ideally for planners, less so for public servants) replaced by movement to new government units in regional 'growth centres' such as Bathurst-Orange or Albury-Wodonga. But Canberra still pulsed with new agencies, acronyms, programs and commitments.[43]

The government spoke of using the public service as an engine for reform not only in policy but in employment conditions, skills recognition, social inclusion and accountability. Wary of senior officials who had served during the Liberal Party's 23 years of unbroken rule, Whitlam wanted change, and power to effect it. The hierarchy of salaries that had once defined rank among Canberra's permanent heads was quickly abolished. All on the same level, departmental secretaries would be easier to move – and in time the majority were. 'Inevitably there have been some conflicts, some areas where we would have wished the service to respond more immediately to our desires', the Prime Minister conceded in May 1973. Ministers began appointing a new breed of 'advisers' from outside to 'supplement' the services provided by their departments. 'The objective', Whitlam explained, 'is to depoliticise the public service' by marking a clear distinction between the role of political guidance and policy administration. But with it, as *Nation Review* noted, came a 'lifestyle' among those staffers – intense, driven, strategic – that was another new ingredient in the Canberra mix.[44]

This new pace inevitably brought tensions: what did it mean to make Canberra more representative of Australia when it was also becoming more specialised? Aboriginal leader Charles Perkins had declared in 1969 that 'if we're not in Canberra, we're history', and on that basis accepted a position in the Office of Aboriginal Affairs established by the Gorton government. Colleagues feared tokenism, and Perkins was frustrated in his desire to achieve 'change from within'. The figure he cut in Canberra's suburbs, in a suit and tie, only compounded a deep popular incomprehension about what Aboriginal policy and politics might mean. Under Whitlam, Perkins seized the opportunity both to bring more Aboriginal staff into his office and to get resources out to Aboriginal communities, but the expectations generated only compounded disappointments and brought a series of public conflicts. In 1975, deeply disillusioned and clouded in controversy, Perkins left Canberra for Alice Springs on extended leave without pay. Elizabeth Reid also resigned as Whitlam's adviser on women's affairs, having endured the pressure of both 'accolades and criticism' in her work. WEL groups around Australia protested that a position offering advice to government on women's affairs must be retained, but it remained unclear what such a job could ever really amount to while the 'system' remained in place.[45]

The representational tasks of the capital acquired many complexities through these years, no less significant because of their symbolic dimensions. Within the parliamentary triangle – still awaiting a clear commitment to build a new parliament house – moves to anchor at least some national institutions, in this new phase of national building, brought a new aesthetics. Denied the uniformity it had sought in the 1960s, the NCDC now advocated 'the drama of calculated irregularity' in preparing briefs for a National Gallery and a permanent home for the High Court. 'We are not overly impressed by excessive formality', Roger Johnson advised, in a marked change from the Commission's view in the past: 'we live', Johnson added, 'in a loosely knit, rapidly evolving society', and the 'asymmetrical siting' now proposed for these two crucial buildings was 'essential to the provision of spatial tension' at the centre of the capital, without which it – and the values to be expressed – would be 'flaccid and dull'. Dull these ventures were not. James Mollison, appointed acting director of the Gallery in 1971 at what seemed an outrageously youthful 40, was committed to a collection that would reach out to audiences, and to a building which 'will not be uptight at all' – visitors would 'be able to wear denims and feel comfortable'. That was not entirely what he felt he got from Colin Madigan's design, brutalist again, which commenced construction in 1973. But for the time being more attention was focused on the Gallery's acquisition program, which included – most notoriously – paintings such as Jackson Pollock's *Blue Poles*, at the then world record price of $1.3 million. Consigned to warehouses around Canberra, works such as this brooded, testament to a new, expansive vision of Australia in international currents, or symptoms of excess.[46]

Inevitably, such activity in Canberra raised questions of its own local political representation. As Minister, Enderby had foreshadowed a move on this issue, having experienced the impossibility of both speaking for a constituency and imposing the dictates of government upon it. From 1973, his successor in the portfolio, Gordon

Bryant, also urged the cause of self-government, although it was unclear whether either minister meant 'greater opportunities for citizen influence' through existing arrangements or new structures with their own legislative power. A Parliamentary Joint Committee examined this question closely and recommended in 1975 that an Australian Capital Territory House of Assembly should be promptly created, with the capacity to legislate free of 'direct ministerial control'. The question remained, however, of how to separate those municipal functions over which territory representatives should have their say, from those which remained Commonwealth responsibilities relating to the role of the national capital. For the time being, an 18-member, fully elected 'Legislative Assembly' – with part-time service and still essentially advisory functions – replaced the old Council in 1974, and filled a range of interlocking boards, authorities and committees with high-minded, ostensibly apolitical appointments poised between patronage and the people.[47]

But if Canberra was not immune to the urgency that characterised government in the early 1970s, neither was it to strains appearing in that mission towards the middle of the decade. Treasury had watched much of Labor's endeavours with a sceptical eye, its tussles with DURD exemplifying a deep culture clash. With rising wages, prices and unemployment through 1974, it advised Whitlam's government to abandon the Keynesian public expansionism which had driven Canberra to that point. Treasury's new counsel for strict deflationary directives exacerbated a pattern of relations with Labor in Power that 'moved between mutual suspicion and downright hostility'. The fight brewing within the parliamentary triangle, however, was far from confined to it. The signals for correction were everywhere. Becoming Commissioner in 1974, Tony Powell found that NCDC staff had grown by 100 per cent under Labor, and that projects under way looked 'extravagant'. He was, his officers observed, a marked departure from the directorial style of his predecessors, who – in typical senior management style – made it clear that more junior staff should not join them in the lift at work. Powell was himself a creation of post-war opportunities in education and professionalism, and appreciated what they could deliver. But while Canberra might have been, as Powell saw it, a 'practical expression of the ideology of the Whitlam government', that sense of the 'practical' did not appear to extend to efficiency in defining or managing business. Others, drawn into Canberra senior circles at that time in an effort at repair, made similar observations – including John Menadue, brought in as head of Prime Minister and Cabinet: there was a pressing need for stock-taking.[48]

Theirs did not begin as an ideological perspective – but it had to recognise the end of an era. Powell's first annual report for the NCDC recorded a 'levelling out' in development in 1974–75, and a marked 'falling-off' in private sector investment. Several major construction firms faced 'financial collapse' given rising costs, industrial unrest and uncertain investment. Many other businesses were likely to leave the city – and to coax them back would 'be very difficult'. And while the Commission had encouraged 'particular interest' groups to participate in planning processes, Powell reflected that the demands on staff to sustain such processes were increasing with the danger that 'the community interest' was being 'submerged' by minority viewpoints. Seeking new directions, Powell turned to American 'management' and 'systems analysis' to help him assess the decisions his officers made rather than traffic engineering to plot the choices of citizens. And still, fundamental aspects of the city remained open to the whim of politics. In a rather perfunctory joint sitting after the election in 1974, Parliament finally determined to lift itself as high as it could over the city and its people, settling on Capital Hill for its new chambers. Even before a crowd of journalists, concerned citizens and public servants gathered on the steps of the old Parliament House on 11 November 1975 to hear of the dismissal of the Whitlam government by the Governor-General, it was clear that any view in the future from that still rabbit-infested hill must be of a different national project and community.[49]

7

You're on your own

PRIMAL SCREAMS

If Canberra, as capital, had presided over the nation until the crisis of the Whitlam government with the increasing if never unchallenged authority of central government, after 1975 it was equally implicated in the new course Australia took, in which governmental power and role were ever more closely scrutinised. Not only that, but the 'laboratory' the capital presented, in which a brave new world of Australian life might be envisaged, became instead a purgatory in which a community, especially one so advantaged, was required to adjust to the end of the boom that had underpinned its existence. That shift heightened the politics of a city that until then had functioned largely in the domain of policy. From 1975 until the late 1980s when, still largely against their will, Canberra's citizens were plunged into the responsibility of governing themselves, the city's story centred on finding a way between the comforts of the past and the stringencies to come.

In 1980, in the midst of this reorientation, Ian Fraser – recently appointed director of the Canberra and South East Region Environment Centre (CSEREC) – published a 'walker's guide' to the city. A community-based group formed in 1974, the Centre was energised by big conservation debates: woodchipping, uranium and 'no dams' on Tasmania's Franklin River. When it came to local issues, however, such as a chairlift proposed to the telecommunications tower on Black Mountain, CSEREC wrestled with a disenfranchisement from the schemes of politicians and bureaucrats. Fraser was aware of the surge of dissent in the Canberra community: a theatre group, for example, neighbouring his office in a decommissioned hostel, ran 'all-day, all-week rehearsals featuring primal screams' – though they sometimes asked him to 'quieten down' the fervent 'gestetnering' that went with building his constituency. He sought an equivalent way of connecting a widespread concern about the state of the world with the strains already evident in the urban fabric around them.[1]

Fraser's guide began, perhaps predictably, by noting Canberra's greater diversity of birds than in any other Australian capital. And there was the splendour of the trees. But when he advised that people with little money might benefit from their edible foods – flour from acorns; nuts from pines; toffee bars from gleditsia pods – a more oblique perspective began infusing his account. Walkers were encouraged to note the taller buildings rising over the city centre, housing the financial and insurance companies that made their money from paper production or supermarkets. They might observe the stylish premises lining Northbourne Avenue, the main route into the city: offices for corporations with clients, contracts and interests to serve in the capital. This one housed the representatives of Rolls Royce, whose nuclear reactors powered Polaris submarines; that one accommodated IBM, which had developed automated battlefield systems for the war in Vietnam. Here was the Queensland Tourist Bureau, promoting tropical holidays while its government threatened to mine the sands of Fraser Island. Further ahead, Sullivan's Creek escaped its concrete embankment under the gentle willows of the Australian National University, to carry into Lake Burley Griffin residues from a new industrial precinct that made it too polluted to irrigate a suburban golf course. A shop selling the latest European wood stoves invited Canberrans to upgrade from their rustic fetish for open fires, moderating the pall of smoke that sank into their valleys and an appetite for wood scrounged from paddocks far out west. Steadily Fraser's itinerary advanced a disarming point. Politics was everywhere: not just in the business of government in the capital, but in the businesses that courted government, and in the choices of citizens themselves.[2]

Pausing in front of the Commonwealth Department of Employment and Youth Affairs, Fraser considered another emerging dimension of the 'ideal city'. For over three decades, unemployment in Canberra had rarely risen above 1 per cent. In 1980, it passed 5 per cent, having spiked at 8 per cent in 1978. Rates would trend past that figure in the next couple of years. Unemployment was higher than in Sydney, higher than the national average, and particularly concentrated among 15–24 year olds. Among the first generation showing significant numbers born in the city, the jobless figure in 1980 exceeded 10 per cent. Celebrated a decade earlier for its 'social mix', Canberra instead was becoming 'polarised'. As the demographer Colin Adrian underscored around the same time, those disparities were 'a direct function of the planned development process' that had guided the city to that point, as the 'neighbourhood units' of the 1960s were starved of the capacity for renewal.[3]

Fraser and Adrian were two among many voices which, by the early 1980s, insisted on the need to look 'beyond the image' of the capital to a disturbing reality. Over three decades Canberra's experiment might have edged aside cynics and cheapskates. But suddenly it had became a crucible of conflict. Contrasts were everywhere. In 1973, the visiting British political scientist David Butler was astonished that Australian colleagues paid so little to attention to the 'gold' that was Canberra. Their ignorance bordered on contempt in dismissing as merely 'parliament' the inherent creativity in government that infused the city. In 1985, the Sydney-based sociologist Michael Pusey took up Butler's challenge. But by then, beginning with extensive interviews with senior public servants, Pusey struck a baser metal. His *Economic Rationalism in Canberra* gained national attention with the message that much was at risk in the 'momentous changes' centring in the capital, as one generation's reformist vocation was swept aside by another's careerist pursuit of market-based discipline. Pusey's characterisation was controversial, but his subtitle – *'A Nation-Building State Changes its Mind'* – captured the extent to which Canberra's dominant narrative was transforming. Not only were the city's defining institutions – parliament and bureaucracy – complicit in the 'hollowing out' of Australian society. Canberra was also being consumed by its own new discipline. When its residents finally acquired self-government in 1989, it was less in fulfilment of their destiny as a progressive community and more in grudging acceptance that they must now 'suffer like the rest of the nation'. Clyde Holding, the Minister overseeing the final stages of that process, was blunt: the Commonwealth was 'shedding Canberra. You're on your own'. Between 1975 and the end of the 1980s, Canberra's walkers entered a straitened path.[4]

SURPLUS TO REQUIREMENTS

A city so closely associated with the agenda of the Whitlam government might have been expected to rally at its dismissal. Instead, a sullen mood descended. In the election of December 1975, the territory voted with a significantly expanded parliamentary representation. In addition to the House of Representatives seat of Fraser, created in 1974 in belated recognition of the size of the Australian Capital Territory electorate and based in Canberra's northern suburbs, two Senate positions – forced through by Labor in a 1974 parliamentary joint sitting – were in contest for the first time. These seats had seen a 'rush of activity' to consolidate the local branches of political parties. The assumption, formulated in 1973 by Don Aitkin, a political scientist with close links to the city, was that a population which 'lives so close to the inanities and hypocrisies of government [would have]...a built-in anti-government majority'. In 1975, however, that hypothesis was tested.[5]

Labor's Ken Fry held Fraser, but against a heavy swing. Fry had begun adapting the staunch local member traditions of the long-serving Jim Fraser, after whom the electorate was named, to issues spanning from access to health and childcare to international human rights. But Kep Enderby, Labor's man in the southern seat of Canberra, lost in a dramatic backlash to a populist Liberal candidate, John Haslem – who frankly admitted he hadn't expected success. Haslem had campaigned on the Whitlam government's failure to meet community expectations, but also urged that the time had come to wean a 'force-fed' city. In the Senate, Labor's Susan Ryan, a candidate reflecting the strength of the local women's movement was elected a distant second place to John Knight, who identified as a 'small-l Liberal' and vowed to restore due process to parliament after the chaos of the previous three years. Canberra seemed to have hedged its bets. Knight, a diplomat, preselected from Saudi Arabia over candidates with deeper local roots, was said to reflect the kindling interest of 'the Liberal Party machine' in the capital. Labor's representatives would equally have to adapt, if they could, to the 'lessons' of their party's fall. Even Haslem – swapping a solicitor's Mercedes for a slogan-daubed Kombi – maintained that the role of a local Liberal must be to moderate the 'kick Canberra syndrome' likely to come from his party in government.[6]

That kick was quick in coming. Deepening economic recession was coupled to the legitimacy the Liberal-Country Party coalition sought to salvage from Whitlam's dismissal by correcting his excesses. At first, Canberra observers judged as 'shrewd' Malcolm Fraser's prime ministerial order to cut ministerial staff and rein in the 'hordes' of task forces Labor had created. These decisions were seen as restoring the public service to its rightful place in policy advice, and proper hierarchy to its chains of influence. It was soon apparent that Fraser's goals went further. Staff ceilings, efficiency reviews and budget cuts became the tools wielded in a sustained campaign of contracting what – at 60 per cent of the workforce – remained the one big industry in town. A cut of $360 million, and a 3.3 per cent decrease in public service staffing, was flagged for 1975–76, then a further 1.5 per cent and, by 1976–77, another 2 per cent – always with the option of 'further review'. In 1981–82 another round of 'razor gang' responses to mounting government deficits led to a 1.6 per cent target for reductions. As Canberra's corridors ran with rumours of 'death lists', the Public Service Board (PSB) conceded that the culling of those judged 'surplus to requirements' was having particular impacts on the capital's central agencies. Early in 1976, the Department of Foreign Affairs, for example, was directed to 'dispense with' 12 per cent of staff.[7]

Morale collapsed. However adroitly a new language sought to neutralise these impacts, the message was blunt. Introducing a centralised computer system, 'Mandata', to calculate 'the manpower implications' of 'the proper use of scarce resources', by 1977 the PSB allowed that the impact of cuts was such that 'low priority tasks may have to be dropped ... or a lower standard of performance accepted'. Even the adoption of 'Flexitime', in part to compensate for clampdowns on overtime and other benefits, generated a cynical response in a popular, locally written cabaret-style farce, lampooning a service that had lost whatever pride it once had.[8]

Malcolm Fraser might have declared a goal of reversing the concentration of power in central government, but this did not diminish the demands made of it. He worked his Cabinet hard, and those pressures spread out into Canberra's departments. Abandoning Whitlam's program of public service transfers to regional growth centres, Fraser began consolidating in the capital the last elements of core departments from Melbourne and Sydney. At the same time, the focus in those departments shifted from policy design to the implementation of measures in accord with government objectives, and increasing the dominance of executive authority. A separate Department of Finance was established in 1976 to secure alternative sources of advice in guiding that process, with a particular emphasis on reducing public sector expenditure. By 1978, the PSB declared its goal must not only be efficiency within departments but also to evaluate the performance of departments against each other. In these processes, the Department of Prime Minister and Cabinet increased its ascendancy. As one of its rising officials, Stephen Sedgwick, recalled, its role was 'to make sure that government worked well...to shake the trees a bit'.[9]

Such cool professionalism changed Canberra's culture. A shift – as textbooks framed it – from 'partner-adviser' to 'assistant' and 'management' roles was under way. Among the most evocative novels of the time, Sara Dowse's *West Block*, set in 1977, reflected this transition, balancing a genuine esteem for the creativity of government observers such as Butler had noted with a creeping sense of disillusion. This process had a generational as well as an ideological dimension. Dowse's portraits include a senior official, resigned to keeping 'an intricate engine turning the wheels of the country', almost regardless of its direction, and salved by the comforts of a good address and a wife sampling the deepening cosmopolitan affluence of the capital: good food, wine and clothes. But there is also a younger man, negotiating issues such as uranium sales and farming subsidies, cautious that small victories led to bigger losses, and juggling parenting with his and his wife's careers. In 1976, Dowse herself had inherited what remained of Whitlam's position of adviser on women's affairs. Determined to keep a low public profile, she anchored her unit in the Prime Minister's Department rather than in his office, framing her advocacy first around questions of women's access to social security rather than the more confrontational abstractions of 'rights'. *West Block* depicts the tensions within a 'Women's Equality Branch' as the pressures of political expedience corrode causes and staff 'gore one another on shards of a broken dream'. Resigning from the public service, also in 1977, Dowse gave as one final reason Fraser's demotion of her office to the Ministry of Home Affairs, in itself a 'most unfortunate choice of name'.[10]

In these relegations, the National Capital Development Commission was early in the new government's sights. Its head, Tony Powell, found Fraser openly 'antagonistic' to the city. The NCDC's expertise might have been sought for the reconstruction of Darwin after Cyclone Tracy in 1974–75, and on the design for Dodoma, the new capital for Tanzania, but the core of its project – the construction of a permanent Parliament House in Canberra – tumbled down the government's 'low priority' list. In 1976, a freeze was placed on all new construction contracts in the capital, and was extended in 1980 to the servicing of new land. Powell had already insisted on a greater 'output' focus for the Commission's work and called Fraser's bluff in sacking 21 staff members in February 1976, forcing an amelioration of the conditions of 'wastage'. But the NCDC still shouldered a 17 per cent cut by 1977, and a 28 per cent cut by 1979. The Commission was in a double bind of accountability: on the one hand, efficiency was the upmost priority, and it sought to demonstrate strict discipline in this respect; on the other, a community in trouble protested at being neglected.[11]

The mounting impact of all these cuts was soon evident. Of residential leases, 42 per cent were passed in at auction in May 1976; the next year saw a 40 per cent drop in private home construction. Population growth halved between 1975 and 1977. By 1978, the NCDC predicted a stabilised growth rate of 3 per cent into the foreseeable future – down from 10 per cent in 1970, and barely that of natural increase. In fact, over the next four years the rate averaged less than 2 per cent, 1981 registering a net 'out-migration' of 262. Canberra was in 'severe downturn'. It was losing skills, especially in construction industries and across the private sector. Even restaurateurs, having seen a 153 per cent boom in the number of licensed premises during the last years of Whitlam's rule (though not, lamented gourmets, an equivalent boost in quality), pleaded in

1976 for some cull in their suddenly struggling ranks. Distortions and dislocations accumulated in once assured programs of growth, and in the lives of those defined by them.[12]

John Knight's Senate campaign had highlighted imbalances in the provision of services in the fast-growing 'new towns' of the early 1970s. The sudden onset of contraction accentuated the problem. To the lack of suburban shopping centres in Belconnen was added the over-provision of office space in the town centre. The sale of the Belconnen Mall – then the largest such commercial complex in the southern hemisphere – was first mooted in 1981, a gust in the rising wind of privatisation. In Tuggeranong, by contrast, where early residents had developed a strong sense of distinctiveness precisely because of their relative distance from the 'old' city and the quality of their setting, the NCDC decided to defer construction of a town centre, leaving suburbs fraying southwards with no 'activity centre' to anchor them. Here was a community caught on the cusp of change – it developed its own momentum, reflected in a mobile, 'cooperating churches' movement, bringing ecumenical services to new settlers, in youth support initiatives and in discussion of the merits of 'open education' in its 'open-plan' schools – but it also wrestled with stagnation.[13]

The internal logic of the Y-plan was unravelling. The NCDC urged instead programs of 'in-fill' to make more efficient use of already serviced areas. But even then what little private investment in residential construction could be lured to such tasks was unprepared to risk experiments in medium density housing, which might not sell – and in any case, existing residents vigorously opposed any initiatives that might further depress property values. More than ever, the Commission expressed 'frustration' and 'disappointment' that citizens were disinclined to engage with any discussion of broad planning objectives. Yet what it saw as an insular defensiveness also carried growing elements of community anxiety and distrust about the shape of the future.[14]

Such pressures encouraged shifting alliances. In 1976, the Liberal Minister for the Capital Territory, Tony Staley, urged Canberra's 'normalisation': more diversification, less planning, 'more grime' – as he put it (along with 'more crime and pollution') – to make the capital a less cosseted part of the nation. Surrounded by fierce debate, a casino entered considerations of what might save the city, in image and revenue, and remained a symbol of what was at stake in its development for trenchantly opposing camps. Soberly, in 1979 the NCDC reversed the optimism of the 1960s, announcing that it had 'no evidence to suggest that Canberra at its present size and with its current employment structure is capable of self-sustained growth'. Believing that only a concerted courting of private enterprise offered salvation, it established a 'Committee of 22' to formalise consultation with industry and commercial interests – at least such a forum might prevent the potential of more open discussion of economic and social projections to be 'counter-productive' to business confidence.[15]

The inclusion of surrounding local government representatives in this committee reflected another aspect of 'normalisation'. Earlier decentralist ideals, or more recent proposals that ACT borders be extended to accommodate an infinite metropolis, assumed a more pragmatic cast in the search for money. For all its difficulties, Canberra was providing services valued in nearby districts enduring their own, often more severe contractions: in primary production (such as Young or Yass), or in local manufacturing (Goulburn). Canberra also underpinned the more robust growth of neighbouring Queanbeyan, if still with that rankling complementarity of their blue- and white-collar labour markets. With its relative salaried and superannuated security, the capital also provided vital, if seasonal, stimulus to holiday trade on the south coast, where older industries, too, were failing and weekender investment was vital. Steadily, the 'Canberra region' became another concept seeking leverage in a search for new directions.[16]

In that search it was clear that established practices and principles were under scrutiny. In 1981, the NCDC conceded that 'the relaxation of some planning and development conditions' must be part of wooing entrepreneurs, especially to the inner city where developers sought the synergy of concentrating tourist, service, financial and commercial functions, arguing that investors needed to be offered an urban model more familiar to them than the satellite form. Already the Parliamentary Joint Committee on the Australian Capital Territory had registered alarm that the Department of the Capital Territory was prepared to 'allow the market to make its own decisions about land use', tolerating businesses to breach the lease clauses that were fundamental to Canberra's planning. Such leniency, the Committee judged, sat awkwardly beside the NCDC's evident determination to maintain its strictures on 'physical planning' – the colours, materials and styles to be used in construction – and its stiff handling of the emerging demands of 'social planning', coming from citizens claiming 'rights' to be heard amid such uncertainty.[17]

Underpinning these trends was the polarisation noted by demographers. At least out in Belconnen and Tuggeranong young families were achieving levels of home ownership (and mortgage indebtedness) that at last approached national averages, if on over 150 per cent of average national incomes. But their Canberra was different from the pockets of disadvantage in older suburbs, such as Narrabundah, Kingston, Griffith, Reid, Ainslie and O'Connor. Even in the first new towns, Woden and Weston Creek, there were areas showing concentrations of those faring less well in these times: the aged, renters, non-nuclear families, divorced and separated people, single parents, those without a car, and younger, more vulnerable adults. Downer, for example, a suburb in the inner north, gazetted in 1960, lost over 8 per cent of its population between 1981 and 1986: those who could moved out; the rest were stuck.[18]

As Tuggeranong clearly demonstrated, the newer suburbs were not immune to slowdown: the construction of schools was deferred, and those completed functioned on the expectation that it would be years before they filled. But in older suburbs, by contrast, student 'catchments' contracted by up to 60 per cent, and some campuses evolving towards the territory's innovative secondary colleges system were threatened with closure. The withdrawal of such infrastructure was compounded by other shifts. John Haslem urged the sale of government housing to those who could afford to make the leap. For those who could not, 'social mix' began shading into 'residential segregation' in what officials began describing as 'welfare' rather than 'public' housing, with its associated stigma. In 1983, 77 per cent of those on priority waiting lists were in receipt of a pension or benefit, a 'dramatic reversal' of the situation existing two decades previously. Stereotypes of Canberra twisted between such extremes: if the narrative of government from the capital was changing, so was that of community.[19]

DELUSIONS OF PURITY

In 1984, an inquiry into welfare services in the Australian Capital Territory declared that 'the political will to develop Canberra had evaporated'. Chaired by Tony Vinson – then Australia's leading researcher in social work (Canberra did not lack the capacity to analyse its predicament) – this investigation was one of several that began itemising failings in areas ranging from homelessness and emergency housing (calculated in 1983 to affect 2396 adults and 276 children) to the absence of facilities for young people requiring psychiatric care. Canberra was then Australia's seventh largest city, sitting between industrial centres Newcastle and Wollongong, with a population passing 220 000. And, Vinson noted, it had acquired 'all the social problems expected in a large urban area'. Funding reductions and policies of 'self-reliance' were found to be exacerbating problems that had long brooded beneath the capital's surface of affluence, and were compounded by other aspects of the city. Without local or municipal government, Canberra had long relied on a dispersed, largely volunteer-driven model of welfare provision. Under unprecedented stress, Vinson found, this system was breeding an 'adversary rather than a cooperative' relationship between unprepared government and professional agencies, and 'amateur' groups close to the issues and pressing for reform.[20]

What resources were available might be deployed with initiative, for – again – Canberra did not lack dedicated administrators. In 1978, the Australian Capital Territory Police Force, having been reprieved – for the time being – from Labor's determination to amalgamate it with an Australia-wide body, built on its connections to the community by introducing 63 'unit beats' to bolster public relations and its grasp of a fragmenting society. But it was responding to alarming trends. Sharp increases in robbery and 'hard drug'-related crime were concentrated among younger offenders in older, inner-suburban areas. The maps of disadvantage and dysfunction overlapped, as did the rising graphs of their incidence.[21]

In 1976, 'Jobless Action' was one of several homegrown groups emerging from this impasse. Its 'direct action' ethic combated a prevailing 'dole bludger' stigma through collective contracting for work, establishing referral services, lobbying for concessions, and offering 'life' if not 'job' skills to its clients in courses from cooking to car maintenance. From 1979, its newspaper, *Hard Times*, reflected an ethic of collaboration embracing charities such as the Salvation Army and St Vincent de Paul. There was, among these networks, a determination not to let go of the 'Whitlam dream', and a sense that Canberra still offered an inter-personal scale of activism and assistance that might not have survived in bigger cities. As the NCDC negotiated programs to 'regenerate' the more disadvantaged areas of Narrabundah in collaboration with large property developers, *Hard Times* argued that residents should at least be given preference for jobs in the demolition of their own homes.[22]

Among Jobless Action's keenest supporters was the Trades and Labour Council (TLC) of the Australian Capital Territory, ramping up its own political activity. Diverse issues readily found a common focus in this context. Dominated by left-leaning construction unions, the TLC was galvanised at this time by the discovery of the extent to which asbestos had been a vital component in building the capital. It entered into its 'most extensive and critical campaign' in dealing with the past exposure of workers, and with clearing asbestos from ostensibly state-of-the-art schools, offices and homes – even the National Library. A fierce critique of managerial indifference generated in this work expanded to encompass other issues in which Canberra's privileges were seen to be a thin veil on the same old face of exploitation: the inadequate provision of low-cost accommodation, for example, and the Council's imposition of a blockade on the construction of another private school at a time of cuts to public education. Such causes also took the trade unions further into the local Labor Party, prompting the formation of factions that would shape its business and raise its temper.[23]

Part of this synthesis was 2XX, one of Australia's most enduring community radio stations. Established out of an ANU-based studio in 1976, in collaboration with welfare and sporting bodies, and funded by subscriptions, 2XX provided training and opportunities to many groups, from ethnic organisations to the elderly to the surge of 'punk' bands in the city – the latter being far from incongruous: here was the personification of the alienation of youth, long associated with the city. These voices were matched by new images when, in 1981, Jobless Action supported the foundation of Bitumen River Gallery in a disused school shed in Manuka.

Run by a collective, Bitumen River reflected the strength of local screen printing, as it evolved from a backyard skill taught in workshops for the unemployed to a vigorous arts movement. Opened by the radical Canberra historian Humphrey McQueen, Bitumen River was, as artist and later filmmaker Tony Ayres recalled, Canberra's first 'cultural fringe'. Its manifesto, opposing 'the terrorism of big business and its concomitant manipulative exploitation mentality' might seem top-heavy in the city, but it cleverly morphed into work using a suburban vernacular to spur consciences on T-shirts, tea towels and posters. Canberra activism specialised in such connections. A youth theatre workshop, established in the early 1970s, similarly fed into productions pushing past primal screams into themes of feminism, violence and sexual stereotyping – never losing touch with a more inclusive sense of the possibility of 'fun' in speaking truth to power in the close proximities Canberra offered. Rallying points included the arrest, under a hastily amended traffic ordinance, of 64 women who sought to join the ANZAC Day march in 1981 to raise awareness of rape in war. The cases against these marchers, eventually dismissed, prompted the formation of the territory's Civil Liberties Council, highlighting the absence of 'mechanisms of accountability'. Always an articulate community, Canberra was increasingly a restless one.[24]

Older issues also edged forward. After more than a century's dispossession and relocation, Aboriginal people in south-eastern New South Wales increasingly turned to Canberra in the search for work or education: it was, after all, a 'regional centre'. A 'scattering' of families could be the price paid for pursuing these opportunities in the city, but they also built deepening networks of support within it. The activist-poet-playwright Kevin Gilbert came to Canberra as one of the founders of the Tent Embassy in 1972 but later settled there, persistently interrogating the national legitimacy the capital represented. Joe Croft, a Gurindji man and a child of the stolen generation, arrived in 1974 as a liaison officer with the Department of Aboriginal Affairs. He soon established social, recreational and sporting facilities, such as Boomanulla Oval in Narrabundah, to assist others to settle in a

Figure 21: Megalo International Screenprinting Collective. An exhibition of postcards and posters by Megalo Unemployment Project, Bitumen River Gallery, 1985. (National Gallery of Australia, Canberra. Gift of the Canberra Contemporary Art Space)

city that was becoming more central to their identities. For Aboriginal people, the communal and the national could bring its own fusion to Canberra. Over 2000 people attended the first National Aboriginal Country Music Festival in 1976, inaugurated by local man Harry Williams and Wilga Munro. The National Aboriginal Conference first met in Canberra in 1978, and brought rising leaders, such as Western Australian Rob Riley, elected in 1981, to test the prospects of influence in the capital. Alongside the Department of Aboriginal Affairs at Woden, from 1980 an Aboriginal Development Commission played a part in Charles Perkins' project – with him as its first chair; in 1984 he was the first Aboriginal secretary of a Commonwealth department – of 'Aboriginalising' his staff. By 1985, a 'Come to Canberra' conference reflected the determination of a self-declared 'flying wedge' of land council negotiators, including John Ah Kit and Pat Dodson, to make sure their point was heard in and beyond the corridors of parliament they walked, both in defiance and in search of influence. In 1971, the territory's Aboriginal population numbered 248; it was 1220 by 1986. If many were recent arrivals, their presence nonetheless assisted local people, as Ngambri-Ngunawal elder Matilda House recalls, in gradually 'piecing everything back together'.[25]

For another Aboriginal community at Wreck Bay, part of the Jervis Bay annex, protest built on a deeper solidarity. In 1979, its 150 residents emerged, the *Canberra Times* noted, from a 'forgotten village', railing against the impact of commercial and recreational fishing on their resources, their declining standard of services and housing, and the trimming of their original reserve to an area leased from the Department of the Capital Territory. Led by George Brown, they imposed a road blockade to highlight the presumption of tourist access over shell middens to a popular beach – and later used a documentary film to oppose plans for a large naval base adjoining their land. As observed by the Aboriginal Treaty Committee, a Canberra-based group of eminent non-Aboriginal men and women chaired by H.C. Coombs, the inconsistencies the Commonwealth applied even in its own jurisdiction at Wreck Bay provided clear evidence of the need for coordinated action on what they already termed 'native title'. Similarly seeking to move the community on from benevolent paternalism, a grant from the territory Schools Authority assisted a teacher, Ann Nugent, to devise a 'community-oriented' program in local Aboriginal language and oral history involving all pupils at the Jervis Bay primary school, including those from Wreck Bay. Considerable progress was made in building understanding among children; relations, however, stalled between groups of parents and the school itself amid the deepening politics of 'land rights'.[26]

These voices, perhaps unexpected in Canberra, nonetheless found a hearing in these years, as did others. Decades of growth had lifted the city's first mass infusion of non-English-speaking immigrants above national averages in literacy and occupational status. Another Schools Authority grant, establishing a 'transfer point' into education for still marginalised people, discovered that there remained many 'drifters between two cultures' in Canberra's suburbs. Among early beneficiaries was a 14-year-old girl, whose immigrant father refused to allow her to attend school because of its 'permissiveness', and several mature women who remained locked within the capital's largely invisible 'ESL ghetto'. A reliance on voluntary services – often provided by the immigrants of the 1950s who understood the challenges to those following them, increasingly from South America and the Middle East – worked to break that isolation. Their efforts proved especially effective in meeting the next challenge of new arrivals.[27]

Several Vietnamese students, studying at the ANU, were among the first refugees from their country in Australia following the fall of the Saigon government in 1975. Marion Roderick, later Marion Lê, a fellow student, was stirred by their plight, and by the pressures evident in the first arrivals of 'boat people'. She led in the foundation of Canberra's Indo-Chinese Refugee Association (ICRA) in 1977, the second such organisation formed after an earlier one in South Australia. Advocating a system of direct settlement in housing supported by community and church-based organisations, ICRA in the Australian Capital Territory averted the dislocation and prejudice associated with the concentration of refugees in government hostel-based accommodation elsewhere. By 1980, with one to two families arriving each week, the association lobbied for access to public housing beyond areas zoned for redevelopment. In part, their practice – providing a national model – was a product of necessity.

Canberra's hostels were gone – or taken over by Jobless Action to provide low-income shelter. In part, Lê noted – as ex-military officers, ASIO operatives, academics and immigration officials gravitated to ICRA in purely voluntary capacities – such community support reflected a sense of implication in the course of the war in Vietnam, keenly felt in Canberra. But, as many volunteers who had arrived in the 1950s argued, this community had also been there before; now it could made a virtue of its own experience in moving past assimilation.[28]

Inevitably Canberra's physical environment also came under critical evaluation. In 1977, George Seddon – then a professor of environmental studies, commissioned to review the NCDC's 'open space system' – returned a mixed verdict. 'It would', he found, 'hardly have been possible to create a more effective set of communication barriers in what began as a fairly open landscape'. A 'keep off the grass' message seemed inscribed in Canberra's public spaces, which might gesture towards order but were deprived of function. Integration was again the message: this was a city, at last, to be used. Pedal Power, a group formed in late 1974, pushed hard to improve the safety of riders; an admirable system of bicycle paths began to thread across Canberra and provided a model of such provision. Under pressure, as urban analyst Paul Mees has shown, the NCDC recognised the need to revise its entrenched 'laissez faire transportation policy', adopting a concept of 'managed demand' that might reduce the environmental and economic costs of private cars and meet diverse needs. Priority and express bus services – conceded to be less than the 'radical' overhaul advocated by some – boosted patronage well into the 1980s, at least until the fleet itself came under the eye of cost-cutters.[29]

Questions of access inevitably raised questions of impact, and of thresholds to continued growth. In a graphic demonstration of these issues, by the 1980s Canberra's dominant landscape and leisure feature was, the NCDC conceded, in a 'critical condition' due to a series of accumulating choices and shortfalls in land use planning. The Lake Burley Griffin Catchment Protection Scheme was, when agreed between the Commonwealth and New South Wales in 1964, a model of collaboration and the largest in the state in extent and expertise. But by the 1980s, the lake's turbidity and nutrient levels reflected strains arising not only from urban run-off and upstream sewerage spills, but from the extent to which rural residential development in that catchment had spurred lifestyle choices and property speculation linked to Canberra itself. These algal blooms symbolised another dimension of Canberra's region, and the accumulating punctures to what the CSEREC's magazine, *Bogong*, called the capital's 'delusions of purity'.[30]

In their own surge of activism, and drawing on a research-skilled constituency, Canberra's environmentalists gained visibility in addressing these delusions. Their campaign to extend the territory's nature reserves led to the declaration in 1984 of Namadgi National Park, taking in the southern third of the territory. They opposed a motor racing circuit, intended to boost tourism, on the grounds of noise pollution. Articles in *Bogong* included a contrast between a city that in 1970 had drawn its power largely from the Snowy Mountains Scheme but by 1980 – consuming more electricity on a per capita basis than anywhere else in Australia, primarily for domestic consumption – had a footprint now reliant on the coal-fired power stations of New South Wales (later reaching further to dirtier sources in Victoria). Wasn't it was time to rethink the options?[31]

The sensibility of the 'bush capital' produced a remarkably creative reflection on such issues. 'Considered as an ecosystem', the poet Judith Wright observed, 'Canberra is impossible'. There was 'no balance between input and output'. Still, Wright was one of several prominent figures who by the 1980s were closely associated with a distinct environmental awareness in and based around the city. Established in 1965, the Australian Conservation Foundation had drawn heavily on the expertise – and caution – of Canberra-based scientists. Over time, that network and base broadened. In 1972, W.K. Hancock's *Discovering Monaro* – as Tom Griffiths argues, a 'foundation text' in Australian environmental history – allowed its author to work through his 'ambivalence' towards Canberra in 'learning' the country to its south. Also ANU-based, philosophers Richard and Val Routley (later Richard Sylvan and Val Plumwood, respectively) developed a trenchant critique of resource management in the south-eastern forests. And while critics resist the reduction to a literal landscape of the pastoral theme in the work of a significant number of self-identifying 'Canberra poets', an engagement with place – 'the streets, the suburbs, the hills' – dominated their work.[32]

If 'aesthetically conservative', as Geoff Page concedes, from the 1970s this group developed a remarkable collegiality across generations and approaches, spanning from the classicism of A.D. Hope and Rosemary Dobson's beguilement by a Canberra bus driver with 'Sartre in his pocket', to more experimental, younger writers. Innovative craft-based publishing was one adaption for this small community, distant from metropolitan centres, and so was a close attention to the juxtapositions at the core of Canberra's 'impossibility'. David Campbell and R.F. Brissenden took courses in the ANU's Human Sciences program, bringing interdisciplinary concepts of ecology into their poetry and – for Brissenden – campaigns for conservation on the New South Wales south coast. There the clustering of Canberrans' beach houses also fostered reflection on their impact and privilege. John Rowland, a retired diplomat, brought his skills to the presidency of the Environment Centre, working with as much as against a community in which, as he wrote:

> ...something in these quiet streets
> Houses at ambush in their drives
> Compels us into separateness.

Breaking out of her own isolation as the wife of an astronomer at Mount Stromlo, Rosalie Gascoigne began assembling discarded objects, gathered from the 'vastness of dry blonde grass' around the city, into artworks that, by 1982 – in an extraordinary acceleration in her career – featured as Australia's entry in the Venice Biennale. Gascoigne's works were meditations on the layering of this landscape, incongruous, already tinged with nostalgia, bare but deep in textuality. 'At first you think there is nothing there', Gascoigne reflected of the country around Canberra, 'and later you learn that there is everything'.[33]

These paradoxes explain the intellectual vitality of the capital: a sense of implication in larger issues, at a scale which seemed to support critical engagement. But there were limitations. Bitumen River began with an anti-careerist ethos but, even so, by 1982 screen-printer Alison Alder reflected that 'because Canberra is such a small place, if you keep doing something then people will think you are OK'. An unspoken expectation that it was enough to remain an 'amateur' in an essentially salaried monoculture meant that 'people burn out fairly quickly', or were taken for granted. A contributor to *Bogong* similarly welcomed the ease of 'social action' embraced by the many groups of which she was a part in the city, but worried at 'a certain "ghetto" consciousness' among them. Was 'an activist lifestyle' in the capital a surrogate for a lack of 'belonging'? This question articulated a particular feature of life in Canberra which was reaching a crucial threshold through the 1980s. The question was: where to next?[34]

HUCKSTERED OUT

Despite government-imposed frugality, Canberra still acquired new – and revealing – trappings. A building for the High Court was completed in 1980 at $49 million, nearly three times the original estimate. Chief Justice Garfield Barwick's ambitions had been trimmed only a little in locking into place the Court's centrality to the business of Australian government. He couldn't, however, secure the full relocation of its functions to the capital, which even his fellow judges argued would deprive them of their connectedness to the nation and their capacity to attract the best officers. The majority of the bench and their staff then joined the city's ranks of transient lives – although at least, in its cavernous spaces, they adopted simplified court attire and found their work gained in press attention and public awareness by being settled in the parliamentary triangle. Adjoining the Court, the National Gallery opened in 1982, its sequence of raw concrete galleries offering a broad, bold and innovative sweep through world art, at once informal and didactic. Both buildings had their origins in the Whitlam years. The recommendation for a Museum of Australia, however, had the misfortune to come from a committee reporting in late 1975. Their vision of encompassing the natural and human history of the continent as well as the nation, of 'mending intellectual rifts' relating to Aboriginal Australians and the impacts of settlement, and of doing so in a series of buildings more gently meshed with a site in the capital to impart ecological awareness, fell into long abeyance.[35]

Two other projects won through with a leaner symbolism. Australia's dismal performance at the 1976 Montreal Olympics spurred the establishment of a national Institute of Sport. Built from 1981, adjacent to the stadium constructed in the suburb of Bruce to host the 1977 Commonwealth Games, the Institute offered scholarships to athletes from around Australia for intensive, scientific training. Reconciling what a series of directors saw as either an overly rigid 'Fortress Bruce' or residual 'lamington-drive' mentality in elite sport proved difficult: their turnover was quick until a more devolved and participatory training model was adopted at the end of the Institute's first decade. In establishing the Australian Defence Force Academy, neighbouring the Royal Military College, Duntroon, the government attempted another delicate balance. The task – as bluntly defined by the Secretary of the Department of Defence, Sir Arthur Tange – was to redress the 'insufficient numbers of officers...with the intellectual bases upon which to analyse issues and contribute to policy'. Intense debate through the late 1970s weighed whether three distinct service identities could be meshed with the provision of 'a balanced and liberal tertiary education'. Sponsorship by the University of New South Wales eventually vouched for the academic integrity of ADFA, which opened in 1986, with 700 cadets, including 52 women. Still, as the *Canberra Times* noted, civilian Canberra regarded this 'tightly-bound sub-culture' with caution, especially as certain city nightclubs became its off-duty haunts. Cadets themselves found their new 'Legoland' very unlike its 'glossy' promotional videos. The Academy was soon clouded by reports of systemic personal harassment, practices judged to have been exacerbated by its objective of going 'further down the road' of integrating military, academic and gender equity requirements than it had the resources to achieve.[36]

Far from the first Canberra laboratories to raise questions of what national institutions should be, these ventures at least added much needed support to the local economy and identity. Overarching them was the matter of a permanent Parliament House. The pressure of nearly 3000 people working in a provisional building intended for a few hundred forced Malcolm Fraser to set aside his concerns at seeming extravagance and announce, in late 1978, a commitment to a new building. A competition, open to architects registered in

Australia, was launched in April 1979, to be overseen by a specially constituted construction authority. Over three hundred entries were received, with the winning design emerging in June 1980. The successful, American-based firm, Mitchell Giurgola Thorp, appealed directly to the 'poetics' of Griffin's plan with a building embedded in Capital Hill, defusing anxieties about parliament's claims to dominate the city. A fusion, as architectural historian Christopher Vernon notes, of 'landscape' and 'architecture', it adapted the apex of the parliamentary triangle to two gracefully arcing forms, defining the legislative and executive quarters and a central mall, and anchoring a soaring flagpole. The building synthesised the city as an ideal, but also as a vernacular, with red-tiled roofs over the chambers and forecourt arcades recalling Murdoch, Sulman and the Federal Capital Commission of the 1920s. Construction began in 1981, its projected budget $220 million. Completed in 1988, at a cost exceeding $1 billion, it made its own significant impact on the fortunes of the city.[37]

Effectively excluded from a project it assumed would be its 'crowning achievement', the NCDC was kept to a bitter diet. In 1982, the government declined to allocate it funds for residential land servicing. The Commission protested: even if private investors could be found to fill the gap, it argued, they could offer no guarantee of the kind of 'balanced' urban development Canberra deserved. The government, however, had already instituted an inquiry seeking to 'eliminate unnecessary regulation' and 'reduce the scope and amount of public sector activity' in Canberra. The NCDC seemed finished. Yet the inquiry committee had a mind of its own. Chaired by George White, architect of the Capitol, Washington, it conceded that the NCDC had made a jerky transition from its undoubted 'greenfields' expertise to the more exacting demands of 'redevelopment and infill'. It questioned whether the Commission's treasured 'independence' continued to be the best way of meeting public opinion, and recommended it 'democratise' its sources of advice. But while it conceded that there must be a considerable diversification away from the reliance on government projects which had plunged the capital into uncertainty, it recommended that there must be no change to the principles of fixed-term and fixed-purpose leasehold that had always guided the planning of the capital. Market-based mechanisms, White argued, tended only to strip assets, including through stigmatising public housing. The Commission's role in social planning was, more than ever, the priority.[38]

Even before this vindication was released, a change of government brought the prospect of relief. Promising an end to national divisiveness, Bob Hawke led Labor to power in March 1983. His victory speech, astutely delivered for the first time in the National Tally Room, from which the 'buzz' of vote counting had been televised since 1963, was celebrated with 'pandemonium' by the thousands of people who queued there. The Australian Capital Territory had emphatically voted Labor, returning sitting members Ken Fry and Ros Kelly (who had defeated John Haslem in 1980) with swings three times the national average. As soon as it could, the NCDC vented its 'outrage' to its new minister at having being subject to inquiry, lamented the 'rock-bottom' condition into which its estate had been allowed to fall, and determined on a renewed program of growth. If Canberra, as journalist Paul Kelly observed, was 'exhausted' and 'demoralised' at the end of the Fraser years, many seemed determined on renewal. Not alone in its confidence that Canberra would return to its best, the Commission was soon similarly to have good company in its disappointment.[39]

Behind Hawke's 'consensus' rhetoric was the recognition that much had changed. Canberra was evolving into a new kind of political theatre, with a more intensely competitive stage. National industry, commercial, professional and other pressure groups ramped up their skills in dealing with politicians and public servants who, in turn, talked of reducing the protection of the state and following – as Treasury put it – the 'self-correcting' instincts of the economy. Fraser's talk of stringency became Labor's creed of efficiency, and new reputations in and out of government would be made in adapting to it. Rick Farley, who came to join the National Farmers' Federation in 1985, on the eve of the protest that brought 45 000 angry farmers to the city in its biggest protest so far, spoke of the inner-south suburb of Barton as 'Bullshit Alley', given the clustering of such 'peak body' expertise in the neighbourhood of the old, and the new, Parliament House, of the Press Club and of the good restaurants where business was done. A master of the 'tipping point' in orchestrating public relations and internal networks, Farley epitomised what it took to work the city, mixing trust and threat in holding the big players – business, unions and government – to the bargains of 'streamlining' and 'rationalisation' with which Canberra was becoming synonymous.⁴⁰

In Hawke's first year, the Public Service Board welcomed a 4 per cent increase in it staff. Under Dr Peter Wilenski, it strengthened its commitment to equal opportunity principles, pledging to make the bureaucracy 'more representative of the society which it serves'. But the Board also began passing on directives for departments to be increasingly responsive to ministerial leadership, to accept the closer involvement of ministers in their management, and for those appointed to the Senior Executive Service to 'think of themselves in terms of the Service as a whole' rather than in terms of the departmental interests of old. Whatever the portfolio into which they were inserted as a kind of shock troop, the SES exemplified the doctrines of 'new public management', answering to those 'who pay for service provision through tax, and politicians who represent the collective will and make policy choices'. The Board itself was abolished in 1987, along with a reduction of the number of Commonwealth departments from 28 to 18 in a two-tier ministry intended to increase policy coordination and the strategic power of Cabinet. The old Canberra – of silos, permanency in leadership, incremental change and the gentle arts of 'log-rolling' influence – was gone.⁴¹

Other institutions, central to the image of the city, also had to adjust. At the ANU, Professor Peter Karmel, as Vice-Chancellor, accepted that the national university must now become part of a 'national tertiary education system', another dimension of Labor's push for accountability. The cuts of the late 1970s had taken more than 10 per cent off the university's budget, and tested the bases on which it could support, and assess, its goals. Past practice, Karmel insisted, could no longer offer a guide through a new landscape of 'change without growth'. As Foster and Varghese record, such self-scrutiny could highlight issues such as the 'systematic discrimination' against women in appointments and promotion, and expose areas where reviews of performance were overdue. But the times were unsettled, and by 1987 the ANU was confronted with its most fundamental challenge. Commonwealth Education Minister John Dawkins urged the amalgamation of the ANU with the Canberra College of Advanced Education (CCAE) to achieve efficiencies, enhance student access, and give the government greater power in setting targets. A strenuous staff campaign defeated this proposal, but was not always diplomatic in acknowledging the standing of the CCAE (which became the University of Canberra under sponsorship from Melbourne's Monash University in 1990) while defending their own integrity. Canberra was a small field for such a battle, and the ANU was not safe from return challenges.[42]

There was a bristling mood in the city. Local Labor moved further left. Succeeding Ken Fry in 1984, John Langmore as member for Fraser, and a former political staffer, openly criticised his government's economic, social and defence policies. Susan Ryan, as Minister for Education, weathered branch hostility over her compromises on university amalgamation and private school funding. On the other hand, local doctors – a tight group, accustomed as eminent figures in the community to their visiting rights in public hospitals – became some of the nation's most militant in long-term strike action, opposing the introduction of sessional contracts in place of fee-for-service as the thin edge of 'socialism' in health. 'Scabs' in hospital wards were treated no more kindly than those in workplaces elsewhere in the city as industrial conflicts became more entrenched. As the local TLC declared, Hawke seemed more prepared that Fraser to 'muzzle the unions' in the name of deregulation.[43]

And behind government 'reform' there was seen to be a face hardly evident in Canberra to this point. While public sector growth slackened in the later 1980s – a reflection of 'efficiency' – entrepreneurs in the finance and business sectors led a surge in private prestige office building, seeking to capitalise in part on providing the services the government no longer provided for itself, and also to take advantage of a new spirit of competition. Rebadging itself as 'a facilitator' of private investment, the NCDC swallowed the argument of this much-courted sector that 'all development should be focused in Civic' as a way of ensuring its profitability and enhancing its image. The city centre, the *Canberra Times*' Jack Waterford declared, was in danger of 'being huckstered out to anyone who says he might spend a bob'. Not only was this development contributing to the imbalance in the progress of Canberra's 'new towns' and undercutting the old ideal of 'dispersal'; it was straining the amenity of Civic and of the suburbs around it. In 1987, the development in Canberra's next 'new town', Gungahlin, to the north, was deferred in the name of consolidation in existing areas, of achieving 'metropolitan' densities and attractions – and assured returns to private investment.[44]

The energy and confidence – the muscle – associated with this investment was, however, infectious: it satisfied a pervasive yearning for reinvention. Another manifestation of this drive was the launching of several high-profile sporting teams, buying into major competitions, testing the capacity of the local community and corporate sponsors to support such expensive undertakings, attract international-level players, and rally to new heroes. The Canberra Cannons went into the National Basketball League in 1979, with several prominent recruits from the United States. The Canberra Raiders entered the Sydney Rugby League competition in 1982. Australian Capital Territory Rugby Union began a longer process of buying into state and national ranks, culminating in the formation of the Brumbies in 1996. These teams, seasoned with recruits from the region, made their mark, providing figures of admiration and a fan-based solidarity Canberra had never had. As business ventures, they brought risks of their own – as the fortunes of the Cannons, privatised in 1986, defunct by 2002, would show – and claims on services, such as the upgrading of public sporting facilities which could distort land use and costs. But through them, the city acquired a 'brand', and one that recognised new areas of achievement, such as when the women's basketball team, the Capitals, launched under the Cannons' wing in 1986, emerged as the city's most successful sporting venture. When Bob Hawke revived the tradition of an annual Prime Minister's XI cricket match at Manuka Oval in 1984, it was with a characteristic zeal of competitiveness and celebrity appeal very unlike the gentlemen's contest Menzies had last presided over in 1965.[45]

The Parliamentary Press Gallery, which took to the wicket against the Prime Minister's team in 1984 (and sent him hurt from the crease) had never warmed to Fraser's aloofness. It was, however, captivated by Hawke, and added its own new spirit to the capital. Far from being a place of exile, Canberra by the late 1980s was the court from which a corps of correspondents – among them Michelle Grattan, Laurie Oakes and Alan Ramsey – had no desire to leave lest something pass them by. Public figures in their own right, they were part of decision-making processes, woven into flows of information defined by an edgy mix of discretion and bravura. Another rising figure, the pollster, perfected its own 'political technology', cultivating telegenic leadership for its clients, exaggerating differences in politics rather than common ground on policy, and playing to 'the most emotive side of the argument' in tapping swinging voters. If this was cynical, it was still creative and not yet formulaic. For a time the satirical magazine *Matilda* – edited from a house opposite the Prime Minister's Lodge by Robbie Swan, who had navigated several of Canberra's organic, esoteric and psychedelic sub-cultures since the 1970s – teased away at the capital's circles of rumour and intelligence, sexual intrigue and pretension with its own home-grown mocking affection. Its circle of contributors included Germaine Greer, Bill Pinwill, Richard Neville, Patrick Cook and Michael Leunig, but the capital was still its focus. It found common cause with the angry frenzy with which the political cabaret of the Doug Anthony All Stars graduated from Canberra's febrile underground to street theatre and national television. Little about the city escaped the magazine's wry attention. A cartoon that appeared in *Matilda* at the time mapped prevailing political and economic mantras ('Wet', 'Dry', 'Crowding Out', 'J-curve', etc.) over bulges in the shorts of the joggers who surged out of government offices every lunch time, proving that the age of the grey cardigan and crumpled suit was gone.[46]

The opening of the new Parliament House in 1988 – 'a luxury Fuhrerbunker', as Mungo MacCallum derided it in *Matilda* – symbolised these trends. The dominance of space allocated to executive over parliamentary functions in the building typified the changing face of government, as did the kind of insularity this world unto itself encouraged among politicians, staffers and journalists, all now with more rooms, even suites, to themselves and none of the old informalities of jostling proximity. The intrigue that toppled John Howard as Liberal opposition leader in 1989, for example, was said to owe much to secrets the new building kept that could never have survived in the old. Segregations inside the building had parallels outside. In 1980, the NCDC had envisaged the parliament on Capital Hill as an apex from which another version of its orderly, urban plaza would proceed to the lake shore. By 1986, this scheme was hollowed out into another gardened landscape. It was becoming harder to envisage the parliamentary triangle as an active theatre of citizenship; the real business was done behind its doors. The people might have been able to climb over Parliament's grassy roof, but its forecourt – while blessed with an extensive, water-framed mosaic by the Walpiri artist Michael Nelson Jagamara – was no place for protest, and was (as Kevin Gilbert pointed out) a sham if it presumed in some way to atone for white theft.[47]

The increasing isolation of parliament seemed to fit the way Canberrans viewed their own political representation. In a referendum of 1978, 64 per cent voted against any form of self-government, concerned at the shift of the costs of the capital onto their shoulders. But this 'fear' – or disdain – of politics, and the desire by many in the burgeoning private and cautious public sectors not to lose the 'backstairs' methods that served them well in local affairs, was tempered by the vulnerability the city had experienced. The most prominent advocates for self-government reflected on the social, welfare and environmental strains of the preceding decade and insisted that Canberrans must gain control over their own circumstances. The lobbying of the local Labor branch saw self-rule written into the party's national platform in 1982, and featured in Hawke's first policy commitments. Successive Labor ministers for the territory spoke of the 'continuing shame' of a mature population being ruled by the 'whim' of others. The clincher for change, however, came from another quarter. A series of inquiries confirmed the increasing extent to which the territory benefited from subsidies from the nation's taxpayers. Its 'featherbedding' was to end under another mantra of the times: 'user pays'.[48]

Steadily in the late 1980s areas of responsibility were transferred from a range of Commonwealth departments to a single Australian Capital Territory Administration, where John Enfield, as Secretary of the Department of Territories and Local Government, determined that budgetary discipline would end an 'inbred' attitude among officers who had faced little accountability in the past. In 1986 the Commonwealth Efficiency Scrutiny Unit recommended that the NCDC be abolished, its work done. A Commonwealth Parliamentary Committee determined that Canberra was to be filleted, with responsibility for 'national areas' going to a National Capital Planning Authority – charged with preserving 'the essential character of the city' – while the rest went to a territory government. So the movement towards self-government grew, structures and concepts being set in place – some truly innovative, such as a constitution for the proposed Legislative Assembly that gave no formal role to a vice-regal representative. But the majority of the people remained opposed to it all. If Canberra was the last national capital among Western democracies to achieve a measure of local representative government, the path scarcely suited the goal.[49]

Deliberations over the form of self-government extended significantly past the final term of the House of Assembly, and in that process the design of an electoral system proved most divisive. Labor proposed the election of representatives from single-member electorates, a model sure to advantage its own candidates. Other parties argued for multi-member electorates, while community interests pushed for a model that would give a breadth of contenders a chance. The D'Hondt system of direct proportional representation was adapted from Europe as a compromise. Modified in protracted negotiations, it was complex enough, with a mix of quota provisions, preference options and deeming rules to be applied in counting the vote. When applied in the first poll, conducted on 4 March 1989, for 17 seats in a single chamber, contested in a territory-wide electorate, it proved deeply confusing, if not ridiculous, for many voters.[50]

At over a metre in length, the ballot paper was the largest ever issued in Australia. It listed 117 candidates, in part the result of an attempt to encourage people to contest the election by setting a low deposit for their registration, but also reflecting significant elements of protest if not sabotage among those running. The paper included groups such as the Sun-Ripened Warm Tomato Party and the Party! Party! Party!, alongside Democrats, National Party, Fair Election and Family Team tickets and several independent and 'community' candidates. Against expectations – and at the end of a counting process that took two months – Labor had won only five seats and the Liberals four, in total just 39 per cent of the vote between them. Government could only be formed in some form of coalition with members of the two other successful parties. One, the Residents Rally, was a coalition of nine candidates who rejected party discipline or a single political philosophy, advocating instead for diverse community grievances. With 10 per cent of the vote, the Rally won three seats. The other, ironically, was the No Self-Government Party, which fielded 17 candidates in a tightly organised campaign on that core platform, winning three seats. Another went to the Abolish Self-Government team.[51]

It would be easy to mock the basis on which Canberra finally emerged as a body politic. Protracted negotiations convinced the Liberals and No Self-Government members to support a minority Labor government with Rosemary Follett, a public servant, as Chief Minister – and the first woman to head a government in Australia. By the end of the year, those bargains broke down and the Liberals' Trevor Kaine, a retired RAAF Wing Commander, assumed leadership of the Assembly. Instability dogged his brief tenure. For a city so associated with the heavy hand of executive government, it was another paradox that its own parliament was born so inherently unstable, and so structurally and temperamentally opposed to majority party rule. But those characteristics also indicated the ways in which Canberra now sought to project itself, in its markedly changed circumstances, into its uncharted future.

8

Feel the power

AN URBAN VILLAGE

In the optimism of the mid-1960s, the National Capital Development Commission (NCDC) had envisaged Canberra's population in 1990 as 500 000. When that year came, the figure was 282 600. Such a shortfall indicates the scale at which visions, and realities, of the city had changed. Briefly, in the mid-1980s, buoyed by a new federal government, the NCDC had been lured back to that half million possibility as a goal to welcome the new millennium – but that was still with a faith that the tasks of national development would inevitably deliver such growth to the capital. By 1990, with the coming of self-government and the end of a deregulation-driven boom grinding into Federal Labor Treasurer Keating's 'recession we had to have', it was clear that Canberra might instead be left to its own devices. The city, as demographers calculate, might then have been on the verge of that long-anticipated threshold at which its size would finally be sufficient to underpin its development. But a number of trends were suggesting that the seeds for such development were fouling. The future to be raised from them might not be pretty.[1]

In 1990, estimates of the Australian Capital Territory's employment growth were nearly halved to 2.8 per cent for the next five years. From 1994 to 1998 its economic activity grew at 1.7 per cent while the Australian average was three times that. Between 1994 and 2006, its population grew at levels consistently below the national rate (0.9 as against 1.3 per cent). When the new millennium came, estimates were for 390 000 residents by 2030; the figure of 500 000 was deferred to 2050. Statistics are not a story in themselves, but they suggest a framework. Having passed through the politicisation of the 1970s and 1980s, the adjustment of expectations, usually downwards, became the overarching priority for a city continuing to find its scale and place in the dynamics of the nation around it.[2]

Relative to that nation, the capital remained undeniably privileged. It was young, with – in 1996 – the second highest national percentage of children zero to four years of age after Darwin. It had by far the highest level of post-secondary qualifications (28 per cent; Sydney coming next with 21 per cent). Its incomes continued well above national averages – the median being up to a third above New South Wales, the next on the rank. Canberra had Australia's largest number of families with dependent children and by 2001 was, again, only just beaten by Darwin in its proportion of DINKs (double income, no kid households). But these two territory capitals – each a 'new town' in its own way – were hardly representative Australian cities, and had other sides to them. Canberrans paid less in rent, but their mortgage repayments were higher than the national average, and for homes with lower occupancy rates. The city had the highest percentage of women single parents at work, but those levels of labour-force participation were proving particularly vulnerable to fluctuations in public service staffing. As Sara Dowse reflected, here was the 'post-' phase of a city that in better times had made strides for 'feminism' in gaining women's access to work combined with motherhood, but now saw that contract unravelling. Unemployment among those aged over 45 might be the lowest in the country, but it was the highest for youth. On several indices through the 1990s, the capital came in fifth relative to state equivalents, behind the rising fortunes of Queensland and Western Australia and just ahead of the doldrums of South Australia and Tasmania. That was a precarious place to be.[3]

This was so especially since, despite its mantra of social and economic diversification, Canberra – unlike the rest of Australia – was distinguished by relatively little shift in its core areas of employment. In fact, contractions in the overall size of the Commonwealth public service across Australia saw increasing proportions of its ranks concentrated in the capital, but also a much greater proportion of its redundancies. Full-time government officials rose from 26 to 33 per cent of the city's workforce in the two decades to 2004; the figures for trades, industry and construction correspondingly declined. Perhaps ironically, approaching its centenary, Canberra was ever more self-conscious of, invested in, and vulnerable due to, its central office status.[4]

Alongside these demographic and economic trends, the city's framework was also under profound reconsideration. Ostensibly, environmental considerations drove a questioning of the dispersed, commuter-driven premises of the NCDC's Y-plan. In its place, the Commission's successor, the National Capital Planning Authority (NCPA), advocated 'a more sustainable and compact city form'. In 1991, it commissioned Western Australian academic planners, Peter Newman and Jeff Kenworthy, to assess Canberra's options for 'sustainable development'. Harvesting conservationist, business and government opinion, they advocated a European model premised on the adoption of light-rail systems, traffic calming and an 'urban village' concept of concentrated residential nodes. Like the NCPA's fascination with the passing comet of the Multi-Function Polis – promising an 'unbroken continuity of closely related urban experiences', a tripling of housing and employment densities, and the transformation of work-life balances – Newman and Kenworthy's manifesto was influential not in implementation so much as in settling into a conversation that informed Canberra's evolution over coming decades. What might a more internationally oriented, service and knowledge-driven city, embracing a 'cosmopolitan lifestyle', look like? With public spending out of the question, the pulse of private investment was key to this speculation. In the process Canberra's landscape was transformed. In part in response to those disturbing statistical trends, in part in defiance of them, a reinvention was envisaged for that nexus of community, environment and government at the heart of the Canberra experiment.[5]

A detailed narrative of recent events can make for tedious history. And in many of its elements, Canberra became more like the wider patterns of Australian experience in the 1990s. Its distinctiveness faded into the broader 'Australian Moment' in which confidence in what had always been the capital's defining trick – 'bureaucratic command' – so political commentator George Megalogenis argues, disappeared to be replaced by other instincts, aspirations and pressures: from the impact of immigration to the awareness of the Asian region; from distrust of the 'magic pudding' of government to the 'cult' of 'bricks 'n' mortar'; from nation-building to market-driven efficiency. This chapter will offer an overview of how, since 1990, Canberra has weathered its times.[6]

POLITICAL CIRCUS

'The unloved status of the ACT legislature has produced strong adaptive reactions from those who have been its members', Gary Humphries reflected in 2000. Emerging from anti-Left student activism at the Australian National University (ANU), he was a prominent member of the first Liberal team elected to the Legislative Assembly in 1989, briefly Chief Minister in 2000–1, and then a senator (2003–13) for the territory. Humphries exemplified the 'small-l' stance his party sought for this community, often at variance from more the conservative leanings of its national body, and keen for adaptations to its circumstances. Why, he argued, should Australia's most internet-savvy constituency not have the option of generating its own referenda on policy reform? At one point an opponent of self-government, he scaled his ambitions to circumstances, understanding that Canberra's deep ambivalence towards its imposed Assembly, coupled to an eccentric voting system, made minority governments the norm. Deftness was required of politicians who usually had minimal opportunities to gain experience before office, and had to negotiate the Assembly's mix of small political groupings and independents.[7]

Adaptability was similarly required of the territory's bureaucracy as it was drawn into the intersection of two rising narratives. There were the expectations of innovation in what was effectively a 'city-state', keen at last to implement its own agendas. There were also the imperatives of accountable management, given the need to adjust the provision of services to a small tax-base. In both areas, Canberra was once again a laboratory.

Commonwealth funding for the Australian Capital Territory was to be preserved for the first three of a projected seven-year period of adjustment to self-government. But with the clock ticking, budgetary discipline added bite to politics from the start – particularly given that, unlike any local government, the ACT government was saddled with maintaining already high standards of provision in areas such as health and education. The first government, a minority led by Labor's Rosemary Follett, fell within eight months. A respected leader, arguing that 'fledging consultative processes' took time and stability to establish, she was dragged down in accusations of 'wheeler-dealer' behaviour among her colleagues. Trevor Kaine's succeeding Liberal-led 'alliance' government was underpinned by a largely opportunist 'accord' with a range of individual members. Mourned by some as bringing two-party polarity into an Assembly many hoped might be a more open chamber of discussion, this arrangement also strained the consciences of those, such as the Residents Rally's Hector Kinloch, an academic historian, who struggled with the pragmatism of holding and using power. One divisive decision was to approve the long-debated issuing of a casino licence – flagged as promising a boost to revenue and development, and bringing 'class' to a new National Convention Centre in the city. The other side of the ledger included cost-driven school closures and an amalgamation of hospital services, resulting in the decommissioning of the Royal Canberra Hospital, on its commanding peninsula in Lake Burley Griffin. Within 18 months Kaine also fell to a no-confidence motion.[8]

Mounting discontent surrounded the return of a Follett-led minority government, which continued an emerging pattern by being skilful in raising taxes and charges, but less so in lowering expenditure or maintaining services in areas such as public transport and health. A plebiscite, held with the 1992 Assembly election, overwhelmingly supported dumping the territory's chaotic electoral system: the single electorate was replaced with three (Brindabella and Ginninderra with five seats, Molonglo with seven) and the D'Hondt method with the Hare-Clark system of a single transferable vote. Locking in place this model, the poll of 1995 delivered an 11 per cent swing to the Liberal Party, saw two independents lose their seats and the emergence of the local Greens as a significant force. Perhaps Canberrans were starting to feel compelled, against their instincts, to trust parties – although never to the same extent as their fellow Australians.[9]

With greater authority, although still in a hung parliament, the Liberals were led by Kate Carnell, a self-declared 'in-your-face' politician. A pharmacist before entering the second Assembly, she demanded the city break out of 'introspection' and embrace 'enterprise'. First to model this virtue was the Australian Capital Territory Administration, becoming an advance guard for public sector contract appointments and performance pay. Some senior officials left, but others – including many recruited from the business sector – were drawn to the prospect of salary packages considerably higher than those paid by the Commonwealth, so long as results were on the board. Contract-based 'purchaser-provider splits' extended the concept of market-driven efficiency into many areas of social welfare delivery. The result, political scientist Roger Wettenhall declared, was 'the most stream-lined and customer-oriented public service in Australia'.[10]

These transformations brought their own points of friction and reflected continuing financial pressure. In the decade from 1989, general-purpose funding to the Australian Capital Territory collapsed from over $600 million to under $300 million. As journalist Crispin Hull argued, cuts cloaked by injunctions to responsible self-government were fundamentally savings-driven on the part of the Commonwealth. Cuts also changed cultures. Seeking efficiencies, the amalgamation of the territory's electricity, water and sewerage assets brought into collision an ethic of cost recovery in power supply and older models of service provision for water, a resource that for some time had been free. In the early years of ACT Electricity and Water (ACTEW), a new identity of 'business units' sat heavily on staff, politicising their work despite high standards of delivery and amid pressures to raise revenue for the ACT government. The national priority on micro-economic reform and of market-based competition between such facilities exacerbated this strain.[11]

From a related perspective, the ACT Council of Social Service (ACTCOSS) had initially welcomed self-government as promising a coordinated 'social justice strategy'. Soon, however, it lamented the impact of diminishing funding in areas such as public housing, and the extent to which the recasting of welfare agencies as 'providers' was constraining their capacity to represent community interests. The scope for advocacy and innovation in such areas narrowed, as did practices of policy development. A good deal of the move towards private sector employment in Canberra was accounted for by the preference of the Commonwealth and territory governments to contract out for services until recently provided in-house. The result was not just the relocation of work, but a recasting of the ethos with which it was done: who got the contract depended in large part on an understanding of what was wanted.[12]

Over-reach was a risk with such a 'can-do' culture. An unauthorised, unbudgeted overspend of $17 million on the redevelopment of Bruce Stadium, in the confidence that it would recoup investment through hosting events such as soccer matches during the Sydney Olympics, exposed limitations in the market-research, consultant-driven methods that were the underside of a lean, entrepreneurial bureaucracy. Similar miscalculations surrounded the territory government's underwriting the costs of a series of V8 Supercar races run around the Parliamentary Triangle, which fell far short of drawing the visitors, international television audiences and dollars anticipated. An attempt to defuse community disquiet at the demolition of the old Canberra Hospital by turning it into a public spectacle was marred when a 12-year-old girl, Katie Bender, was killed by flying debris – a coronial inquiry finding that planning for the demolition had been flawed by the 'intrusion' of inexpert officials in the Chief Minister's office. Amid accumulating scrutiny of her competence, Carnell resigned in 2000, her position passing to Humphries. An election the next year saw all independents lose their seats in an expression of the need to tighten up the practices of government. Labor's Jon Stanhope, a former political adviser to Federal Opposition leader Kim Beazley, formed another minority government with the Greens' support.[13]

For the next 10 years, Stanhope made his own mark – equally driven, if less charismatic – on the territory. Where Carnell had criticised the staying power of community consultation processes, he cultivated such forums, projecting an image of a party now less dominated by the factions and union influence and determined to improve a range of welfare and infrastructure services. Both endorsed the last attempt by the Commonwealth to use Canberra to push a reform agenda, when the Hawke government legalised the sale of X-rated material in the territory in the late 1980s – a move that at least gave the capital one new lucrative niche industry.

Zoned only in light manufacturing and hardware areas (a revealing association, perhaps), Canberra's sex shops were soon said to have the largest mailing and product lists in the country, and in 1992 the territory became the third Australian jurisdiction to decriminalise brothel and escort work. Carnell supported this reform as recognition of women's rights to health and safety in work. Stanhope – with a much less tolerant Federal Liberal government, led by John Howard, watching him – expanded the agenda into areas of civil liberties, introducing legislation to remove sexual or gender-based discrimination, to enable same-sex couples to marry and adopt children, and to implement Australia's first Bill of Rights.[14]

In 2004, with soaring approval ratings, Stanhope formed the territory's first majority government. When, in 2005, he placed the Prime Minister's draft anti-terrorist legislation on his personal website, to prompt debate over unprecedented powers conferred on intelligence and law-enforcement agencies, spice was added to the already 'provocative relationship' existing between the two governments. As it had in relation to Carnell's prescription heroin trial, the Commonwealth vetoed Stanhope's bill on civil unions as well as Australian Capital Territory and Northern Territory legislation on euthanasia. But what Howard and his ministers derided as Canberra's 'dishonourable political circus' also reflected a desire – as the territory's chief justice, Terrence Higgins, put it – to test 'the way we think'. Reflecting different aspects of their constituencies, Carnell and Stanhope both reaffirmed a distinct identity for Canberra, and a determination to reflect it in political innovation.[15]

Many factors continued to erode that image. An inquiry of 1998, chaired – perhaps appropriately for Canberra – by an ANU philosopher of republicanism, Philip Pettit, diagnosed an entrenched cycle of minimal public regard for the Assembly. Its members had little direct connection to defined constituencies, and its voters were chronically under-represented relative to the rest of Australia. (The territory then had one member for 14 500 voters; the national average was one to 2250 – but still a third House of Representatives seat, Namadgi, proclaimed in 1994, won by Labor in 1996, was abolished the following year given falling population projections.) Pettit found a 'disputatious' community, alienated from government invocations, such as the 1997 attempt to create a new mood with a 'Feel the Power' Canberra campaign. Against a range of largely Liberal-initiated ideas of defusing politics into more consultative processes, Pettit advised instead that what was required was not diminution of political contest in the assembly, but more scrutiny of its policy formulation processes.[16]

By 2006 an expanding deficit, a threatened credit-rating downgrade, and the calculation that services in the capital cost 20 per cent more than elsewhere, led to a 'horror budget' proposing measures such as the closure of 39 schools, an increase in government charges, and another round of public service restructuring. Local business leaders dismissed as 'left-wing bullshit' the proposition that these were necessary corrections: the problem remained chronic mismanagement. The severity of cuts was moderated in response to loud community protest, but the message remained the same: Canberra must live within its own, not the nation's, means.[17]

These local messages were echoed higher up. Paul Keating, more than any other recent prime minister, might have been 'present' in Canberra, working from home, walking with his family around shops, or calling on Manning Clark. But his 'big picture' vision extended well beyond the capital, and seemed even to diminish it. He resisted, for example, reviving the dormant project of a national museum as another 'mausoleum by the lake', not only on grounds of cost but believing that the city offered meagre soil to nourish a representation of national social history. If Canberra was to have no more monuments, a different political landscape was under construction. Formal negotiations between government departments were giving way to 'whole of government' approaches in which small groups of advisers, select senior public servants and co-opted academics worked intensively, discretely, and in close contact with relevant politicians. This new paradigm of public policy, driven by budget scrutiny, refining the arts of influence and implementation, reshaped the power associated with the city, and the careers it made.[18]

In gaining government in 1996, John Howard had seized on popular discontent with schemes spun in these 'secret rooms'. His attitude to the city seemed clear in his decision to make Kirribilli in Sydney his official residence, and in his prompt dismissal of a third of Canberra's departmental heads. The following year public service redundancies in the capital peaked at 4200 – representing 40 per cent of all Commonwealth public-sector jobs lost. But the new Prime Minister continued using specially constituted, flexible task forces to push policy, ever more tightly under his gaze and that of his departmental secretaries: the impatient Max Moore-Wilton and the 'consummate fixer', Peter Shergold. Unprecedented accountability devolved down the ranks to officers for the advice they offered and the calls they made. The televised appearance of mid-level officials, giving evidence to parliamentary committees on matters of political controversy, was a new, not necessarily ennobling view the nation gained of its servants in the capital. When Kevin Rudd led Labor back into Federal government in 2007 it might have been with a determination to revive the capacities required to support an expansive policy agenda within departments, but that brought its own demands. Soon Rudd was publicly deriding officials for their poor work ethic in supporting his '24/7' commitment. In less than a year the Prime Minister's own office went through a 53 per cent staff turnover – a statistic of which Rudd seemed proud.[19]

As political scientist Chris Beer argues, there was a synergy between these shifting modes of government and moves to raise revenue by selling off Canberra's government offices. The 'statement' style of earlier department headquarters made a point about permanence, status and the integrity of portfolios. Steadily they were being replaced by new, leased constructions in an anonymous, generic modernism, after 9/11 hedged with security bollards. Leadership became less about competitiveness between departments within Canberra's 'league table' – the narrative of the 1950s to the 1970s – and more narrowly about managing resources to achieve results sought by the 'stakeholder' – the citizen – or 'the client'. Exceptions could serve to prove the rule. When the National Museum finally opened in 2001, on the site of the demolished hospital and in an over-wrought building of jigsaw postmodernism, it was soon to demonstrate the limits within which diversity was tolerated. Amid controversy over whether the museum reflected the spirit of Australian acheivement, Howard commissioned a review to ascertain 'whether the Government's vision in approving funding for [its] development ... has been realised'. Duly chastised, the museum became a caution to other cultural institutions for which a place in the city, once coveted, could also be a place under scrutiny.[20]

The capital could still produce countervailing voices. Since the constitutional crisis of 1975, successive Governors-General had sought to reposition their authority, conscious that their official residence would never make that symbolic as well as physical move into the executive centre of the city that had once been promised. Yarralumla, instead, as historian Robert O'Shea observes, became the margin from which Sir Ninian Stephen (1982–89) and his successors (most prominently Sir William Deane, 1996–2001) 'reported to' rather than 'addressed' the nation, as citizens not subjects, and exerted a distinct influence over a range of social justice concerns. But their voices were, in a way, raised in compensation to the tide of change.[21]

Inevitably, the wider image of Canberra was defined by these transformations. Under a 'civics education' program, since 2006 increasing numbers of schoolchildren (nearly 100 000 in 2011) have received assistance to travel to their capital, on condition that they visit Parliament House, the National Electoral Education Centre or (after it opened in 2009) the Museum of Australian Democracy (MOAD) and the Australian War Memorial (AWM). 'Doing Canberra' built familiarity with these affirming aspects of government. But how deeply did their messages penetrate, and what did they seek to control? MOAD offered digital interaction and role-play in exploring what democracy means; the AWM found a kind of closure in 1993 in opening the Tomb of the Unknown Soldier – finally brought home from Flanders fields – and, after 1998, the inclusion of 'wars and war-like operations' in its Vietnam and peacekeeping galleries. But there were limits to what could be said. Amid controversy, the AWM stood firm in opposing arguments that it should recognise Australia's own frontier conflicts. Across the lake the Howard government sought to contain Reconciliation Place, built in 2002, within 'some artistic impressions' relating to Aboriginal Australians but with no 'memorial' to their suffering. No official permission was ever given for the Uniting Church–coordinated erection at Weston Park, on the lake shore, of 353 crosses to mark those who disappeared with the sinking of an asylum-seeker boat in 2001. Since 1992 on Anzac Parade, in its silent embrace of stone, the Vietnam Memorial carried among its inscriptions: 'I don't seem to have many friends since I came home'. Amid the many tributes to valour and national dedication that thickened Canberra's official landscape, and in televised national spectacles such as, from 2004, 'Australia Day Life' from the lawns of Parliament House, which trade in a celebrity-driven sense of pride, few unsettling national reflections have been entertained.[22]

VALUE FOR MONEY

Through these years Canberra's community itself negotiated mixed signals. Newman and Kenworthy's 'new urbanism' had many versions, advocates calling for a return to the 'Griffin legacy' and 'a cosmopolitan lifestyle', for departures from the NCDC's linear model for a 'compact city' radiating around one 'thriving and vibrant' centre. These options touched all aspects of life, including equity, inclusiveness, and economic and environmental impacts. When, in 2002, the OECD selected Canberra as the third candidate in its 'urban renaissance' program – following Belfast and Krakow – it was not as a public planning ideal but an example of the transformations involved in embracing the 'new economy' of enterprise-driven imperatives. A survey in 1996 found many Canberrans to be living with a sense of imminent 'crisis', recognising the need to change their behaviours and shoulder their costs. What they wanted was a clear sense of direction, and an end to being 'derogatively lumped together with politicians and the machinery of federal government'. They were not confident about receiving either.[23]

Those doubts were particularly grating, given mounting signs of a 'waning Commonwealth interest' in the capital. The NCPA began with the aspiration of re-energising the city. Slow growth and investment made its programs piecemeal; a high turnover of senior staff undermined its authority; and the lack of mechanisms through which Canberrans could influence its actions compounded the problem. New buildings for the Department of Defence, conceived as finally anchoring the third, municipal axis of Griffin's scheme, left it still a largely insular, martial precinct – an effect accentuated by the later, nearby location of new headquarters for the Australian Security and Intelligence Organisation. To mark Australia's bicentennial,

Japan gifted a building for the Science and Technology Centre on the other side of the lake. Yet there were no funds for a new central home for the National Archives and its holdings, proposed for an adjoining site. Pointedly, a review of the NCPA in 1995, shadowed by the Commonwealth Department of Finance, roped it back to a pursuit of 'value for money' activities, to be 'tested against the market' and deferred wherever possible to the Australian Capital Territory Administration. The NCPA (National Capital Authority after 1996) was never adequately resourced to discharge its functions. It was not, as an inquiry judged in 2011, simply that no unified plan coordinated Canberra's development, but that the trajectories of the capital, the city and the community had become so divergent as to dismantle the wisdom of such goal. Even when the Commonwealth led all state and territory governments to agree on a National Capital Strategic Planning System in 2009 – aimed at fostering 'competitive, productive, liveable' cities – Canberra was conspicuously without mechanisms to move along that path.[24]

Whether driven by 'crisis' or opportunity, the community sought its own initiatives. The 'new economy' was envisaged in 'innovative and high tech' projects. The reality was a private sector essentially defined by small-scale units, of which – by 2007 – over 88 per cent employed fewer than 20 people and were often run from homes, with the second worst 'survival rate' (after the Northern Territory) in Australia. There were success stories: Michael McGoogan established Aussie HQ, a prominent software, web and cloud services provider, while still a school student in the early 2000s. But overall Canberra's businesses were 10 per cent above the national average in reporting vulnerability to economic conditions, and the slowest in their investment in innovation.[25]

Still, a home-grown stratum of senior entrepreneurs – Jim Service and John Hindmarsh prominent among them – made their money in property development and project management. They had big schemes. In the most expansive formulation of the concept so far, a 'Canberra Capital Region' was declared in 1996, encompassing surrounding local government areas in 'the largest inland growth area in Australia'. Encouraging investment in areas from tourism to education, the concept was also aimed at recouping the costs the region was placing on the capital in the provision of services increasingly unaffordable in, or stripped from, its smaller communities. As part of this vision, VFT became the city's 'hardest working acronym' throughout the 1990s, as a series of ventures canvassed a Very Fast Train – travelling at over 350 kilometres an hour – to link Melbourne and Sydney via Canberra, and potentially to extend to Brisbane. High-level corporate backing, surges of political enthusiasm, and support from businesses seeking the benefits of unprecedented economic integration kept the idea in play, and even brought it to tender at several junctures. The stumbling point remained government insistence that the project must involve no net cost to the public purse, and no concessions. The prospect, however, was still factored into the schemes of Canberra's only entrant into Australia's 'Richest 200' list, locally born Terry Snow. In 1998 he gambled on purchasing the privatised Canberra Airport, turning it into an international facility in the hope that the VFT might come. In the interim, the airport became the hub for a business park that made a stylish, lucrative statement about what private enterprise could do.[26]

Snow was one enthusiast for urbanism, but his 'Brindabella Park' complex still tugged at the centre of gravity for the 'compact city'. As Tony Powell, an NCDC commissioner through an earlier period, regretted in 2003, coherent concepts of urban form – once vital to Canberra's planning – were compromised in such driven ventures. The same trend was evident in the suburbs. Since the late 1980s, parcels of unserviced land had been auctioned to firms with demonstrated capacity to develop it, given the lack of public funds. In 1994, a shortage of affordable housing prompted the Follett government to resume public land development, including in joint ventures aimed at retaining a measure of public control. But in the new town of Gungahlin an entire suburb was handed over to corporate developers. Auctions for tranches of Palmerston began in 1991, an ethos of consolidation encouraging bidders to propose residential densities up to 40 per cent above required minimums. Their targets were second-, third- or fourth-time home-owners, seeking bigger homes on smaller blocks. Critics noted the crowding resulting from such 'hands-off' planning, and calculated that, while governments received quicker returns from selling these 'raw' blocks, releasing fully developed stock would have been more lucrative. The pursuant density could also be used as an excuse for not providing a balance of infrastructure – schools, shops and so on. It certainly did little for social mix. Whether in the pace of redevelopment or dual occupancy construction in established suburbs, or the densities prevailing in the new, Canberra's fundamental asset of land was shifting its currency.[27]

Shifting, not only in value and control, but in the relationships it mediated. Canberrans have been found to extend less 'licence' to their children to negotiate their suburbs than British or German parents, a paradox perhaps of planning or a consequence of the increasing disjunction between public and private space. They also began demanding more police visibility, to bring a sense of safety into a gap between such spaces that was widening in the 1990s. Rates of domestic violence, rape and drug- and alcohol-related offences were rising sharply by the end of the decade. Whatever social stresses might contribute to such trends, there was a basic issue of capacity. The capital, Australian Federal Police Commissioner Mick Palmer observed in 1997, had effectively become 'a satellite of Sydney' in illegal drug trafficking: dealers could be in and out in 15 minutes; the same applied to burglary and armed robbery. Police could do little to control it. In what some urban enthusiasts foresaw as a '24-hour international city', two-thirds of women reported feeling unsafe after dark. Concerted policing programs, with new powers and surveillance methods, were introduced to curb antisocial behaviour, especially around the nightclubs in some shopping centres, which were themselves products of loosening regulation.[28] A significant factor in the continuing liberalisation of the territory's sex industry was to counteract threatened incursions by organised crime into one of the capital's booming fields of business. Opening its own prison in 2009, so that local offenders could serve out their sentences in their community, the Australian Capital Territory was the first in Australia to introduce a trial syringe exchange program in such a facility. Amid controversy over costs and delays, and the fact that no-one wanted the prison sited near them, the complex was built in a paddock as far from Canberra as possible – but very close to Queanbeyan.[29]

Amid these strains, the political volatility of the 1980s – which had drawn a remarkable number of young people from Canberra's suburbs into punk, poster art and radical performance – subsided into something less energising. From 1985, Splinters Theatre of Spectacle had formed as a group of young performers who practised a 'crowd theory' of audience interaction in productions that were 'self-conscious, carefree and serious'. Yet by 1997, as one founder, the younger Patrick Troy, remembers, this 'collective of idealist artists had completely dissolved'. Professionalism and careers elsewhere claimed some; the pressures of forming families and relationships others. Some were consumed by the demons they taunted in drugs. Beyond personal factors, the Canberra public school system that produced much of this generation in itself lost its experimental edge amid cutbacks and closures, in courting more aspirational students in niche programs, or in parental choices that steadily favoured the perceived rigour of private schooling, or systems – Steiner or Montessori – with alternative philosophies. Again, a polarisation became evident in the lives of some of Canberra's youth – familiar enough elsewhere, but conspicuous in these designed spaces. In her arresting account of one of Canberra's more symbolic crimes – a lover overdosed by an obsessional partner, caught in a spiral of self-doubt and self-importance – Helen Garner recorded parallel lives in the capital in the late 1990s. These were the 'bored, under-occupied undergraduates', taking to suburban share houses and circles where 'heroin is cheaper and more readily available than in any other city', given the heavy recreational drug-use stimulated by a ready, unspoken market around places such as Parliament House. Other lives ran in close proximity, in the plazas of Civic, for example, which Garner saw as 'swarming with junkies – gap-toothed, lank-haired, tattooed, with bruises and scabby lips'. Both were aspects of a city to which people gravitated, either out of ambition or finding themselves stranded under its 'beautiful...cloudless skies'.[30]

Other, less graphic contrasts, tracked this steady adjustment of expectations and experience. The activism driving the community radio station, 2XX, for example, broadened to serve an increasing range of ethnic and special interest groups. The station's impact was no doubt small when set against the generic fare offered by the expansion of commercial television licences after 1989 – both going to broadcasters based outside Canberra, trading on new 'regional' identities. But it still offered a perspective on local diversity. While levels of immigration to the territory declined significantly into the 1990s, groups from Asia and Africa became a much larger percentage of the whole. In 2006, Sudanese joined the station's list of language offerings, as its programs promoted the work of Companion House, established by volunteers in 1989 to support refugees who had survived torture and trauma. *Deadly Sounds* occupied another new slot, serving Canberra's Aboriginal population. This group, too, was benefiting from new services in the community, including the provision of full-time, designated Aboriginal health services and the development of specific educational resources at Narrabundah Primary School, where around a quarter of the enrolment identified as indigenous. There might not have been the over-arching solidarity of the social movements gravitating to 2XX in the past, but these were still voices to be heard.[31]

Advocates for reform also emerged from more established areas of the community. Appointed Catholic Auxiliary Bishop of Canberra and Goulburn in 1986, Cooma-born, Canberra-educated and Queanbeyan-ordained Pat Power was prominent in discussions of poverty, the impact of drugs, the pursuit of international peace and reform in the clergy. Recalling his early ministry to the Causeway, Power spoke of hidden strength among the more disadvantaged local communities and strenuously opposed dogmas of economic reform which affronted 'people's dignity'. Owen Dowling, elected Anglican Archbishop of Canberra and Goulburn in 1983, campaigned vigorously for the ordination of women priests, surmounting legal challenges in 1992 and placing the cause firmly in the context of entrenched gender bias in society. Sharing ecumenicalism, and with significant levels of congregational support, both leaders worried about the relevance of churches that would not confront social problems.[32]

There were significant areas of growth in other faiths. A Buddhist Centre, established primarily by Vietnamese immigrants in 1984, supported a monastery which, into the 1990s, engaged with environmental and social welfare issues and assisted refugees to settle in the 'freedom country'. Between 1996 and 2006, the number of Buddhist adherents in the Australian Capital Territory grew by 84 per cent to 7117. In the same period the number of Muslims grew by 78 per cent to 4364. Canberra's first mosque had been constructed in 1960 as an initiative of the Pakistan, Malaysian and Indonesian Embassies, supporting an Islamic school pledged to 'teachings that are compatible with contemporary world views'. By the 1990s, local donations contributed to the building of an Islamic Centre and Library, dedicated to developing a common 'culture of belonging' among a local diversity of Muslim national and ethnic groups, including recently arrived Kosovar refugees. Now committed to 'removing stereotyping' among Canberrans, this centre was the subject of vandalism as its leaders entered into debates over anti-terrorism laws and the status of Israel. But its community grew in strength, establishing its own fully credentialled primary school in 2005 and seeking approval to build another mosque in Gungahlin.[33]

Not even Canberra's most august institutions escaped adjustment. Entering the 1990s, the ANU put its best face on conscription into the Hawke government's national 'relative funding model'. All Australian universities were now to be rewarded on their 'outputs', and the 'quality' the ANU had cultivated had to be translated into numbers. New courses in subjects such as Information Technology and Resource and Environmental Management, and new areas such as Engineering, and centres for Aboriginal Economic Policy Research, Middle Eastern and Central Asian Studies, reflected a search for relevance. In 1990, the bastion of the Institute of Advanced Studies – the ANU's assembled Research Schools – was directed to become 'a resource for the Australian research system as a whole'. Enduring rolling cuts, the university stepped into the ruck for grants, fellowships and international rankings. Prizes – such as the Nobel to astronomer Brian Schmidt in 2011 – always helped, but pressure for more fundamental change was undeniable. As Vice-Chancellor from 2001 to 2011, Ian Chubb demanded that his charge become 'an education-intensive research university', seeking to force at last a fusion between the two sides of the university. Tapping the vein of property development, he also sought to integrate the campus into the city through a residential precinct – focused on international students – in place of a barren moat of car parks. As protests against the budget-driven assaults on the School of Music by Chubb's successor would show, Canberra remained sensitive to the role of its first university as a cultural institution in the community.[34]

Less captive to reputation, the University of Canberra (UC) moved from its initial dependency on Monash University in 1993, and a transfer from Commonwealth to territory government responsibility in 1997, to explore the possibilities of professionally oriented education. Over- rather than under-enrolment marked its adjustment to the national system, and a 'continuous process of course revision and quality enhancement' in response to employer needs set its pace. Astute chancellorial and vice-chancellorial appointments, including those of the eminent social commentator Donald Horne; the activist, entrepreneur and 'change agent' Wendy McCarthy; and the indefatigable Don Aitkin, worked to boost academic morale and performance, always a little in the shadow of the ANU. UC's fields broadened to include management, health, business, law, international studies, creative practice, and social and economic modelling. The balance between the 'applied' and 'academic' could be strained in these ambitions, and 'relevance' a fickle goal. The Canberra Institute of Technology – evolving from a college of technical and further education in 1988 – tapped a deeper current in the capital's 'learning community'. It grew rapidly to meet emerging local priorities in areas such as project management (responding to the demands of business restructuring and contracting), tourism and hospitality. Across all three institutions, education remained Canberra's best bid into the 'new economy'.[35]

Picking winners clearly remained a challenge, not least in respect to how the capital wanted to be seen. The attempt to hold in Canberra 'the biggest display of military equipment ever to be held in the southern hemisphere' – the Australian International Defence Exhibition (AIDEX), reflecting the Commonwealth government's desire to boost military exports – attracted concerted protest in 1989 but much more organised opposition in 1991 from diverse environmental, social and religious groups. Their tactics of obstructive direct action were matched by aggressive police action, resulting in an event that cost a great deal more than it added to territory revenues and that produced images of the city no-one wanted to see repeated. There was no third AIDEX. More enduring initiatives arose from the decision in 1992 to base the annual National Folk Festival in Canberra. Attendances rose from 8000 that first year to 38 000 in five years, and 50 000 by 2001, with a corresponding expansion in a program including workshops, lectures, dances and performances from groups such as the Canberra Gay and Lesbian Choir (later Qwire – established in 1993), dancers from Mornington Island, and musicians from Ghana, Hawaii and the Middle East. A rather different clientele came for Summernats, a 'street machine' car festival held in Canberra after 1988. From an initial 2000 cars and 50 000 spectators, by 2005 nearly 120 000 people watched 1600 cars cruise, 'shine and show', run a slalom or burn out tyres. The biggest event of its kind outside the United States, Summernats was, to one critic, 'a savage, drunken, topless, five day party' in which the crowd echoed with ritual calls of 'show us your tits' amid the stench of exhaust and flaming rubber. But it was also, a government inquiry found, 'a successful commercial venture' in which the $12–$15 million spent each year, during a quiet time in Canberra's calendar, translated – after costs – into a significant economic benefit. Such events brought people to the city and became part of its brand and its enduring enigma.[36]

GRAFITTI, FUNDAMENTALISM, SHOPPING TROLLEYS

At the end of the 20th century it was still possible to look over Canberra's valleys and not see the city they contained – except, perhaps, for the sentinel of the Telecom Tower. With that exception, at least some of Griffin's precepts that related to keeping the hills and ridges undeveloped had been observed. But how was that landscape seen? That the Australian Capital Territory was Australia's most urbanised state or territory was not itself surprising, but with 98 per cent of the population in 1991 characterised as urban, with a fall of 2 per cent in rural dwellers since 1971, the imbalance was stark. Proclivities for rural residential settlement in the region were judged as threatening scarce stocks of arable land, though the focus was no longer on pastoralism but on specialised organic farming, serving new markets and tastes. Extended in 1991, Namadgi National Park made up 46 per cent of the territory, and within it remnant pine plantations were removed, active pastoralism ceased and brumbies were eradicated – all in the cause of arresting soil erosion but also marking a clear break with the past. Employment in forestry and agriculture in the territory was minuscule and falling. By contrast, the CSIRO scientists who led in establishing the Canberra region's burgeoning wine industry in the 1970s did so as a hobby, and with the insight that better use might be made of degraded land. The reputation local growers and producers built from the 1990s onwards in premium cool climate wines neatly reflected the transformation of Canberra's productive landscape, along with the city itself: a sheep station spoiled for Riesling and Shiraz rather than parliament was perhaps more palatable.[37]

Affluent and well-educated, some Canberrans' attention to 'lifestyle' increasingly encompassed their own environmental impacts. Population growth might have seemed vital to the 'cultural depth' and revenue flows some commentators looked for, but at what cost to equity and coherence? An expressway serving Gungahlin, cut through native parkland, was one among many issues that galvanised community debate: whose interests, and amenity, came first? ACTEW trialled projects to generate power from methane in landfill, a hydroelectric station fed by a water treatment plant and a solar farm in Queanbeyan. Although it might have been cheaper to buy green power from elsewhere, that was beside the public relations point. Water tanks and solar panels – installation of the latter boosted by Australia's second (after South Australia) and most generous electricity buy-back scheme in 2008 – reflected citizens' choices and government incentive. Making good use of leverage over minority governments, the Greens' Legislative Assembly member Kerrie Tucker proved particularly effective in campaigning for energy ratings for houses and consumption audits for households. Local Landcare groups also took pride in the extent to which Canberra enabled them to work at a fragile urban–rural interface, and at small, inclusive scales, that were hard to replicate elsewhere.[38]

Such initiatives drew on distinctive capacities. Robert Boden came to Canberra as a forestry student in the early 1950s. He relished the opportunity of working with 'practical people' in planting the 'garden city', studied recreational use of the country around the city, became the first Director of the National Botanic Gardens in 1979, and built upon this experience and respect in popular and expert writing for Canberrans about the 'urban forest' they loved, and the mounting cost-driven threats to its maintenance and diversity. This sense of a fragile heritage acquired urgency during an extended drought from 1997 to 2009 – the most sustained in Australian history. A 50 per cent reduction in inflows into catchments prompted the introduction of potentially permanent water restrictions, forcing consumption down 35 per cent. With no agricultural industry to speak of, the drought had relatively little economic impact in the Australian Capital Territory, especially in comparison to neighbouring centres such as Goulburn, which faced the prospect of running out of water. The psychic bite, however, went deeper: trees died, gardens withered, lawns baked hard.[39]

On 8 January 2003, a lightning strike in the Brindabella Ranges to the south-west of Canberra ignited desperately dry forest. A series of bushfires commenced, were noted over the coming week, and watched – although not comprehensively fought in remote and difficult country. The sunsets, Canberra residents noted, became 'full of gorgeous colour' in this accumulating pall of smoke and ash. However, on 17 January, prevailing conditions drew the fires into a consolidated front that began heading east with speed. On 18 January, when ferocious winds and heat took the territory to the 'extreme' end of the fire index, Canberra was in grave danger. Residents noticed burnt leaves among the debris swirling into gardens, and saw nearby ridgelines in flames. The air yellowed, reddened, then blackened. Local radio stations broadcast advice to evacuate from the most vulnerable suburbs in Tuggeranong, Woden and Weston, but confusion mounted as that advice turned into an unearthly wail of emergency sirens, familiar from television dramas but never expected in reality, and soon lost in a sound like 'jet engines taking off as trees exploded in the path of the flames'. At 2:45 p.m. the city was declared in a state of emergency, as a major firestorm jumped from nearby pine plantations and grasslands into residential streets. On that afternoon, four lives were lost and over 500 homes were destroyed, 414 of which were in suburbs, and many others damaged. Around the city, 70 per cent of the territory's pasture, forest and nature parks were incinerated. The toll included major losses to government infrastructure and facilities, most graphically the destruction of much of the Mount Stromlo Observatory. The Canberra area had experienced major fires in the past: in 1903, 1926, 1927, 1939, 1952 and 2001. That of 2003 was the worst, and prompted the most far-reaching questions.[40]

An early official inquiry into the disaster found that the Australian Capital Territory community had 'not been sufficiently well prepared to understand the nature of the bushfire risk that exists as a consequence of the siting of the city in a bushland setting'. As some residents reflected, many of those areas most affected were vulnerable precisely because 'the aspect, trees and environment were what we wanted'. The legacy of those choices was compounded by the finding that – for all the dedication shown in fighting the fires – it was doubtful whether the Australian Capital Territory, given its limited population and budget, possessed the resources to meet the challenge of living in an environment prone to such events. Others contended that Canberra's vulnerability had been accentuated by the failure to properly manage the forests around it, given a desire to keep them a 'natural' backdrop rather than recognise that they were once, and had long been, a resource shaped by practices of controlled burning. Debate would continue over liability for the impact of the fires, spurred by a coroner's report which criticised a lack of early action, coordination and capacity. It was 'a miracle' that more lives had not been lost. A consensus emerged: on the day, the fires were 'unstoppable', but no simple formula of recurrence or prevention could be deduced. For many, the city found, or finally proved, a real solidarity in the shared experience of the fires. The bonds forged in suffering or assistance, judged Jennifer Horsfield – drawing on her own experience – should see 18 January enter Canberra's calendar as 'community day'. But some found those bonds to be exclusive as well as inclusive, as hierarchies of 'being there' seemed to develop in some groups. Others noted the irony that a disaster, so much a product of a place, should serve to confirm a spirit among the people in it.[41]

The drought, and the fire, did draw forth action. Investment in a new dam on the Cotter River (with 20 times the capacity of the old one) commenced with the promise that it would curb the need to impose serious water restrictions in the future – but with what impact on environmental flows in that larger river system, the Murray–Darling Basin, within which Canberra sits? And since 2005, a 250-hectare National Arboretum has been established by the Australian Capital Territory Government on an extensive site, once planted at Burley Griffin's direction but burnt out in 2003. A defiant riposte to the destruction of so much of the territory's forests, including early experimental arboreta in the Brindabellas, this project reaffirms Canberra's love of trees. But a future in which drought and fire are likely to become more frequent and severe looms, and the potential of ecosystems to recover from such events is correspondingly reduced. For environmental scientist Stephen Dovers, a more evocative representation of the learning Canberra needs is the rehabilitation since 1995 of grassy woodlands at Mulligan's Flat, on the fringes of Gunghalin, where native species are being reintroduced into a fenced area that is returning quickly to a pre-European settlement state. Like the 300-year-old trees that endure, and provide precious habitat in some of Canberra's suburbs, this work seeks not to the hold the line for some version of the ideal city, but to recover what came before it.[42]

Such fine-grained rehabilitation has its corollary in the convening in 1999 of the first Weereewa Festival, taking the Ngunawal name for Lake George for a program combining 'artists, academics, Indigenous and other local communities' in their responses to the cultural and ecological significance of the area. At the ANU's School of Art an Environment Studio combines scientists, historians, artists, landholders and local schools in an exploration of the diversity of landscapes readily accessible from Canberra, from the alpine to the semi-arid. But the city, in the thrall of promoters and developers, still struggles for an equivalent imagination. Each year since 1988, the beds and exotic bulbs for Floriade, a festival of flowers, are laid down in a selected theme, then scraped away, appealing more to locals yearning for what might remain of a 'garden city' than the desired tourists, who hesitate still about a side trip to the Australian capital. As regretted by Romaldo Giurgola – who remained after seeing to completion his firm's design for the new Parliament House – Canberra's turn to shopping malls and spectacle has exemplified a shift from the realm of public planning and coherence to that of a privatised consumption, at variance with 'the very nature of this city and its heritage'. Much the same might be said of the pockets of intricately designed, up-market 'renewal' in certain areas of the city, complete with laneways, mews and even marinas. These developments fill the aspirational void left by those unacted projects of integrated, urban expansion envisaged by earlier optimists.[43]

In this – as always – Canberra is perhaps not an aberration from the nation, but its child. In 1997 Wendy McCarthy, while lamenting the federal government's 'rejection' of Canberra, still felt that visitors can 'enjoy [here] vicariously a quintessential Australian experience. One that few places can offer. You can see Australian icons and you can dream of a lifestyle that now eludes most of us'.

Nearly two decades on, that judgement may still ring true – although with increasing qualifications. The nature of Australia's economic development from the 1990s onwards questions one coherent national view. As academic lawyer Greg Craven observes, 'What is correct thought in Sydmelberra – that fashionable strip that runs from the North Shore, through the staff bar of the Australian National University, stopping a decent distance from Geelong – is social death in Perth', or probably Brisbane, where a different tune in called. Equally, as Canberra-born photographer Lee Grant records in her 2012 visual essay, it is with some pride that residents of sections of Belconnen present their claim to be citizens of Australia's generic 'western suburbs', of 'grafitti, fundamentalism, shopping trolleys and immigrants'. Christie Thompson's 2013 novel, *Snake Bite*, set in the suburbs of Tuggeranong in Canberra's south, offers a similar stage for a coming-of-age story. No doubt, still well below its half-million benchmark, Canberra gives more space, amenity and ease of mobility to its workers and residents. But in those rewards – whether as a lifestyle or a symptom – the city continues to worry over questions of coherence, sustainability and purpose that have troubled it from the start.[44]

CONCLUSION

A child, just learning to talk, points from her pram as she is pushed towards the Floriade NightFest, at the sudden swell of colour and the roar of flame in the belly of a hot air balloon. 'Skywhale!' she exclaims. And there it is by the lake shore: a bright orange swag of fabric, slowly taking shape, its 10 pendulous breasts filling and its lips, against the Canberra twilight, the august National Library spotlit in the background.

The child was about to move with a crowd into a night-time viewing of Canberra's annual festival of flowers, this year featuring a laser-lit spectacular in a gentle glade originally conceived in 1965 by Dame Sylvia Crowe, eminent British landscape architect, to help meld the Griffins' long-delayed lake into a city that had taken a different course. Crowe's commission was not without its own provocation, as part of a tussle between the National Capital Development Commission and the Commonwealth Department of the Interior over whether an Australian (so the latter maintained), and even a local, could have done the job as well and cheaper. In the endless theatre of Canberra, *Skywhale* had also been controversial since its unveiling. It had been commissioned by Robyn Archer, the creative director of the yearlong festival to celebrate 100 years since Canberra's foundation. It was the creature of multimedia artist Patricia Piccinini, born in Sierra Leone, a graduate in Economic History from the Australian National University and then of the Victorian College of the Arts. Her balloon was seen as an indulgence, an exemplar of a contracting-out culture. (It was paid for,

Figure 22: Patricia Piccinini's *Skywhale*, afloat over Canberra, 2013. (Reproduced with permission of Martin Ollman)

but not owned, by the Australian Capital Territory government – and the price itself was the subject of some fudging.) As some wits commented, it was a perfect symbol for a city 'always on the tit'. But that child embraced it as a familiar thing, and entered into its fantasy. And to that extent she verified Piccinini's rationale – to provide a figure that would engage people with the puzzle of evolution: things that find their course through chance, impact and adaptation over time. As Piccinini explained 'Coming from a place like Canberra where it's a planned city that's really tried to integrate and blend in with the natural environment, it makes a lot of sense to make this sort of huge, gigantic, but artificial and natural-looking creature'. *Skywhale* offended many, until they saw it. And then, its gentle, benevolent gaze and ample nurturing presence tended to win them over.[1]

The centenary of Canberra in 2013 prompted extended reflection on a city that still emerged from most accounts as a paradox. A city 'conspicuously self-conscious', as one of its most recent students, Paul Daley, has put it: 'hyper-sensitive', 'accidental' but still – if simply in its landscape – capable of generating unexpected intimacy despite neatness and order. Like many accounts of the capital, Daley's was autobiographical in its emphasis. The first-hand account, it seems, is needed to give Canberra authenticity, to establish the scale at which the city has meaning. Ruth Hingston and Mary Hutchison's *Shaping Canberra* exhibition – also mounted for the centenary – centred on the 'lived experience' evoked in the sensory, tactile, found object and craft aesthetic that has a particular resonance in Canberra: lives put together from what was carried in, available, not planned. I began this book in the same way, with my convict ancestor. And Archer's festival program – diverse and inspired – has equally proved successful in filling the spaces left void in Canberra's development, bringing people to its centre: light-shows and cocktails in the parliamentary triangle; a ballet celebrating the architecture of the new Parliament House; the stories people tell of trees.[2]

The first-hand, and the familiar, however, reach only so far back, and do not always make for good history. And they can settle on a sense of what an occasion deserves, which can leave out a good deal of the past. It is striking that in a set of booklets, published by the Chief Minister Katy Gallagher to commemorate the centenary, the past seemed to run up to 1913, and end with the foundation of the city. An exhibition at the Canberra Museum and Gallery leaped ahead, challengingly, to envisage the city in 2113 as another 'place imagined'. In between, however, there has been much silence. A festival cannot be encyclopaedic, and has an imperative to celebrate. But why – between the pioneer and the present – has Canberra's been left to personal reflection? 'Confident, bold and ready' was the slogan, derived from Canberra's baggage tag acronym 'CBR' in a tourist campaign launched in November 2013. Again, it seems, Canberra waits for its destiny. But its history, like *Skywhale*, is worth contemplating beyond first impressions of the bizarre, with considered reflection on the phases, and causes, of its evolution.[3]

The cosmopolitanism of 'Canberra 100' sits on the shoulders of a community of pragmatically managed, even exploited, cultural diversity and reluctant mobility. An image of Walter Burley Griffin printed on street swags for the homeless made an arresting point going into the centenary year: what of his ideal is relevant to those who fall short of, or out of, its assumptions? The experimental flair in government that created the capital has been defused, as journalist Chris Hammer insists, in 'a thousand debates, power plays and turf wars'. The result is that nothing is quite where it was meant to be. Nor should the city's fidelity to the great gift of its landscape obscure the damage done in the processes of settlement, or the extent to which environmental values are symptoms of historical change. Canberra's 2012 planning strategy sets aside much of the 'new urbanism' that gripped the capital in the 1990s. Not only does this new strategy aim to address the inequities urbanism entrenched in relation to the young, the old, the ill and the economically disadvantaged, it is also way of pitfalls that higher densities might create as climate change leads to an increasing frequency of heat waves and places a premium on the simple necessities of shade and the circulation of air. The strategy's formula of 'the capital in the bush' serves different needs from those of 'the bush capital', and teaches different lessons. The authenticity that is bestowed on Canberra by fond accounts, shaped by personal reflection – 'the city I know' – too easily leaves the politics of these and other iterations aside.[4]

There is much to be learned from these politics, locally, nationally and beyond. This book has sought to emphasise that Canberra's evolution was not smooth, and that the attributes selected along the way – in government, community or environment – were often tactical adaptations, deals and roadblocks, the consequences of which endure. The city continues to present the opportunities that enthused the Griffins: what would an ideal city be? It also continues to wrestle with the factors that caused it to be chosen as a site for a national capital – primarily, in Karl Fischer's phase, the poverty of its economic geography: that there was nothing much to supplant, buy out, or suppress. Entering its record fourth term in 2012, the Australian Capital Territory's Labor government maintained its pace on nation-leading reform, whether in advancing protections for 'whistleblower' disclosure, the online delivery of 'open government' resources, or in commitments to legislate for marriage equality. It also continued to wrestle with the entrenched problems of health provision and affordable housing, the first reflecting the challenges of a relatively small population and taxation base, the second a pattern of economic growth particularly dependent on population increase and construction. Also, with a change to a Liberal federal government in 2013, came the reminder that any public service 'downsizing' would fall especially heavily on the capital. But whatever party is in power, the discipline of public sector 'efficiency dividends' remains the mantra of a government town, and conditions its aspirations for the future.[5]

In these evolutions, and politics, there is a more fundamental point. The problem with seeking the real Canberra is that, for all its layered histories, the concept is itself inconsistent with its history, and its peculiar purpose. The authentic is hard to find in such a place, and harder still to use. For years, for example, Aboriginal peoples have been divided in Canberra by the question of who has the right to speak as traditional owners of the land. Deep tensions have arisen between the organised representatives of the Ngunawal and Ngarigu people as to who should be identified in that role, given the privileges attaching to that standing and its place in building community wellbeing. On the one hand, over that debate sits the profound artificiality of the Australian Capital Territory itself, and its arbitrary intervention into the lives of many generations of those who have lived in its mountains and valleys. The recovery of a claim over such lost histories is an inherently fraught, often confrontational act: it speaks to the present as much as to the past. On the other is the fact that, at several points, Aboriginal people have come to the capital, itself an attempt to create a coherent sense of the nation, to protest, to work, to hear, to demand (as in the early days of the Australian Institute for Aboriginal Studies) that they not be seen simply as the subjects of curiosity or benevolence, or (in the current programs of the Australian Institute for Aboriginal and Torres Strait Islander Studies) just that they be included in programs of recovering language and culture that will enrich the nation. Many people, prominent or not, women and men, local or new to country, have shaped these processes. It is in embracing as much as we can of those who have found or not found a voice in Canberra, that the capital can continue to tell its best story.

NOTES

INTRODUCTION
1 Bruce Moore, *The Lanyon Saga* (Canberra: Moore, 1982), p. 198; Bruce Moore, *Cotter Country: A History of the Early Settlers, Pastoral Holdings and Events in and around the County of Cowley* (Canberra: Moore, 1999), p. 73.
2 Paul Daley, *Canberra* (UNSW Press, 2012), p. 105.
3 *Canberra Times*, 1 June 2013; *Age*, 22 October 2009; Don Watson, *Recollections of a Bleeding Heart: A Portrait of Paul Keating PM* (Sydney: Vintage, 2003), p. 249; Jeanne MacKenzie, *Australian Paradox* (Melbourne: Cheshire, 1961), p. 32.

1 NGUNAWAL COUNTRY AND THE LIMESTONE PLAINS
1 Walter Burley Griffin, *New York Times*, 2 June 1912; T.A.G. Hungerford, *A Knockabout with a Slouch Hat* (Fremantle Arts Centre Press, 1985), p. 102.
2 M. Owen et al., *Geological Monuments in the Australian Capital Territory* (Canberra, Geological Society of Australia, 1988); D.M. Finlayson, *A Geological Guide to Canberra Region and Namadgi National Park* (Canberra: Geological Society of Australia, 2008).
3 W.G. Woolnough, 'Structure and Scenery of the Federal Capital Territory' in *Commonwealth Year Book* (Melbourne: Government Printer, 1929), no. 22, p. 631.
4 L.D. Pryor and J.C.G. Banks, *Trees and Shrubs of Canberra* (Sydney: Little Hills Press, 1991), p. 15; Ian Fraser, *A Bush Capital Year: A Natural History of the Canberra Region* (Canberra: CSIRO, 2011), pp. xi, xii.
5 John Mulvaney and Johan Kamminga, *The Prehistory of Australia* (Sydney: Allen and Unwin, 1999), pp. 297–9; Sandra Bowdler, 'The Empty Coast' in S. Haberle et al., *Altered Ecologies: Fire, Climate and Human Influence on Terrestrial Landscapes* (Canberra: ANU ePress, 2010),

pp. 177–85; Debbie Argue, 'Aboriginal Occupation of the Southern Highlands', *Australian Archaeology*, no. 41, 1995, pp. 30–6.
6 Harry Lourandos, *Continent of Hunter Gatherers: New Perspectives on Australian Prehistory* (Cambridge: CUP, 1997), pp. 237, 243; Josephine Flood, 'Man and Ecology in the High Country of Southeast Australia' in Nicolas Peterson (ed.), *Tribes and Boundaries in Australia* (Canberra: AIAS, 1976), p. 14.
7 Ann Jackson Nakano, *The Kamberri: A History of Aboriginal Families in the ACT and Surrounds* (Aboriginal History Monograph 8, 2001); Peter Rimas Kabaila, *Belconnen's Aboriginal Past* (Canberra: Black Mountain Projects, 1997; Harold Koch, 'Aboriginal Languages and Social Groups in the Canberra Region: Interpreting the Historical Documentation', in Brett Baker et al. (eds), *Indigenous Language and Social Identity (Canberra*: Pacific Linguistics, 2010), pp. 131–53; *Understanding the Land Through the Eyes of the Ngunnawal* (Canberra: ACT Department of Environment, Climate Change, Water and Planning, nd), p. 3.
8 Vivienne Parsons and Charles Throsby, *Australian Dictionary of Biography* (Melbourne University Press, 1966), vol. 2, 1967, p. 531; Grace Karskens, *The Colony: A History of Early Sydney* (Sydney: Allen and Unwin), p. 497.
9 John Ritchie, *Punishment and Profit* (Melbourne: Heinemann, 1970), vol. 1, p. 180.
10 George Main, *Heartland: The Regeneration of Rural Place* (UNSW Press, 2005), p. 17; Stephen Dovers, 'Still Discovering Monaro' in Stephen Dovers (ed.), *Australian Environmental History* (Oxford University Press, 1994), p. 120; Stephen H. Roberts, *The Squatting Age in Australia* (Melbourne University Press, 1964), p. 4; Bill Gammage, *The Biggest Estate on Earth: How Aborigines Made Australia* (Sydney: Allen and Unwin, 2011).
11 Peter Read, *A Hundred Years' War* (Canberra: ANU Press, 1988), p. 1; Ian Clark (ed.), *Journal of G.A. Robinson* (Melbourne: Heritage, 1998), vol. 4, p. 205; Gwendoline Wilson, *Murray of Yarralumla*, Oxford University Press, 1968), p. 85; Jackson Nakano, *The Kamberri*, p. 36; Frederick Watson, *A Brief History of Canberra* (Canberra: Federal Capital Press, 1927), pp. 8, 13.
12 John Lhotsky, *A Journey from Sydney to the Australian Alps* (Hobart: Blubber Head Press, 1978), pp. 55, 67.
13 ibid., pp. 67–9.
14 ibid., pp. 55, 56, 58, 61.
15 David Meyers, *Lairds, Lags and Larrikins: An Early History of the Limestone Plains* (Canberra: Sefton, 2010), pp. 28, 32; (Canberra: Moore, 1999), p. 3; W. Davis Wright, *Canberra* (Sydney: Andrew, 1923), p. 22.

16 Meyer, *Lairds*, p. 62; *Canberra Times*, 25 November 1939, p. 2.
17 Meyer, *Lairds*, p. 66; Moore, *Cotter Country*, pp. 9, 22.
18 Edward John Eyre, *Autobiographical Narrative of Residence and Exploration in Australia 1832–1839* (London: Caliban, 1984), pp. 86–8.
19 Lyall Gillespie, *Canberra 1820–1913* (Canberra, AGPS: 1991), p. 16; Frederick Watson, *History*, p. 27; Eyre, *Autobiographical Narrative*, p. 83; Wilson, *Murray*, p. 110; David Neal, *The Rule of Law in a Penal Colony* (Cambridge University Press, 2002), p. 136; Bruce Moore, *The Lanyon Saga* (Moore: Canberra, 1982), p. 198.
20 Eyre, *Autobiographical Narrative*, p. 83; Wilson, *Murray*, p. 110; W.K. Hancock, *Discovering Monaro: A Study of Man's Impact on his Environment* (Cambridge University Press, 1972), p. 34; Lyall Gillespie, *Early Verse of the Canberra Region* (Canberra Local History Series no. 3, 1994), p. 71; Kabaila, *Belconnen's Aboriginal Past*, p. 24.
21 *Sydney Gazette*, 26 April 1832.
22 *Colonist*, 11 July 1838; *Sydney Gazette*, 4 August 1840.
23 L.F. Fitzhardinge, 'Old Canberra and District 1820–1910' in H.L. White, *Canberra: A Nation's Capital* (Sydney: Angus and Robertson, 1954), pp. 21–2; Samuel Shumack, *Tales and Legends of Canberra Pioneers* (ANU Press, 1977), p. 1.
24 Patricia Clarke, '"Big Tancred from the South": The Crossed Paths of Terence Murray and Daniel Deniehy', *Canberra Historical Journal*, no. 58, 2007, pp. 9–10; Wilson, *Murray*, pp. 133–4.
25 Wilson, *Murray*, pp. 146, 184; Richard Waterhouse, *The Vision Splendid: A Social and Cultural History of Rural Australia* (Fremantle Arts Centre Press, 2005). p. 78; Wright, *Canberra*, pp. 33–4.
26 Iain Stuart, Squatting Landscapes in South-East Australia 1820–1895, PhD thesis, University of Sydney, 1999, p. 104; Gillespie, *Canberra*, pp. 33–4.
27 Linda Young, *Lost Houses of the Molonglo Valley* (Canberra: Ginninderra Press, 2007); Bruce Moore, 'Land Settlement and Use' in *The Development of Land Settlement and Its Effects on Local History* (Canberra: CDHS, 1978), pp. 13–15.
28 Hancock, *Discovering Monaro*, p. 42; Wright, *Canberra*, pp. 33–4.
29 Gillespie, *Canberra*, pp. 83–4; Lyall Gillespie, *Early Education and School in the Canberra Region* (Canberra: National Capital Printing, 1999), pp. 11–12; Fitzhardinge, 'Old Canberra', p. 24.
30 Gillespie, *Canberra*, pp. 83–4; Gillespie, *Early Education*, pp. 11–12; Fitzhardinge, 'Old Canberra', p. 24; Shumack, *Tales*, pp. 4, 24; Gillespie, *Early Verse*, p. 2; Moore, *Cotter Country*, p. 32.
31 John Gale, *Canberra: History and Legends* (Queanbeyan: Fallick, 1927), pp. 127–8; Hancock, *Monaro*, pp. 37, 57–8.
32 Rebecca Lamb, *Macquoid of Waniassa* (Canberra: Waniassa Publications, 2006), p. 153; Hancock, *Monaro*, pp. 37, 57–8.

33 Wright, *Canberra*, p. 59; Eyre, *Autobiographical Narrative*, p. 89; W.E. Riley (1831) in Lamb, *Macquoid*, p. 257.
34 Robinson, *Journal*, vol. 4, p. 200; Wilson, *Murray*, p. 85; Wright, *Canberra*, pp. 15, 84; Meyers, *Lairds*, p. 13; Bruce Moore, *The Lanyon Saga*, p. 29.
35 Dale Middleby, *2113: A Canberra Odyssey* (Canberra: CMAG, 2013), p. 8.
36 Wright, *Canberra*, pp. 28–9, 65–6; Ron Winch, 'A Tale of Two Halls', *Canberra Historical Journal*, no. 16, 1985, p. 18; Kabaila, *Belconnen's Aboriginal Past*, p. 22.
37 Frederick Watson, *History*, p. 69.
38 Jim Hagan and Glenn Mitchell, 'The Southeast' in Jim Hagan (ed.), *People and Politics in Regional Australia* (Sydney: Federation, 2006), p. 115; Theo Barker, 'Growth and Decline in Rural Communities' in *Development of Land Settlement*, p. 3.
39 W.J.M. McIntyre, *Thomas Southwell of Parkwood* (Canberra, Federal Capital Press, 1938); *The Register*, 28 March 1913, p. 5; Gerald Walsh, *Pioneering Days: People and Innovations in Australia's Rural Past* (Sydney: Allen & Unwin, 1993), p. 198; Lyall Gillespie, 'If Ginninderra Creek Could Speak', *CHJ*, no. 2, 1978, p. 23.
40 Errol Lea-Scarlett, 'The Improbable Culture of Gundaroo', *Journal of the Canberra and District Historical Society*, no. 1–2, 1972, pp. 1–11; Gillespie, *Canberra*, pp. 163–4; Jill Roe, *Stella Miles Franklin* (Harper Collins, Sydney, 2008), p. 8.
41 Shumack, *Tales*, pp. 45, 138; Gillespie, *Canberra*, p. 149.
42 Hancock, *Discovering Monaro*, pp. 90–4.
43 Stuart, Squatting Landscapes, pp. 212–36, 256–7; Canberra Stories Group, *Settlers' Stories (1913–1975)* (Littlewood, Murrumbateman, 2000), pp. 1–2; Shumack, *Tales*, pp. 45–6.
44 Shumack, *Tales*, pp. 37, 46; Gillespie, *Canberra*, p. 156.
45 Matthew Higgins, *Rugged beyond Imagination: Stories from Australia's Mountain Region* (Canberra: NMA Press, 2009), pp. 26–9; *Town and Country Journal*, 2 November 1888, p. 833; Gillespie, *Canberra*, p. 173.
46 John Merritt, *The Making of the AWU* (Oxford University Press, 1986), pp. 51, 108; *Pastoralists Review*, 15 May 1991, p. 61; *Queanbeyan Age*, 5 November 1987; 9 November 1887.
47 Jennifer Horsfield, *Mary Cunningham: An Australian Life* (Canberra: Ginninderra Press, 2005), pp. 62–5; Bruce Mansfield, Edward William O'Sullivan, *Australian Dictionary of Biography*, vol. 11 (Melbourne University Press, 1983), pp. 107–8; W.C. Andrews, 'Roads and Bridges', W.C. Andrews et al. (eds), *Canberra's Engineering Heritage* (Sydney: Brown Prior, 1990), p. 9.
48 Gillespie, *Canberra*, p. 164; Wright, *Canberra*, pp. 46–7; R.S.C. Newman, 'Frederick Campbell of Yarralumla: A Forgotten Pioneer

Pastoralist', *Journal of the Royal Australian Historical Society*, June 2007, p. 31; *Canberra Times*, 23 August 1928, p. 6; Stuart, Squatting Landscapes, pp. 258; Shumack, *Tales*, pp. 152–3, 158, 161.
49 Dovers, 'Still Discovering Monaro', pp. 126, 135.
50 Jackson-Nakano, *The Kamberri*, pp. 108–59; Kabaila, *Belconnen's Aboriginal Past*, pp. 22–5; Gillespie, *Canberra*, p. 149; Gale, *Canberra*, pp. 123–4.
51 Shumack, *Tales*, p. 15.
52 *Queanbeyan Age*, 3 March 1988; Glenn Rhodes, The Australian Federation referenda 1898–1900: a spatial analysis of voting behaviour, PhD thesis, London School of Economics and Political Science, 1988.
53 *Queanbeyan Age*, 13 May 1899, 14 October 1899, 4 November 1899; Gillespie, *Canberra*, pp. 228–9.

2 NOT LIKE ANY OTHER

1 Lawrence J. Vale, *Architecture, Power and National Identity* (London, Routledge, 1992), p. 54; John Hirst, *Sentimental Nation: The Making of the Australian Commonwealth* (Oxford University Press: 2000); Helen Irving, *To Constitute a Nation: A Cultural History of Australia's Constitution* (Cambridge University Press: 1999).
2 John Quick and Robert Garran, John Quick and Robert Randolph Garran, *The Annotated Constitution of the Australian Commonwealth* (Sydney: Legal Books, 1995), p. 542.
3 Mark Haefele, Ideal Visions of Canberra, MA thesis, Australian National University, 1995, pp. 19–20; Karl Fischer, *Canberra: Myths and Models* (Hamburg: Institute of Asian Affairs, 1984), p. 10; *Report of the Commissioner on Sites for the Seat of Government* (Sydney: Government Printer, 1900), p. 3; *Proceedings at the Congress of Engineers, Architects and Surveyors and Others Interested in the Building of the Federal Capital of Australia* (Melbourne, Stephens, 1901); Robert Freestone, *Model Communities: The Garden-City Movement in Australia* (Melbourne: Nelson, 1989), pp. 72, 79.
4 A. Oliver, *A Short Review of the Contents of the Report of the Commonwealth Commission on Sites for the Seat of Government* (Sydney: New South Wales Government Printer, 1903), pp. 10–11.
5 John Reps, *Canberra 1912: Plans and Planners of the Australian Capital Competition* (Melbourne University Press: 1997), p. 1.
6 *Report of the Commissioner on Sites*, pp. 18, 33, 38; Roger Pegrum, 'Canberra: The Bush Capital' in Pamela Stratham (ed.), *The Origins of Australia's Capital Cities* (Cambridge University Press, 1989), pp. 320–2.
7 Haefele, 'Ideal Visions', p. 31; O'Malley, *CPD*, 19 July 1901, p. 30; Pegrum, 'Canberra', pp. 322–4; Ken Inglis, 'Ceremonies in a Capital Landscape', *Daedalus*, vol. 114, no. 1, 1985, p. 88; Terry Birtles, *Charles Robert Scrivener* (Melbourne: Arcadia, 2013), pp. 82, 84, 89, 91.

8 Lionel Wigmore, *The Long View* (Melbourne, Cheshire, 1963), p. 41; Haefele, 'Ideal Visions', p. 26; Frank Brennan, *Canberra in Crisis* (Canberra, Dalton, 1971), p. 30.
9 Pegrum, 'Canberra', pp. 326–31; Wigmore, *Long View*, p. 42.
10 Pegrum, 'Canberra', pp. 331–2; Birtles, *Scrivener*, p. 109; Griffith Taylor, *Journeyman Taylor* (London: Robert Hale, 1958, p. 125); Reps, *Canberra 1912*, p. 56.
11 Vale, *Architecture*, p. 104.
12 Brennan, *Canberra*, pp. 9, 14, 15, 19, 22–4, 35; Freestone, *Model Communities*, p. 116.
13 Susan Mary Withycombe, 'Women in Canberra, 1911', *CHJ*, no. 67, 2011, pp. 1–7; *Queanbeyan Age*, 30 August 1906.
14 Jan Blank, 'The Voteless Years, 1911–1928', *CHJ*, no. 65, 2010, p. 8.
15 Michael Roe, *Nine Australian Progressives* (St Lucia: University of Queensland Press, 1984), pp. 189–90; *Age*, 25 April 1915, p. 2.
16 *Pastoralists Review*, 15 November 1910, pp. 974–8; J.R. Brackenreg, 'Brackenreg Lives and Times', *CHJ*, no. 15, 1985, pp. 1–12; John Gray, 'The Initiation of Planning, Afforestation and Conservation at the Federal Capital Site', *CHJ*, no. 67, 2011, p. 28.
17 Charles Daley, *As I Recall* (Canberra: Mulini, 1994), pp. 33–4; James Collet, 'The Heritage of Acton', *CHJ*, no. 67, 2011, p. 33.
18 Brian Maher and Greg Wood, 'Title Fights: Jeremiah Keeffe and the Federal Capital Territory Vigilance Association', *CHJ*, no. 62, 2009, pp. 19–24; Susan Mary Withycombe, Building communities: Women in the making of Canberra, PhD (History), Australian National University, 2008, p. 39; Samuel Shumack, *Tales and Legends of Canberra* (Canberra: ANU Press, 1977), 165–6; Alfred Body, *Firm Still You Stand* (Canberra: St John's Parish Council), 1986, p. 111.
19 C.D. Coulthard-Clark, *Duntroon: The Royal Military College of Australia* (Sydney: Allen & Unwin, 1986), pp. 31–8.
20 Ross McMullen, *Farewell, Dear People: Biographies of Australia's Lost Generation* (Melbourne: Scribe, 2012), pp. 115, 123; W.C. Andrews et al., *Canberra's Engineering Heritage* (Canberra: Institution of Engineers, 1990).
21 Humphrey McQueen, 'Navvies Rocked This City: Canberra 1911–12', *CHJ*, no. 67, 2011, pp. 17–22.
22 Collet, 'Acton', pp. 33–4; Susan Mary Withycombe, Building communities, p. 74; H.M. Rolland, 'From Country to City', pp. 14–16.
23 Freestone, *Model Communities*, p. 117; Paul Reid, *Canberra Following Griffin* (Canberra: NAA, 2002), p. 23; Peter Harrison, *Walter Burley Griffin: Landscape Architect* (Canberra: NLA, 1995), pp. 6–7.
24 Federal Capital Design Competition material, J.S. MacDonald Papers, Noel Butlin Archives, ANU, MS 129.
25 Reps, *Canberra*, pp. 85–9; Alasdair McGregor, *Grand Obsessions: The Life and Work of Walter Burley Griffin and Marion Mahony Griffin* (Melbourne: Penguin, 2009), pp. 142–3.

26 Reps, *Canberra*, p. 100.
27 William Cronon, *Nature's Metropolis: Chicago and the Great West* (New York: Norton, 1991), pp. 341–4; Paul Kruty, 'Chicago 1900: The Griffins Come of Age' in Anne Watson (ed.), *Beyond Architecture: Marion Mahony and Walter Burley Griffin: America, Australia, India* (Sydney: Powerhouse, 1998), p. 12; McGregor, *Grand Obsessions*, pp. 36–9, 56, 69, 109; Harrison, *Griffin*, p. 25; Reid, *Canberra*, pp. 41–3; Peter Proudfoot, *The Secret Plan of Canberra* (Sydney: UNSW Press, 1994), p. 10.
28 Harrison, *Griffin*, p. 26; Reid, *Canberra*, p. 48; James Weirick, 'Spirituality and Symbolism in the Work of the Griffins' in Anne Watson (ed.), *Beyond Architecture*, pp. 64–7.
29 Reid, *Canberra*, p. 101; W.B. Griffin, *The Federal Capital: Preliminary General Plan, October 1913*, p. 13, MacDonald papers; McGregor, *Grand Obsessions*, p. 117; D.I. McDonald, 'Architect J.S. Murdoch and the Provisional Parliament House', *CHJ*, no. 15, 1985, pp. 22–3.
30 Gibbney, *Canberra*, pp. 7–8; Inglis, 'Ceremonies', pp. 86–7; Richard Broinowski, *A Witness to History: The Life and Times of Robert Broinowski* (Carlton: Melbourne University Press, 2001), p. 106.
31 *Advertiser*, 13 March 1913; *Courier*, 13 March 1913; Greg Murphy, 'Canberra. What's in a Name?', *CHJ*, no. 19, 1987, pp. 14–17.
32 Reps, *Canberra*, pp. 252–3; *Report of the Royal Commission into the Federal Capital: Matters Relating to Mr W.B. Griffin* (Melbourne: Government Printer, 1917), p. 7.
33 Gibbney, *Canberra*, p. 29; McGregor, *Grand Obsessions*, pp. 187–92.
34 Harrison, *Griffin*, pp. 33–4.
35 Reid, *Canberra*, pp. 109–15; Harrison, *Griffin*, p. 35; Fischer, *Canberra*, pp. 28–30, 34.
36 Commonwealth Year Books; Brennan, *Canberra*, p. 52.
37 McDonald, 'Murdoch', pp. 18–25; Reid, *Canberra*, p. 69.
38 D.I. McDonald, 'Architect J.S. Murdoch and the Provisional Parliament House', *CHJ*, no. 15, 1985, pp. 18–25; Barry Price, 'The Tuggeranong Town that Never Was', *CHJ*, no. 58, 2007, pp. 17–28; Alan Foskett, *The Molonglo Mystery* (Canberra: Elect, nd).
39 Jennifer Horsfield, *Mary Cunningham* (Canberra, Ginninderra, 2004), pp. 104–5; Coulthard-Clark, *Duntroon*, pp. 79–82; Blank, 'Voteless Years', pp. 8–9.
40 Tony Rout, 'Growing with the Capital', *CHJ*, no. 5, 1980, pp. 24–30; Harrison, *Griffin*, p. 47.
41 Charles Daley, *As I Recall*, pp. 35–6; Reid, *Canberra*, p. 121; *Report of the Royal Commission on Wasteful Expenditure at Canberra* (Melbourne, Government Printer, 1917), pp. 17–19.
42 Reid, *Canberra*, p. 145; David Carment, 'The Forgotten Founder', *CHJ*, no. 1, 1978, pp. 1–7; Harrison, *Griffin*, pp. 30, 49.

3 A DOCUMENT OF AUSTRALIAN IMMATURITY

1 *Register* (Adelaide), 18 April 1921; Gavin Souter, *Acts of Parliament* (Melbourne: Melbourne University Press, 1988), p. 216.
2 Dustin Griffin (ed.), *The Writings of W.B. Griffin* (Cambridge: Cambridge University Press, 2008), p. 79.
3 *Queanbeyan Age*, 15 June 1920; Frank Brennan, *Canberra in Crisis* (Canberra: Dalton, 1971), p. 58.
4 Chapman, *CPD*, 3 August 1922, p. 1098; John Livingston, 5 August 1922, p. 1482; West, p. 1482.
5 *SMH*, 5 April 1922.
6 *Argus*, 21 September 1922; *SMH*, 20 October 1922; *Daily News* (Perth), 14 July 1922.
7 David Lee, *Stanley Melbourne Bruce: Australian Internationalist* (London: Continuum, 2010); Michael Roe, *Australia, Britain and Migration* (Cambridge: Cambridge University Press, 1995), p. 48.
8 Charles Daley, *As I Recall* (Canberra: Mulini Press, 1994), p. 48; McGregor, *Griffin*, p. 340.
9 Peter Freeman, 'John Sulman and Town Planning in Australia' in Sulman, *An Introduction to Town Planning in Australia* (Sydney: National Trust of Australia NSW, 2007), pp. 1, 28; Sulman, 'The Laying Out of Towns', AAAS, *Report of the Second Meeting* (Melbourne: Australasian Association for the Advancement of Science, 1890), p. 735; McGregor, *Griffin*, p. 337; Reid, *Canberra*, p. 152; Charles Daley, *As I Recall*, pp. 42, 44.
10 *Official Year Book of Australia* 1922, p. 947.
11 Reid, *Canberra*, pp. 162, 164, 167.
12 D.I. McDonald, 'Architect J.S. Murdoch and the Provisional Parliament House', *CHJ*, no. 15, 1985, p. 22.
13 Jill Adams and Chris Oakes, *Serving the Nation* (Canberra: PSMPC, 2001), pp. 36–7.
14 *The Griffin Legacy: Canberra, the Nation's Capital in the 21st Century* (Canberra: National Capital Authority, 2004), pp. 60–2.
15 Freestone, 'Planning Suburban Canberra', p. 26.
16 Frank Brennan, *Canberra in Crisis* (Canberra: Dalton, 1971), pp. 60–4.
17 Freestone, 'Planning Suburban Canberra', pp. 15–16.
18 Charles Daley, 'The Growth of a City' in H.L. White (ed.), *Canberra: A Nation's Capital* (Sydney: Angus and Robertson, 1954), p. 36; Brennan, *Canberra*, pp. 64–6.
19 Greg Murphy, 'Thirty Green Years', *CHJ*, no. 4, 1979, pp. 34–43; Charles Daley, 'The Growth of a City', p. 52.
20 Graeme Taylor, The Federal Capital Commission 1925–1930, MA thesis, Australian National University, 1974, pp. 14, 52, 56; G.A. Mawer, *Canberry Tales: An Informal History* (Melbourne: Arcadia, 2012), p. 94.

21 Lionel Wigmore, *The Long View* (Melbourne: Cheshire, 1963), pp. 99–100; Brennan, *Canberra*, pp. 80, 85–6; Frederick Watson, *A Brief History of Canberra* (Canberra: Federal Capital Press, 1927), p. 202; Taylor, FCC, pp. 78–9.
22 Foreword, *Canberra Illustrated*, 1925, p. 10.
23 Jill Waterhouse (ed.), *Canberra: Early Days at the Causeway* (Canberra: ACT Museums Unit, 1992), pp. 3–4; Harry Trevillian in Val Emerton (ed.), *Past Images, Present Voices* (Canberra: Canberra Stories Group, 1996), p. 25.
24 Tim Reeves and Alan Roberts, *100 Canberra Houses* (Canberra: Halstead, 2013), p. 13; Ann Gugler, *True Tales from Canberra's Suburbs* (Canberra: Gugler, 1999), p. 19; Taylor, FCC, p. 91; Ken Dinnerville in Emerton (ed.). *Past Images*, p. 40; *Year Book of Australia 1928* (Melbourne: Green, 1928), p. 606.
25 *Argus*, 30 January 1924; Emerton (ed.), *Past Images*, pp. 25, 27, 40; Alan Foskett, *You May Have Lived Here for a While* (Canberra: Aussie Print, 2002), p. 10; Richard Broinowski, *A Witness to History* (Melbourne: Melbourne University Publishing, 2001), p. 114.
26 Ken Charlton, Rodney Garrett and Shibu Datta, *Federal Capital Architecture* (Canberra: National Trust of Australia, 2001).
27 CCN, 11 November 1925; Alison Bashford, 'Karl Haushofer's *Geopolitics of the Pacific Ocean*' in Kate Fullager (ed.), *The Atlantic World in a Pacific Field* (Cambridge: Scholars Press, 2012), p. 136.
28 CNN, 14 October 1925; Freeman Wyllie, Constructing a community: The Canberra Social Service Movement 1925–1929, MLitt, Australian National University, 1994, pp. 12, 23; CCN, 11 November 1925, pp. 1–2; Taylor, FCC, p. 84; Waterhouse, *Canberra*, p. 67.
29 Wigmore, *Long View*, p. 111; Broinowski, *Witness*, p. 118; Maryrose Casey, 'Disturbing Performances of Race and Nation', *International Journal of Critical Indigenous Studies*, vol. 2, no. 2, 2009, p. 31.
30 Frank C. Green, *Servant of the House* (Melbourne: Heinemann, 1969), p. 73; *A Descriptive Guide to Canberra* (Melbourne: Brown Prior, 1927), p. 3.
31 C.J. Lloyd, *Parliament and the Press* (Melbourne: Melbourne University Press, 1988), pp. 72, 92.
32 P.W.E. Curtin, 'The Seat of Government' in White (ed.), *Canberra*, pp. 69–71; Warren Denning, *Capital City* (Canberra: Hewitt, 1944), p. 35.
33 Nick Swain, 'Barton – a 1920s Garden Suburb', *CHJ*, no. 64, 2010, pp. 35–41.
34 Helen Crisp and Loma Ruddock, *The Mothering Years: The Story of the Mothercraft Society 1926–1979* (Canberra: Mothercraft Society, 1979), p. 4; Gibbney, *Canberra*, pp. 132–3; Charles Daley, *As I Recall*, p. 65; Adams and Oates, *Serving the Nation*, p. 89.

35 Taylor, FCC, p. 118; Gibbney, *Canberra*, pp. 115–18; Crisp and Ruddock, *The Mothering Years*, p. 20; CNN, 9 May 1927; Patricia Clarke, 'The Journos' Pub: The Hotel Wellington 1927–1984' in Shirley Purchase (ed.), *Canberra's Early Hotels: A Pint-sized History* (Canberra: Canberra District Historical Society, 1999), p. 90.
36 Brennan, *Canberra*, p. 96; *Canberra Times*, 15 April 1929; Michael McKernan, *Here Is Their Spirit* (St Lucia: University of Queensland Press, 1991), pp. 106–11; Gibbney, *Canberra*, p. 142; Kel Robertson, The Federal Capital Territory Unlawful Assemblies Ordinance of 1937, MLitt, Australian National University, 1995, p. 2.
37 Warren Denning, *Caucus Crisis* (Sydney: Hale and Iremonger, 1982), p. 23.
38 J. Brackenreg, 'Brackenreg Lives and Times', *CHJ*, no. 15, 1985, p. 10; Wendy A. Way, Canberra in the Depression Years 1930–31, MA (Qual), Australian National University, 1975, pp. 10, 13, 41, 49; C.D. Coulthard-Clark, *Duntroon* (Sydney: Allen & Unwin, 1986), pp. 113–14.
39 W.K. Hancock, *Australia* (London: Benn, 1930), pp. 277–82.
40 Charles Daley, *As I Recall*, p. 150; Broinowski, *Witness*, pp. 173–4; G. Temperly, 'Canberra's Ideological Climate in the 1930s', *Canberra and District Historical Society Newsletter*, March 1985, p. 8; M.J.S. Knowles, 'Canberra in the Early Government Period', *CHJ*, no. 19, 1987, pp. 3–8; Robert Garran, *Prosper the Commonwealth*, Angus & Robertson, Sydney, 1958, p. 286; Anne Edgeworth, *The Cost of Jazz Garters* (Canberra: Canberra Repertory Society, 1991), pp. 9–21; John Farquarson, 'Lewis Windermere Nott', *Australian Dictionary of Biography* (Melbourne: Melbourne University Press, 2000), vol. 15, p. 501.
41 Way, Canberra, pp. 7–72.
42 Kate Power and Lyall Gillespie, *A Pictorial History of Telopea Park School* (Canberra: Telopea Park School, 1983), pp. 11–12; Patience Wardle, 'The National Capital 1928–1931', *CHJ*, no. 4, 1979, p. 7; Hope Hewitt, 'Lady Callers: Canberra Daughters and the Barrier of Convention', *CHJ*, no. 8, 1981, pp. 16–17; Jenny Hocking, *Gough Whitlam: A Moment in History* (Melbourne: Miegunyah Press: 2008), pp. 32, 40–1.
43 Eric Martin, 'Albert Hall', *Heritage in Trust*, Autumn 2005, pp. 5–6; Lenore Coltheart, 'Grand Days at the Albert Hall', *CHJ*, no. 60, 2008, pp. 2–9.
44 Gwen Cameron, *Canberra: A City of Flowers* (Canberra: Department of the Interior, nd); Hocking, *Whitlam*, p. 48; W.M. Rolland, *Growing Up in Early Canberra* (Adelaide: Kangaroo Press, 1988), pp. 51, 66; Frank Dunshea, 'Old Acton' in Ann Gugler (ed.), *True Tales From Canberra's Vanished Suburbs* (Canberra: On Demand, 1999), pp. 368–9; Hocking,

Whitlam, p. 48; Barbara Malpass, *Cycling Canberra* (Canberra: Ginninderra Press, 1999), p. 32; Stanley Ray in Louise Lyon (ed.), *Voices of Old Ainslie* (Canberra: Canberra Stories Group, 1995), p. 9.

45 Mary Hutchinson (ed.), *Tracks through Time* (Canberra: Canberra Stories Group, 1997); *Canberra Times*, 28 September 1933; Eirene Mort, *Old Canberra* (Canberra: National Library of Australia, 1987).

46 Brian Egloff, *Wreck Bay* (Canberra: Australian Institute of Aboriginal Studies, 1981); Egloff, 'Aboriginal Landscapes and Seascapes' in George Cho (ed.), *Jervis Bay* (Canberra: Australian Nature Conservation Agency, 1995), pp. 14–15; Lee Chittick and Terry Fox, *Travelling with Percy* (Canberra: Aboriginal Studies Press, 1997); Peter Kabaila, *Belconnen's Aboriginal Past* (Canberra: Black Mountain Projects, 1997), p. 30; Gugler (ed.), *True Tales*, p. v.; Peter Read, *A Hundred Years' War* (Canberra: Australian National University, 1988), pp. 19, 53.

47 J.W. Evans, *The Life and Work of Robin John Tillyard* (St Lucia: University of Queensland Press, 1963), pp. 24–5; John Dargavel, *The Zealous Conservator* (Perth: University of Western Australia Press, 2008), pp. 85–6; 118–20, 153.

48 Libby Robin, *How a Continent Created a Nation* (Sydney: UNSW Press, 2007), pp. 84–7; Charles Daley, 'Administrative History', pp. 70–1; James Gillespie, *The Price of Health* (Cambridge: Cambridge University Press), pp. 53–4; Crisp and Ruddock, *Mothering Years*, p. 41.

49 Colin Foster and Cameron Hazlehurst, 'Australian Statisticians and the Development of Official Statistics', *Year Book: Australia 1988* (Canberra: Government Printer, 1988), pp. 69–73; George Caiden, *Career Service* (Melbourne: Melbourne University Press), p. 244; S.G. Foster and Margaret Vargese, *The Making of the Australian National University* (Sydney: Allen & Unwin, 196), p. 145.

50 Editorial, *ANR*, vol. 1, no. 1, 1937, p. 5; C. Lane-Poole, 'Trees Have No Votes', *ANR*, vol. 1, no. 1, pp. 45–53; C.E.W. Bean, 'Problems of Australian Literature', *ANR*, vol. 1, no. 3, 1937, pp. 35–7; E.H. Burgmann, 'The Future of Democracy', *ANR*, vol. 1, no. 2, p. 16; 'Letter from a Machine Age Politician', *ANR*, vol. 1, no. 1, p. 66; 'A Young Australia', *ANR*, vol. 3, no. 4, p. 73; Wigmore, *Long View*, pp. 143–4.

51 Gavin Souter, *Acts of Parliament* (Melbourne: Melbourne University Press, 1988), pp. 265, 300, 309; David Day, *John Curtin* (Sydney: Harper Collins, 1999), pp. 312–13; Diane Langmore, *Prime Ministers' Wives* (Melbourne: McPhee Gribble, 1992), p. 92; Lloyd, *Parliament and the Press*, p. 118; Robertson, *Unlawful Assemblies Act*.

52 Susan Mary Withycombe, Building communities p. 204; M. Barnard Eldershaw, *Plaque with Laurel* (London: Harrap, 1937), p. 250.

53 *Canberra Times*, 13 January, 16 January 1939; Tom Griffiths, 'An Unnatural Disaster', *History Australia*, vol. 8, no. 1, 2009, p. 35;

L. Pryor, 'The Bush Fire Problem in the ACT', *Australian Forestry*, vol. 4, no. 1, 1939, p. 37.

4 UNREAL CITY

1 *Sydney Morning Herald*, 14 April 1945; Warren Denning, *Capital City* (Canberra: Hewitt, 1944), p. 85.
2 Ric Throssell, *My Father's Son* (Melbourne: Heinemann, 1989), pp. 204, 248.
3 Tim Rowse, *Nugget Coombs: A Reforming Life* (Cambridge University Press, 2001), p. 154; F.A. Bland, 'Public Administration in Wartime', *Australian Quarterly*, vol. 14, no. 4, 1942, p. 52; P.W.E. Curtin, 'Politics and Administration II', *Public Administration*, vol. 8, no. 1, 1949, p. 18.
4 Paul Hasluck, *The Government and the People 1939–41* (Canberra, Australian War Memorial, 1952), pp. 475–7.
5 G.C. Remington, 'The Cry for Better Men in Government', *Australian Outlook*, vol. 12, no. 3, 1940, p. 39.
6 Gavin Souter, *Acts of Parliament* (Melbourne: Melbourne University Press, 1988), p. 326.
7 Curtin, 'Politics and Administration', p. 18; W.E. Dunk, *They Also Serve* (Canberra: Dunk, 1974), p. 43; Giblin in F.R.E. Mauldon, 'The University Man in Public Administration', *Australian National Review*, vol. 5, no. 30, 1939, p. 28; Sir Roland Wilson, interviewed by Cameron Hazlehurt and Colin Foster, NLA TRC 1612, p. 10; Hasluck, *Government and People*, pp. 484–6.
8 Wilson, NLA, p. 2; Charles Daley, 'The Administrative History of Canberra and its Development' in Kenneth Binns (ed.), *Handbook for Canberra* (Canberra: Government Printer, 1938), p. 67; H.C. Coombs, *Trial Balance* (Melbourne: Macmillan, 1981).
9 Hasluck, *The Government and the People 1939–42*, p. 470; Wilson, NLA, p. 2; Sir Keith Shann, interviewed by Ken Henderson, 21 August 1985, NLA TRC 1857, p. 22.
10 Geoffrey Sawer, *Australian Federal Politics and Law 1929–1949* (Melbourne, Melbourne University Press, 1963), p. 149; Sir Alan Watt, interviewed by Bruce Miller, 11 December 1974, NLA TRC 306, p. 9; Sir Frederick Wheeler, author interview, 3 July 1997; Shann, interview, p. 3.
11 Shann, interview, pp. 3, 17, 19.
12 F.R.E. Mauldon, 'The University Man in Public Administration', *Australian National Review*, vol. 5, no. 30, 1939, pp. 29–30; Wilson, interview, p. 13.
13 F.A. Bland, 'Public Administration in Wartime', *Australian Quarterly*, vol. 14, no. 4, 1942, pp. 50–8; K.H. Bailey, 'The War Emergency Legislation of the Commonwealth', *Public Administration*, vol. 4, no. 1, 1942, p. 12.
14 Rowse, *Coombs*, p. 154.

15 Bland, 'Public Administration in Wartime', p. 51.
16 Hasluck, *Government and People 1939–42*, p. 243; Ross Fitzgerald and Stephen Holt, *Alan 'The Red Fox' Reid* (Sydney, NewSouth, 2010), pp. 21–9.
17 Souter, *Acts*, pp. 324–5, 348; Bailey, 'War Emergency Legislation', p. 11; L.F. Crisp, *The Parliamentary Government of the Commonwealth of Australia* (London: Longman, 1949), p. 161.
18 David Day, *John Curtin: A Life* (Sydney: Harper Collins, 1999), p. 473; C.J. Lloyd, *Parliament and Press* (Melbourne: Melbourne University Press, 1988), pp. 131, 138.
19 Michael McKernan, *Here Is Their Spirit* (St Lucia: University of Queensland Press, 1991), pp. 4–5.
20 *Canberra Times*, 11 November 1941.
21 Don Whitington, *Rings the Bells* (Melbourne: Georgian House, 1956), p. 70; Hasluck, *Government and People 1942–45*, pp. 125, 135.
22 Marion Douglas and Fionna Douglas, *Not without My Corsets* (Canberra: ACT Government, 1996), p. 33; *Canberra Times*, 20 November 1941, 23 December 1941; Watt, NLA interview, p. 15; E.H. Frohlich in *My First Home in Canberra* (Canberra Stories Group: Murrumbateman, 1994), p. 33.
23 Rae Else-Mitchell in Judith Baskin (ed.), *Wartime in Canberra* (Canberra: National Trust, 2005), p. 89; Sir Peter Lawler, author interview, 15 June 1994; Paul Hasluck, *Diplomatic Witness* (Melbourne, Melbourne University Publishing, 1980), p. 49.
24 *Canberra Times*, 28 March 1942, 26 February 1943; Barry York, 'A Happy and a Hard Time', *CHJ*, no. 25, 1990, pp. 23–7; Jim Gibbney, *Canberra 1913–53* (Canberra: AGPS, 1988), p. 223.
25 *Canberra Times*, 9 October 1943; Jean Salisbury, Ruth Masel, Stan Goodhew and Nancy Sutherland in Baskin (eds), *Wartime in Canberra*, pp. 43, 64, 94, 101; Helen Tracey, *The Y-Generation* (Canberra: YMCA, 2011), pp. 13–15.
26 G.A. Mawer, *Canberry Tales* (Melbourne; Australian Scholarly Publishing, 2012), pp. 156–9; Ginette Snow, *Canberra Airport* (Canberra: Goanna, 2009), pp. 11–2.
27 Rowse, *Coombs*, p. 159; Diane Langmore, *Prime Ministers' Wives* (Melbourne: McPhee Gribble, 1992), pp. 132–3; Patricia Clarke, *Eilean Giblin: A Feminist Between the Wars* (Melbourne: Monash, 2013), pp. 112–13.
28 Paul Hasluck, *Diplomatic Witness* (Melbourne University Press, 1980), p. 51; L.F. Crisp, *Ben Chifley* (Croydon: Longmans, 1961, pp. 257–8; Nicholas Brown, *Richard Downing: Economics, Advocacy and Social Reform* (Melbourne University Press, 2001), pp. 106, 114–15, 118.
29 G.E. Caiden, *Career Service* (Melbourne: Melbourne University Press, 1965), p. 265; Hasluck, *Government and People 1942–45*, p. 471.

30 Eilean Giblin, Diary 1940–43, NLA MSS 366, entry for 24 October 1941; Clarke, *Giblin*, pp. 107–25.
31 Watts, *The Foundation of the National Welfare State* (Sydney: Allen & Unwin, 1987), p. 111; Ministry of Post-War Reconstruction, 'Preliminary Report on a Plan for the Development of the ACT' at www.archives.act.gov.au/__data/assets/pdf_file/0008/155762/Plan_for_development.pdf; S.G. Foster and Margaret M. Varghese, *The Making of the Australian National University* (Sydney: Allen & Unwin, 1996), pp. 3–42.
32 Gwenda Tavan, *The Long, Slow Death of White Australia* (Melbourne: Scribe, 2005), p. 42.
33 Nicholas Brown, 'Sir William Ernest Dunk', *Australian Dictionary of Biography* (Melbourne: Melbourne University Press, 2008), vol. 17, pp. 343–5; Public Service Board, *Report on the Public Service of the Commonwealth* (Canberra: AGPS, 1947), pp. 17–18.
34 Ian Hancock, *National and Permanent* (Melbourne: Melbourne University Press, 2000), pp. 31–3; Crisp, *Parliamentary Government*, p. 64.
35 Peter Kabaila, *Wiradjuri Places* (Canberra: Black Mountain Project, 1998), vol. 1, p. 24.
36 Frank Brennan, *Canberra in Crisis* (Canberra: Dalton, 1971), p. 151.
37 Lionel Wigmore, *The Long View* (Melbourne: Cheshire, 1963), pp. 154–5; Alan Foskett, *Homes for the Workers* (Canberra: Narrabundah Pre-Fabs History Group, 2–11, pp. 27, 127.
38 Anne Edgeworth, *The Cost of Jazz Garters* (Canberra Repertory Society, 1992), p. 43; Donald Horne, *Confessions of a New Boy* (Melbourne: Viking, 1985), pp. 130, 140.
39 *Canberra Times*, 16 December 1947, 22 December 1947; Meryl Hunter, *Over My Shoulder* (Canberra: Canberra Stories Group, 1998), p. 117.
40 Helen Crisp and Loma Ruddock, *The Mothering Years* (Canberra Mothercraft Society, Canberra, 1979), p. 52; *Canberra Parents Bulletin*, March 1945, April 1945; Minutes of the Griffith Progress and Welfare Association, 13 January 1944, 28 October 1946; Minutes of the Canberra Citizens' Rights League, 25 July 1944: Bill Fanning Papers, NLA MS 7881, Box 4; Don Selth, *More Than a Game* (Canberra: Ginninderra Press, 2010), pp. 175–9.
41 *Canberra Times*, 11 August 1947, 1 November 1947, 9 December 1949, 12 December 1949; Public Service Board, *Annual Report*, 1949, pp. 3–4; Warren Denning, *The Road to Canberra* (Sydney: Australasian Publishing, 1947), p. 238; Hungerford, *Knockabout in a Slouch Hat* (Fremantle Arts Centre Press, 1984), p. 108.

5 MOVING UP, AND MOVING IN

1 *Digest of the Australian Citizenship Convention* (Canberra: Department of Immigration, 1950), p. 3.

2 Hugh Stretton, *Ideas for Australian Cities* (Adelaide: Griffin Press, 1970), p. 103; Eric Sparke, *Canberra 1954–1980* (Canberra: AGPS, 1988), p. 20.
3 Alan Foskett, *A Capital Change: Some Recollections of the NCDC* (Canberra: Foskett, 1996), p. 8; *Canberra Times*, 23, 31 January 1950.
4 *Canberra Times*, 27 January 1950; *Daily News* (Perth), 6 December 1949; *New Australian*, January 1950, p. 3.
5 *Inside Canberra*, 8 June 1950; C.J. Lloyd, *Parliament and the Press* (Melbourne: Melbourne University Press, 1988), p. 190; Peter Edwards, *Arthur Tange: The Last of the Mandarins* (Sydney: Allen & Unwin, 2006, p. 83; Frederick Wheeler, 'The Professional Career Public Service: Some Reflections of a Practitioner', *Australian Journal of Public Administration*, vol. 39, no. 2, 1980, p. 173.
6 W.E. Dunk, *They Also Serve* (Canberra: Public Service Board, 1974), p. 82.
7 Menzies, *CPD*, 2 October 1951, p. 184; *Nation*, 4 July 1959, pp. 14–15.
8 P.W.E. Curtin, 'The Seat of Government' in H.L. White (ed.), *Canberrra: A Nation's Capital* (Sydney: Halstead, 1954), p. 79; *SMH*, 28 August 1950.
9 Stephen Foster and Margaret Varghese, *The Making of the Australian National University* (Sydney: Allen & Unwin, 1996), pp. 73–4; Milton Cameron, *Experiments in Modern Living: Scientists' Houses in Canberra 1950–1970* (Canberra: Australian National University e-Press, 2012), p. 14.
10 Bruce Wright, *Cornerstone of the Capital: Public Housing in Canberra* (Canberra: ACT Government, 2000), pp. 39, 41; Max Neutze, 'Planning and Land Tenure in Canberra after 60 Years', *Town Planning Review*, vol. 58, no. 2, 1987, p. 152.
11 H.J. Gibbney 'Awful Tales of a Canberra "Pioneer"', *CHJ*, no. 7, 1981, p. 7; Alan Foskett, *You May Have Lived Here for a While* (Canberra: Foskett, 2002), pp. 87, 111, 126–9; Foskett, *The Memories Linger On* (Canberra: Foskett, 2010), p. 86; *My First Home in Canberra* (Murrumbateman: Canberra Stories Group (1994)), p. 49.
12 Frederick Howard, *Kent Hughes: A Biography of Colonel the Hon. Sir Wilfrid Kent Hughes* (Melbourne: Macmillan, 1972), p. 156.
13 Barry Price, 'The Tocumwal Houses in Canberra', *CHJ*, no. 62, 2009; Stretton, *Ideas*, pp. 71, 118.
14 *Australian Women's Weekly*, 1 May 1957; T.R.S. Gibson, 'Canberra Today and Tomorrow' in *1951 Federal Congress on Regional and Town Planning* (Canberra: Planning Institute of Australia, 1951), pp. 13–14; Tim Reeves and Alan Roberts, *100 Canberra Houses* (Canberra: Halstead, 2013), p. 91; *Commonwealth Year Book 1957* (Canberra: AGP, 1957), p. 113.

15 Sparke, *Canberra*, pp. 8–10; Gibson, *Senate Select Committee on the Development of Canberra: Evidence* (Government Printer: Canberra, 1957), vol. 1, p. 74.
16 Robin Boyd, *The Australian Ugliness* (Melbourne: Penguin, 1960), p. 154.
17 Robert Bolland and Erik Eklund, 'The Hidden Proletarian Past of Canberra' in Bobbie Oliver (ed.), *Labour History in the New Century* (Perth: Black Swan, 2009), pp. 104–7; *Canberra BWIU News*, September 1953, p. 3; Wright, *Cornerstone of the Capital*, p. 41.
18 *Sun-Herald*, 15 May 1955.
19 Betty Kavunenko, Italians in Canberra and Queanbeyan: the post-war immigration, BLitt thesis, ANU, 1983; Rochelle E. Ball, *Worlds Turned Upside Down* (Canberra: Ginninderra Press, 2005), pp. 82–5; Salvatore Gambale et al., *Canberra: Our Italian Heritage* (Canberra: Italo-Australian Club, 1988), pp. 6, 15–16, 32.
20 *Canberra Times*, 1 April 1949; Foskett, *You May Have Lived Here for a While*, pp. 58, 61–2; Don Garden, *Builders to the Nation: The A.V. Jennings Story* (Melbourne: Melbourne University Press, 1992), pp. 104–5; *Canberra BWIU News*, August 1953, pp. 7, 10; December 1953, p. 14.
21 C.I. Fleming, *A History of the Good Neighbour Council of the Australian Capital Territory* (Canberra: GNC, nd), pp. 2, 4; Bruce Juddery, 'The Seat of Adminstration', *Canberra: A People's Capital* (Canberra: Australian Institute of Urban Affairs, 1988), p. 29.
22 Patricia Frei, *Canberra, the City on the River: the Austrian Migrant Experience* (Canberra: Ginninderra Press, 2005), pp. 58–67; *Australian Home Beautiful*, March 1955, p. 55.
23 Cameron, *Experiments*, p. 36; Adele Rosalky, *The Jewish Community of Canberra* (Canberra: Jewish Community Inc., 2000), pp. 15, 32; *Australian Women's Weekly*, 1 May 1957; Vladimir Bondarenko, 'The Windwalkers of Westlake' in Ann Gugler (ed.), *True Tales From Canberra's Vanished Suburbs* (On Demand, Canberra, 1999), p. 19; Ann-Mari Jordens, 'Migrants and their Contributions to Canberra', *CHJ*, September 2003, p. 10; Nick Guoth, 'Ethnicity and Soccer in Canberra', *CHJ*, September 2003, pp. 29–31; *Age*, 18 August 1979, 5 December 1979.
24 Ken Charlton, Bronwen Jones and Paola Favaro, *The Contribution of Enrico Taglietti to Canberra's Architecture* (Canberra: RAIA, 2007).
25 O.H.K. Spate, 'Social Structure and Function' in H.L. White (ed.), *Canberra: A Nation's Capital* (Sydney: Angus & Robertson, 1954), p. 288; A.W. Martin, *Robert Menzies: A Life* (Melbourne: Melbourne University Press, 1999), vol. 2, pp. 270, 381–3; Clarrie Harders, NLA Oral History, trs. 3537, p. 8; Paul Hasluck, *The Public Servant and Politics* (Canberra: Royal Institute of Public Administration, 1968), p. 15.

26 Jane Connors, The glittering threat: the 1954 Royal Tour of Australia, PhD, UTS, 1996, pp. 201, 210; Shibu Datta, *Reid: ACT* (Canberra: Reid Residents Association, 1980), p. 8; Patricia Frei, *Mervyn Jones and the Capital and Civic Picture Theatres* (Canberra: Frei, 2008), p. 38; Martin, *Menzies*, vol. 2, p. 248; K.S. Inglis, 'Ceremonies in a Capital Landscape', *Daedalus*, vol. 11, no. 1, 1985, p. 107.

27 Hal Myers, *The Whispering Gallery* (Sydney: Kangaroo Press, 1999), pp. 121–2, 143, 152–3; Robert Manne, *The Petrov Affair: Politics and Espionage* (Sydney: Pergamon, 1987), p. 43; Vladimir and Evdokia Petrov, *Empire of Fear* (London: Praeger, 1956), p. 237; Throssell, *My Father's Son*, p. 208; *Courier-Mail*, 14 April 1954.

28 *Canberra Times*, 28 Mary 1952; Peter Worsley, *An Academic Skating on Thin Ice* (London: Berghahn, 2008), pp. 95–6; *Australian*, 14 January 2012; *Sydney Morning Herald*, 30 May 1952.

29 *Canberra Times*, 20 October 1950; Michael Thwaites, *Truth Will Out: ASIO and the Petrovs* (Collins, Sydney, 1980), pp. 66–7; Amirah Inglis, *The Hammer and Sickle and the Washing Up* (Melbourne: Hyland, 1995), p. 166.

30 *Sun-Herald*, 15 May 1955; McCallum, *CPD*, 16 September 1954, p. 359, 3 November 1954, p. 1191; Michael Easson, John Archibald McCallum (1892–1973), *Australian Dictionary of Biography* (Melbourne: Melbourne University Press, 2000), vol. 15, pp. 164–5.

31 Senate Standing Committee on the Planning and Development of Canberra, *Report* (Canberra: Government Printer, Canberra, 1955), pp. 15–16, 18–20; *Minutes of Evidence* (Canberra: Government Printer, 1955), vol. 1, pp. 490, 1118–9.

32 Senate Select Committee, *Report*, pp. 16, 25, 32–4, 53; *Minutes*, pp. 103, 1856; Sparke, *Canberra*, pp. 39–49.

33 Martin, *Menzies*, pp. 385–7.

34 ibid.; Sparke, *Canberra*, pp. 42–54.

35 *Canberra Times*, 21 June 1957; Sparke, *Canberra*, p. 91; William Holford, *Observations on the Future Development of Canberra* (Canberra: Government Printer, 1958), p. 9.

36 Holford, *Observations*, pp. 5, 6, 7, 9, 10, 11; *Canberra Times*, 21 June 1957; Paul Reid, *Canberra Following Griffin* (Canberra: NAA, 2002), p. 226.

37 NCDC, *Annual Report*, 1957, p. 3; John Overall, *Canberra: Yesterday, Today, Tomorrow* (Canberra: Federal Capital Press, 1995), pp. 39–40, 50; K.F. Fischer, *Canberra: Myths and Models* (Hamburg: Institute of Asian Affairs, 1984), pp. 70–1; Harrison, NLA interview, p. 72.

38 NCDC, *Annual Reports*, 1957–58, pp. 9, 12; 1958–59, p. 9; Overall, *Canberra*, p. 51; Lindie Clark, *Finding a Common Interest* (Cambridge: Cambridge University Press, 2002), pp. 94–5; Garden, *Builders*, p. 169; Stretton, *Ideas*, p. 76.

39 Fischer, *Canberra*, pp. 72–4; Stretton, *Ideas*, pp. 78–9; NCDC, *Annual Reports*, 1958–59, p. 10; 1959–60, p. 20; 1960–61, p. 7; Reeves and Roberts, *100 Canberra Homes*, p. 124.
40 Alan Foskett, *The Campbell Community* (Canberra: Foskett, 2009), pp. 61, 76; Christine Cannon, 'A "Most Pressing Problem": Housing and the National Capital Development Commission 1955–62', *UEP Working Paper*, no. 66, 1999, pp. 7, 9, 12, 13, 19; Wright, *Cornerstone*, pp. 57–8.
41 Bernadette Hince, A Pryor commitment: Canberra's public landscape 1944–58, MSc thesis, ANU, pp. 18, 26; L.D. Pryor, 'Landscape and Trees in Canberra' in *Federal Congress*, pp. 20–2; Matthew Higgins, 'Skis on the Brindabellas' in Ian Fraser and Margaret McJannet (eds), *Brindabella Heritage* (Canberra: Canberra and South-East Region Environment Centre, 1994).
42 *Conservation of the Soil* (Canberra: Department of the Interior, nd), pp. 2, 6, 22, 24; Soil Conservation Council (ACT), *Annual Report 1957*, pp. 17–18; Neville Esau, 'Gudgenby Wilderness' in G. Mosely (ed.), *Fighting for Wilderness* (Melbourne: Australian Conservation Foundation, 1984), p. 107; NCDC, *Annual Reports*, 1957–8, p. 8; 1962–3, p. 17.
43 Stretton, *Ideas*, p. 123.
44 *Australian Women's Weekly*, 1 May 1957, p. 1; W.D. Borrie, H.W. Arndt and G. Rudduck, *Canberra; The Next Decade* (Canberra Sociological Society, 1962), p. 8; *BWIU News*, November, 1953, p. 61; W.A. Cramond, *An Appreciation of the Psychiatric Services of the ACT* (Canberra: Department of Health, 1967), p. 3; NCDC, *Planning Report 1959–64* (Canberra: NCDC, 1959), p. 2; Charles Price, *Report on Departing Settlers* (Canberra: Good Neighbour Council, 1963).
45 *Observer*, 18 February 1961, p. 16; Jeanne MacKenzie, *Australian Paradox* (Melbourne: Cheshire, 1961), p. 36; 'Canberra – A Continuing City', *Walkabout*, vol. 23, no. 12, 1957, p. 11; Patricia Ann Dalgarno (1909–1980), *Australian Women's Register* at www.womenaustralia.info/biogs/AWE0773b.htm; Susan Mary Withycombe, Building communities: women in the making of Canberra 1911–1958, PhD, ANU, 2008, p. 298.
46 Bruce Harding, 'Canberra – A Continuing City', *Walkabout*, vol. 23, no. 12, 1957, p. 12; Foskett, *Campbell*, p. 73; Clark, *Common Interest*, p. 96.
47 *Catholic Weekly*, 20 June 1957, p. 5.
48 Peter Hempenstall, *The Meddlesome Priest: A Life of Ernest Burgmann* (Sydney: Allen & Unwin, 1993), pp. 266, 287.
49 Hempenstall, *Burgmann*, pp. 289, 303.
50 Hector Harrison, NLA interview, 2 October 1973, TRC 121/46; *Presbyterian Life*, 5 November 1965, pp. 7–8.

51 Public Service Board, *Annual Reports*, 1959–60, p. 50, 1961–62, p. 108; Committee of Enquiry into Public Service Recruitment, *Report* (Canberra: Government Printer, 1959), pp. 9–10; Gerald Caiden, 'Administrative Reform', *Australian Journal of Public Administration*, vol. 29, no. 3–4, 1980, p. 441; *Nation*, 4 July 1959, p. 15.
52 NCDC, *Annual Report*, 1961–62, pp. 7, 20; *Bulletin*, 24 April 1957, p. 6; *Nation*, 26 April 1961, pp. 7–9, 3 March 1963, pp. 12–13; Rod Chalmers, *Inside the Canberra Press Gallery* (Canberra: ANU e-Press, 2011), pp. 61–2; Lloyd, *Parliament and the Press*, pp. 192–3.
53 Foster and Varghese, *The Making of the ANU*, pp. 105, 125, 155.
54 ibid., p. 186.
55 R.F. Brissenden, NLA interview, TRC 1/207, 30 March 1967; Mark McKenna, *An Eye for Eternity* (Melbourne: Melbourne University Press, 2011), pp. 300, 304.
56 Frederick Colin Courtice, 'Bede Morris 1927–1988', *Historical Records of Australian Science* at www.asap.unimelb.edu.au/bsparcs/aasmemoirs/morris.htm; NCDC, *Planning Report*, p. 9.

6 QUIET REVOLUTION

1 Frank Clune, *Journey to Kosciusko* (Sydney: Angus & Robertson, 1964), pp. 329, 244, 245–6, 264; Donald Horne, *The Lucky Country* (Melbourne: Penguin, 1964), p. 64.
2 *Australian*, 28 April 1965.
3 *Australian*, 15 July 1964.
4 William Holford, 'The Growth of Canberra', *Town Planning Review*, vol. 38, no. 1, 1967, p. 8; *Tomorrow's Canberra* (Canberra: NCDC, 1970), pp. xvii–viii.
5 Edmund Bacon, 'Canberra as Statement of World Culture', *Architecture in Australia*, vol. 57, no. 4, p. 625.
6 Graeme Davison, *Car Wars* (Sydney: Allen & Unwin, 1990), p. xii; Peter Harrison, interviewed by James Weirick, 30 September 1990, NLA TRC 2635, p. 108.
7 Paul Reid, *Canberra Following Griffin*, p. 258; G.J.R. Linge, *Canberra: Site and City* (Canberra: Australian National University Press, 1975), p. v.
8 NCDC, *Annual Report 1963–64*, p. 13; Karl Fischer, *Canberra: Myths and Models* (Hamburg: Institute of Asian Affairs, 1984), pp. 82–90; Reid, *Canberra*, p. 257.
9 Holford, 'The Growth of Canberra', p. 6; NCDC, *Planning Report 1959–64* (Canberra: NCDC, 1959), p. 7; P.N. Troy and N.G. Butlin, *The Cost of Collisions* (Melbourne: Cheshire, 1971), p. 73; *Canberra Times*, 25 October 1965; Fischer, *Canberra*, p. 81.
10 *Tomorrow's Canberra* (Canberra: NCDC, 1979), pp. 188, 221; Bacon, 'Canberra', p. 626.

11 John Gilchrist, Woden–Weston Creek New Town: Concepts, Techniques, Processes, MSc (Arch) thesis, University of Sydney, 1985, p. 316.
12 Stretton, *Ideas*, pp. 119–21.
13 Roger Johnson, *Design in Balance: Designing the National Area of Canberra* (University of Queensland Press, 1974), pp. 23, 26, 67–9; Reid, *Canberra*, p. 284.
14 Richard Clough, 'Landscape of Canberra', *Landscape Australia*, no. 3, 1982, pp. 196–206; Jane Correy and Allan Correy, 'The Landscape Treatment of Canberra', *Architecture in Australia*, vol. 57, no. 4, 1968, p. 627; George Clarke and Tom Heath, 'Canberra Observed', *Art in Australia*, vol. 1, no. 3, 1963, p. 179; Margaret Hendry, 'Canberra – A City Within the Landscape', *Landscape Planning*, no. 6, 1979, pp. 277–8.
15 *Canberra Times*, 2 July 1966; Bruce Juddery, 'Prices in Canberra', *Nation*, 6 August 1966, p. 4; Barbara Higgs, 'Going to Canberra', *Nation*, 17 September 1966, p. 6.
16 ACTCOSS, *Annual Report*, 1966, p. 2; *ACTCOSS Newsletter*, July 1967.
17 Richard Kingsland, *In the Midst of Things* (Canberra: Air Power Defence Centre, 2010), pp. 163–7; Sir Richard Kingsland, interviewed by Robert Hyslop, 26 June 1990, NLA TRC 2595.
18 Larry Sitsky, interviewed by Hazel de Berg, 4 November 1967, NLA TRC 313–314; Ruth Atkins, *The Government of the Australian Capital Territory* (St Lucia: University Queensland Press, 1978), pp. 108–10, 119–20; Bill Tully, in Lizz Murphy and Sarah St Vincent, *The Pearly Griffin* (Canberra: ACT Government, 2006), p. 31; J.D.B. Miller, 'Self-Government for Canberra', *Public Administration*, vol. 26, no. 3, 1967, pp. 218–26.
19 ibid., pp. 269–70; Christopher Monnox, *ACT Labour 1929–2009* (Canberra: Ginninderra Press, 2013), pp. 19–21; Malcolm Mackerras, 'The ACT: What Sort of Electorate', *The Hub*, vol. 1, no. 1, 1969, pp. 15–16.
20 Graham Freudenberg, *A Certain Grandeur* (Ringwood: Penguin, 1987), pp. 66–7; Ian Hancock, *John Gorton* (Sydney: Hodder, 2002), pp. 103, 114–16.
21 Max Neutze, 'Planning and Land Tenure in Canberra', *Town Planning Review*, vol. 58, no. 2, 1987, p. 161; Patrick Weller, Joanne Scott and Bronwyn Stevens, *From Postbox to Powerhouse* (Sydney: Allen & Unwin, 2011), pp. 67–8; Gavin Souter, *Acts of Parliament* (Melbourne: Melbourne University Press, 1988), p. 480; *Inside Canberra*, 7 March 1968.
22 Public Service Board, *Annual Report*, 1963–4, pp. 5–7; 1964–5, p. 14; Bruce Juddery, *At the Centre: The Australian Bureaucracy in the 1970s* (Melbourne: Cheshire, 1974), pp. 81–2; Tom Sheridan, 'Regulator Par

Excellence': Sir Henry Bland and Industrial Relations 1950–1967', *Journal of Industrial Relations*, vol. 41, no. 2, 1999, pp. 228–55; *Canberra Times*, 13 November 1997; *Financial Review*, 12 November 1965.

23 Patrick Weller, *Australia's Mandarins: The Frank and the Fearless* (Sydney: Allen & Unwin, 2001), pp. 54–60; L.F. Crisp, *Peter Richard Heydon* (Canberra: Crisp, 1972), pp. 27, 32–3; *Inside Canberra*, 16 May 1968; *SMH*, 29 January 2003; Bruce Juddery, *At the Centre: The Australian Bureaucracy in the 1970s* (Melbourne: Cheshire, 1974).

24 Foster and Varghese, *ANU*, p. 203.

25 *Bulletin*, 13 January 1968; Coral Bell, 'Strategic Thought and Security Preoccupations in Australia' and T.B. Millar'; 'Strategic Studies in a Changing World' in Meredith Thatcher and Desmond Ball (eds), *A National Asset* (Canberra: Strategic and Defence Studies Centre, 2006), pp. 11, 18–22.

26 Stuart Macintyre, *The Poor Relation: A History of the Social Sciences in Australia* (Melbourne: Melbourne University Press, 2010), pp. 109–10, 147, 150–1; *Inside Canberra*, 15 February 1968.

27 Foster and Varghese, *Making of the ANU*, pp. 197–8, 218; *Worhoni Soitharunka*, 11 May 1967, pp. 2, 16; Patricia Dobrez, *Michael Dransfield's Lives: A Sixties Biography* (Miegunyah, 1999), p. 493; Tim Rowse, *Nugget Coombs*, pp. 318, 371; L.F. Crisp, *Gravediggers and Undertakers* (Canberra: ANU, 1974), pp. 7, 12.

28 Clifford Burnett, 'How the ACT Schools Authority Came into Being', *Australian Education Review*, no. 10, 1978, pp. 13–17.

29 *An Independent Education Authority for the ACT* (Canberra: ANU, 1967) pp. 5–7, 14; *Secondary Education for Canberra* (Canberra: AGPS, 1973), pp. 10, 12–15, 21–4.

30 Barry Price, 'Planning a New School System', *CHJ*, March 2004, pp. 23–34; Grant Harman, 'The New ACT School System', and Hedley Beare, 'Developments and Major Issues', *Australian Education Review*, no. 10, 1978, pp. 89, 75; Biff Ward and Harry Oldmeadow (eds), *Starting Again* (Canberra: SWOW, 1974), p. 15.

31 Atkins, *Government*, pp. 85–92; Susan Mary Withycombe, *Ethos and Ethics* (Canberra: ACT Law Society, 1993), pp. 44–6; *Canberra Times*, 27 October 1969, 15 December 1971; Thomas Mautner papers, NLA Ms 8898, Box 1, Folder 2.

32 *Australian*, 21 October 1969; Canberra Times, 2 July 1969, 2 November 1971; *Camp Ink*, October 1971, p. 13; November 1971, p. 11; February 1972, p. 11; May 1972, p. 8.

33 Susan Ryan, *Catching the Waves* (Sydney: Harper Collins, 1999), pp. 75, 128; Suzanne Dixon, 'Confessions of a Sisterhoodlum' in Jocelyn Scutt (ed.), Different Lives (Ringwood: Penguin, 1987), p. 201; Lorraine Merrony, 'Women in Canberra', *Canberra Women's Liberation Newsletter*, no. 12, 1971, np.

34 Marian Sawer, *Making Women Count: A History of the Women's Electoral Lobby in Australia* (UNSW Press, 2008), pp. 8–9, 22, 33, 37, 40, 94.
35 *Canberra Times*, 23 August 1972, 5 November 1972; Scott Robinson, 'The Aboriginal Tent Embassy', *Aboriginal History*, vol. 18, no. 12, 1994, pp. 51–2, 60; Pat Eatock, 'Minorities within a Minority' in Scutt (ed.), *Different Lives*, pp. 25–6; Eatock, 'A Small but Stinging Stick', *Politics*, vol. 8, no. 2, 1973. p. 152.
36 *Advertiser* (Adelaide), 1 June 1979; *Bad Luck, Dead Duck* (Canberra: SSRS, 1970); *What a Mess, Let's Confess* (Canberra: Dalton, 1971).
37 *Canberra Times*, 3 November 1970; 17 February 1996; NCDC, *Annual Report 1962–63*, p. 31; W.K. Hancock, *Battle of Black Mountain* (Canberra: RSSS, 1974), pp. 1–2; Reid, *Canberra*, p. 256.
38 Kep Enderby, interviewed by Mel Pratt, 14 May 1975, NLA TRC 121/79, p. 28; *Age*, 25 May 1973; Sparke, *Canberra*, p. 204; C.J. Lloyd and Patrick Troy, *Innovation and Reaction*, 33, 47.
39 National Council of Women (ACT), *Annual Report 1973–74*, p. 4.
40 Robert Freestone, *Urban Nation: Australia's Planning Heritage* (Melbourne: CSIRO, p. 196, 200; *Urban Change in Canberra* (Canberra: NCDC, 1975), np; Mikal Skeats-Udy, 'The Squats' in Annie Bolitho and Mary Hutchison (eds), *Stories of the Inner South* (Canberra: Arts Council, 1992), p. 39.
41 NCDC *Annual Report*, 1972–73, pp. 1, 3, 17–18; 1973–74, pp. 6, 12; Sparke, *Canberra*, pp. 231, 243; *How to Build a Utopia – or Not Bomb Out by Much* (Canberra: NCDC, 1975), pp. 5, 7; *The Future Canberra* (Canberra: NCDC, 1975), pp. 3, 6.
42 *Belconnen Town Centre: Social Facilities and Factors* (Keys Young Planners: Sydney, 1974), pp. 1, 6, 67–8.
43 Souter, *Acts of Parliament*, p. 518; Sparke, *Canberra*, p. 213.
44 *Canberra Survey*, 6 April 1973; Public Service Board, *Annual Report*, 1972–73, pp. 1, 47; *Nation Review*, 29 June 1973.
45 Peter Read, *Charles Perkins: A Biography* (Ringwood; Penguin, 2001), pp. 140–1, 148, 177, 190–1, 199; Sawer, *Making Women Count*, p. 134.
46 Reid, *Canberra*, p. 293; Johnson, *Design*, p. 81; *Canberra News*, 28 October 1971; *Canberra Times*, 11 December 1971; *National Times*, 22 January 1973.
47 Atkins, *Government*, pp. 122, 126–9; Bruce Juddery, 'Australian Capital Territory: Social Democrats' in Andrew Parkin and John Warhurst (eds), *Machine Politics in the Australian Labor Party* (Sydney: Allen & Unwin, 1983), p. 215; Phillip Grundy, Bill Oakes, Lynne Reeder and Roger Wettenhall, *Reluctant Democrats: The Transition to Self-Government in the Australian Capital Territory* (Canberra: Federal Capital Press, 1996), p. 12.

48 Sparke, *Canberra*, p. 211; Tony Powell, interviewed by Margaret Park, 19 October 2005, TRC 5532, p. 8; John Menadue, *Things You Learn along the Way* (Melbourne: Lovell, 1999), pp. 120–4.
49 NCDC *Annual Report*, 1974–75, pp. 5–7.

7 YOU'RE ON YOUR OWN

1 Ian Fraser, 'Some Musings on Earlier Days', *Bogong*, no. 21, no. 1, 2000, p. 13; Kerrie Tucker, 'Twenty Years of Environmental Campaigns in the Australian Capital Territory', pp. 9–10.
2 Ian Fraser, *Canberra's Environment: A Walker's Guide* (Canberra: CSEREC, 1980).
3 Colin Adrian, *Canberra: A Social Atlas* (Canberra: ABS, 1981), pp. viii, ix.
4 David Butler, *The Canberra Model* (London: Macmillan, 1973), pp. 4–6; Michael Pusey, *Economic Rationalism in Canberra* (Cambridge: Cambridge University Press, 1991), pp. 8, 24–5, 43, 168, 183; Phillip Grundy et al., *Reluctant Democrats* (Canberra: Federal Capital Press, 1996), p. 203.
5 Ruth Atkins, *The Government of the Australian Capital Territory* (St Lucia: University of Queensland Press, 178), p. 141; *National Times*, 22 January 1973.
6 Ken Fry, *A Humble Backbencher* (Canberra: Ginninderra Press, 2002), p. 64; *Canberra Times*, 13 October 1975, 7 November 1975, 15 November 1975, 4 June 1976, 20 April 1979, 17 April 1983; *National Times*, 7 July 1979, 24 October 1977.
7 *Canberra Survey*, 16 January 1976, p. 2; 16 July 1976, p. 3; PSB, *Annual Report*, 1976, pp. 1, 3; ibid., 1977, pp. 1, 2; ibid., 1981, p. 1.
8 ibid., 1977, p. 2.
9 Gavin Souter, *Acts of Parliament* (Melbourne: Melbourne University Press, 1999), pp. 551–3, 557; Greg Whitwell, *The Treasury Line* (Sydney: Allen & Unwin, 1987), p. 238; Patrick Weller, Joanna Scott and Bronwyn Stevens, *From Postbox to Powerhouse* (Sydney: Allen & Unwin, 2011), pp. 88, 99.
10 Catherine Althaus and John Wanna, 'The Institutionalisation of Leadership in the Australian Public Service' in Paul 't Hart and John Uhr (eds), *Public Leadership: Perspectives and Practices* (ANU e-Press, 2008), p. 119; Paul Kelly, *The Hawke Ascendancy* (Sydney: Angus & Robertson, 1984), p. 424; Sara Dowse, *West Block* (Ringwood: Penguin, 1983), pp. 20, 71, 73, 234–5; *SMH*, 31 May 1976; *Canberra Times*, 21 December 1977.
11 Tony Powell, interviewed by Margaret Park, 19 October 2005, NLA TRC 5532, p. 47; *Canberra Survey*, 16 July 1976, pp. 2–3; NCDC, *Annual Report*, 1976, p. 5; 1977, p. 8; 1979, p. 5.
12 NCDC, *Annual Report*, 1977, pp. 4, 6; ibid., 1978, p. 10; *Canberra Times*, 23 August 1976.

13 NCDC, *Tuggeranong: The Early Views of Some Residents* (Canberra: 1977), p. 15; *Murrumbidgee*, 31 August 1975; 6 November 1977.
14 NCDC, *Annual Report*, 1976, p. 18; ibid., 30, 39; ibid., 1977, p. 12; ibid., 1978, p. 15.
15 Phillip Grundy et al., *Reluctant Democrats*, p. 89; NCDC, *Annual Report*, 1979, pp. 8–9; ibid., 1981, p. iii.
16 Jim Hagan and Glenn Mitchell, 'The Southeast' in Hagan (ed.), *People and Politics in Regional New South Wales 1950s–2006* (Sydney: Federation, 2006), pp. 105, 107, 108, 125.
17 NCDC, *Annual Report, 1981, p.* 2; Joint Committee on the Australian Capital Territory, *Planning in the ACT: Procedures, Processes and Community Involvement* (AGPS, 1979), pp. 47–51, 79, 109.
18 Adrian, *Social Atlas*, pp. ix, 22, 28.
19 Madeline Drake, Brian Rope and Robyn Walmsley, *Homelessness: A Capital Problem* (Canberra: AGPS, 1984), p. 9.
20 Tony Vinson, Victor Coull and Robyn Walmsley, *Review of Welfare Services and Policies in the Australian Capital Territory* (Canberra: AGPS, 1985), pp. 4, 6–8, 9, 11, 42.
21 ACT Police, *Annual Report*, 1978, pp. 6–7.
22 *Hard Times*, no. 1, p. 1; ibid., no. 14, p. 12; ibid., no. 16, p. 7.
23 ACT Trades and Labour Council, *Annual Report*, 1982–83, pp. 33–4, 36; 1985, pp. 23; *Canberra Times*, 24 July 1983; Chris Monnox, *ACT Labor 1929–2009* (Canberra: Ginninderra Press, 2103), pp. 36–9.
24 *Hard Times*, no. 12, 1980, p. 2; Anni Doyle Wawrzynczak, 'Canberra's Bitumen River Gallery', *Art Monthly*, no. 259, 2013, pp. 35, 38; *Canberra Times*, 3 March 2012; Inge Kral, 'Fools Gallery' in Julia Church and Alison Alder (eds), *True Bird Grit: A Book about Canberra Women in the Arts 1982–83* (Canberra: ACME Ink, nd), p. 19.
25 Peter Kabaila, *Survival Legacies* (Canberra: Canprint, 2011), pp. 403–4, 544; *Canberra Times*, 9 September 1988; *Nation Review*, 26 January 1979; Quentin Beresford, *Rob Riley: An Aboriginal Quest for Justice* (Canberra: Aboriginal Studies Press, 206), pp. 130–1; Kevin Keefe, *Paddy's Road: Life Stories from Patrick Dodson* (Canberra: Aboriginal Studies Press, 2003), p. 276.
26 *Canberra Times*, 29 April 1979; Ann Nugent. 'Language-Cultural Program: Wreck Bay', *Community Liaison*, vol. 3, no. 2, 1980, pp. 5–6; Stewart Harris, *It's Coming Yet: An Aboriginal Treaty Within Australia Between Australians* (Canberra: Griffin, 1979), pp. 1, 49.
27 Frederika Steen, 'Canberra's Introductory Education Centre' in John Nicholas (ed.), *The ACT of Educational Innovation* (Canberra College of Advanced Education, 1979), pp. 32–7; Ann-Mari Jordens, *Hope: Refugees and their Supporters in Australia* (Canberra: Halstead, 2012), pp. 48–50, 169.

28 Ann-Mari Jordens, *Hope*, pp. 172–5; Marion Lê, interviewed by Ann-Mari Jordens, 4 June 2004, NLA, TRC 5159; Nancy Viviani, *The Indo-Chinese in Australia 1975–1995* (Melbourne: Oxford University Press, 1996), p. 103; ICRA (ACT), *Newsletter*, December 1979, February 1980.
29 George Seddon, *An Open Space System for Canberra* (NCDC, 1977), pp. 18, 65, 67; Barbara Malpass, *Cycling Canberra* (Canberra: Ginninderra Press, 1999), pp. 42–3; NCDC, Intertown Public Transport (Canberra, 1876); Paul Mees, 'A Centenary Review of Transport Planning in Canberra, Australia', *Progress in Planning*, vol. 87, no. 1, 2014, pp. 1–32.
30 NCDC, *Annual Report*, 1979–80, p. 30; Peter Fogarty, 'Soil Erosion and Soil Catchment in the Lake Burley Griffin Catchment', *Australian Journal of Soil and Water Conservation*, vol. 2, no. 2, 1989, pp. 28–30; Ian Morison, 'Beyond the City-State – Metropolitan Canberra', *Urban Policy and Research*, vol. 13, no. 2, 1995, p. 118.
31 Rolf Gerritsen, 'Natural Gas and the ACT's Medium Term Energy Future' *Bogong*, vol. 1, no. 5, 1980. p. 6.
32 Judith Wright, 'Ecological Comment', Phillip Mackenzie (ed.), *The Poetry of Canberra* (Canberra: Polonius, 1990), p. 21; Tom Griffiths, 'Discovering Monaro', *Journal of Australian Studies*, no. 62, 1999, p. 180; David Books, Editorial, *Canberra Poetry*, Winter 1975, p. 43.
33 Geoff Page, 'Spitting Out Poems' at http://www.irmagold.com/2/post/2013/03/spitting-out-poems-an-interview-with-geoff-page.html; John Rowland, 'Canberra Suburbs' in Phillip Mackenzie (ed.), *Poetry of Canberra*, p. 59; Janet Hawley, *Artists in Conversation* (Melbourne: Slattery, 2012), pp. 178, 183.
34 Alison Alder and Julie Miller in Julia Church and Alison Alder, *True Bird Grit*, pp. 14, 29; Skyda Hopkins, 'A Community of Activists', *Bogong*, vol. 3, no. 8, 1982, p. 5.
35 Peter Durack, 'Court's move to Canberra' in Michael Coper, Tony Blackshield and George Williams (eds), *Oxford Companion to the High Court of Australia* (Oxford University Press, 2001), pp. 80–2; P.H. Pigott et al., *Museums in Australia* (AGPS, 1975), pp. 70–81.
36 Grant Nihill, *Australian Institute of Sport: Celebrating Excellence* (Sydney: Focus, 2006), pp. 10, 12, 39, 53–5; Hugh Smith, *The Battle of ADFA* (ANU, 1989), p. 5; *Canberra Times*, 4 December 1988; *Report of the Review into Policies and Practices to Deal with Sexual Harassment and Sexual Offences at the Australian Defence Force Academy* (Canberra: Defence Equity Organisation, 1998), p. xiv.
37 Paul Reid, *Canberra Following Griffin* (Canberra: NAA, 2002), pp. 305–17; Christopher Vernon, 'A Chosen City' in David Headon and Andrew Mackenzie (eds), *Canberra Red* (Sydney: Allen & Unwin, 2013), p. 89.

38 NCDC, *Annual Report*, 1982, pp. ii–iii; Committee of Review of the Role and Functions of the NCDC, *Canberra: Planning and Development* (AGPS, 1983), pp. 10, 35, 63, 98.
39 NCDC, *Annual Report*, 1983, pp. ii, 8; Paul Kelly, *The Hawke Ascendancy* (Sydney; Angus & Robertson, 1984), p. 424.
40 Whitwell, *Treasury Line*, p. 232; Nicholas Brown and Susan Boden, *A Way Through: The Life of Rick Farley* (Sydney: New South, 2012), pp. 117, 134–5.
41 Public Service Board, *Annual Report*, 1984, pp. 4–5, 36; Jill Adams and Chris Oates, *Serving the Nation: 100 Years of Public Service* (Canberra: ASMPC, 2001), p. 100.
42 Stephen Foster and Margaret Varghese, *The Making of the Australian National University* (Sydney: Allen & Unwin, 1996), pp. 308, 313, 340–5, 349–50.
43 Keith Powell, *Canberra's Health 1950–1994* (Canberra: Brolga, 1999), p. 220; Peter Hughes, *Medical and Party Politics* (Canberra: Hughes, 2012), pp. 88–9; 157, 164; ACT TLC, *Annual Report*, 1986, pp. 3–4.
44 NCDC, *Annual Report*, 1988, pp. 5, 7; NCDC, *Civic Centre Canberra: Policy Plan* (1987), pp. 9–17; Jack Waterford, 'Canberra Leasehold Administration' in Shelley Schreiner and Clem Lloyd (eds), *Canberra: What Sort of City?* (ANU, 1987), p. 34.
45 *Cannons Yearbook 1983*, pp. 2, 4; *Canberra Raiders: The First Three Years* (Canberra: Paragon, nd), pp. 6–8; Jenny Lee, 'Basis for Success in Women's Sport' in Helen Lumby (ed.), *Empowering Women in Sport* (Canberra: O'Connell Education Centre, 1990), p. 22; Don Selth, *The Prime Minister's XI* (Canberra: Selth, 1990), pp. xii, 90.
46 Derek Parker, *The Courtesans: The Press Gallery in the Hawke Era* (Sydney: Allen & Unwin, 1990), pp. 2, 9, 34–6, 52–5; Stephen Mills, *The New Machine Men: Polls and Persuasion in Australian Politics* (Melbourne: Penguin, 1986), pp. 30–1; Robbie Swan, interviewed by Daniel Connell, 10–11 December 2003, NLA TRC 5098; 'Joggers around parliament', *Matilda*, no. 11, 1985, p. 5.
47 Mungo MacCallum, 'The New Parliament House', *Matilda*, no. 7, 1985, p. 5; *Bulletin*, 17 May 1988; *Age*, 18 May 1988.
48 Alan Fitzgerald, Introduction, *Self-Government for the ACT* (Canberra: Department of the Capital Territory, 1981), pp. 11–13; Phillip Grundy et al., *Reluctant Democrats*, pp. 92, 132, 137, 141.
49 *Canberra Times*, 1 July 1988; 12 August 1992; Phillip Grundy et al., *Reluctant Democrats*, pp. 141, 170–1.
50 David M. Farrer and Ian McAllister, *The Australian Electoral System* (UNSW Press, 2006), p. 73; *Report of the Select Committee on Self-Government* (Canberra: Legislative Assembly, 1990), pp. 1–2; Bruce Juddery, 'Self-Government for the ACT', *Australian Journal of Public Administration*, vol. 48, no. 4, 1989, pp. 419–20.
51 Phillip Grundy et al., *Reluctant Democrats*, pp. 196–200.

8 FEEL THE POWER

1 *Civic Centre Canberra: Policy and Implementation Plan* (Canberra: NCDC, 1987), p. 21; Commonwealth of Australia, *Year Book 1990* (Canberra: AGPS, 1990), p. 808.
2 *Canberra at the 2006 Census* (Canberra: ACTPLA, 2006), p. 4; Alison Taylor and Denise Carlton, 'Canberra Celebrates its Centenary' at http://adsri.anu.edu.au/population-change-in-canberra-seminar.
3 Dalma Jacobs, *Canberra: A Social Atlas* (Australian Bureau of Statistics, 1998), pp. 6, 18, 21–2, 26, 35; *Population Growth and Distribution in Australia* (Australian Bureau of Statistics, 1994), pp. 7–12; Sara Dowse, 'Canberra' in Susan Hawthorne and Renate Klein (eds), *Australia for Women* (New York: Feminist Press, 1994), pp. 364–5.
4 *Government Staff Cuts in the ACT* (Canberra: Chief Minister's Department, 1999), pp. ix, 19, 38; Julian Fitzgerald, *Lobbying in Australia* (Sydney: Rosenberg, 2008), p. 31.
5 Peter Newman and Jeff Kenworthy, *Towards a More Sustainable Canberra* (Perth: Murdoch University, 1991), p. vii.
6 George Megalogenis, *The Australian Moment: How We Were Made for These Times* (Melbourne: Penguin, 2012), p. 367.
7 Gary Humphries, 'Ten Years in the City State' in John Halligan and Roger Wettenhall (eds), *A Decade of Self-Government in the ACT* (University of Canberra, 2000), p. 74; *Canberra Times*, 28 November 1984; 10 December 1989.
8 David Hughes, 'Australian Capital Territory', *AJPH*, vol. 42, no. 2, 1996, pp. 245–8.
9 ibid., pp. 245–6.
10 Kate Carnell in *Proceedings of the National Capital Futures Conference* (ACT Government, 1997), p. 3; John Halligan and Roger Wettenhall, introduction, Halligan and Wettenhall (eds), *A Decade*, pp. 21–2.
11 *Canberra Times*, 4 April 1998; Peter Donovan, *Lights, Water, ACTEW!* (Canberra: ACTEW, 1999), pp. 164, 175, 199.
12 ACTCOSS, *Annual Report*, 1992, p. 11; 1993, p. 14; Lyn Morgain, 'And when they got there', Halligan and Wettenhall (eds), *A Decade*, p. 103.
13 David Hughes, 'Australian Capital Territory', *AJPH*, vol. 43, no. 2, 1997, p. 225.
14 Fiona Patten, 'The Economy of Pleasure and the Laws of Desire' in Jill Julius Matthews (ed.), *Sex in Public* (Sydney: Allen & Unwin, 1997), pp. 42–3; Gwyn Singleton, 'Australian Capital Territory', *AJPH*, vol. 8, no. 2, 2002, p. 297; Janine Flynn, 'Australian Capital Territory', *AJPH*, vol. 50, no. 4, 2004, pp. 636–7; vol. 51, no. 2, 2005, p. 623.
15 Janine Flynn, 'Australian Capital Territory', *AJPH*, vol. 52, no. 2, 2006, p. 334; vol. 52, no. 4, 2006, pp. 685–7.
16 Philip Pettit, 'Three Problems with Self Government', Halligan and Wettenhall (eds), *A Decade*, pp. 95–8.

17 Flynn, 'Australian Capital Territory', *AJPH*, vol. 52, no. 4, 2006, p. 689.
18 Don Watson, *Reflections of a Bleeding Heart* (Sydney: Vintage, 2011), pp. 134, 514; Meredith Edwards, *Social Policy, Public Policy* (Sydney: Allen & Unwin, 2001), pp. 182–7.
19 Patrick Weller, *From Postbox to Powerhouse* (Sydney: Allen & Unwin, 2011), pp. 126–7, 135–6; Paul Malone, *Australian Departmental Heads Under Howard* (ANU e-Press, 1996), p. 7; Public Service Commissioner, *Annual Report*, 2009–10, p. 7; Mark Evans, 'The Rise and Fall of the Magic Kingdom' in Chris Aulich and Mark Evans (eds), *The Rudd Government* (ANU e-Press, 2010), p. 271.
20 Chris Beer, 'Accommodating Bureaucrats in Canberra', *Australian Journal of Public Administration*, vol. 66, no. 1, 2007, pp. 53, 56; James Walter, 'Is There a Command Culture in Politics', Paul 't Hart and John Uhr (eds), *Public Leadership*, pp. 190, 198; John Carroll, *National Museum of Australia: Review of Exhibitions and Programs* (Canberra: Department of Communication and the Arts, 2003), p. 74.
21 Robert O'Shea, The Australian Governor-Generalship: sources of authority and identity, MA thesis (History), University of Melbourne, 2012, p. 85.
22 K.S. Inglis, 'The Unknown Australian Soldier', *Journal of Australian Studies*, vol. 23, no. 60, 1999, p. 17; Elizabeth Strakosch, 'Counter-Movements and Nation Building in Australia', *Peace Review*, vol. 22, no. 3, 2010, pp. 272–3; Godden Mackay Logan, *Western Park: Conservation Management Plan* (Canberra; TAMS, 2011), p. 21.
23 *The Griffin Legacy: The Nation's Capital in the 21st Century* (NCPA, 2004), p. vi; *Urban Renaissance: Canberra – A Sustainable Future* (Paris: OECD, 2002), pp. 15–16; *Facing Our Future* (Canberra: NCPA, 1996), pp. iv, 16.
24 Paul Stein, Patrick Troy and Robert Yeomans, *Report into the Administration of ACT Leasehold* (ACT Govt. Printer, 1995), p. 50; *Review of the Functions and Resourcing of the National Capital Planning Authority* (Canberra, 1995), pp. 2–4; NCPA, *Annual Report*, 1991–92, p. 6; 1995–96, pp. 4, 31; Allen Hawke, *Canberra: A Capital Place* (NCA, 2011), pp. iii, 3, 52.
25 *SMH*, 21 September 2012; *ACT in Focus* (Canberra: ABS, 2007), pp. 144–6.
26 David Hughes, 'Australian Capital Territory', *AJPH*, vol. 43, no. 3, 1997, p. 381; Paula Williams, *Australian Very Fast Trains: A Chronology* (Canberra: Parliament of Australia, 1998).
27 Tony Powell, 'Real Town Planning', *Urban Policy and Research*, vol. 21, no. 1, 2003, p. 114; Steven Bourassa, Max Neutze and Ann Louise Strong, 'Managing Publicly Owned Land in Canberra', *Land Use Policy*, vol. 13, no. 4, 1996, pp. 276, 280–1, 283; Stein, Troy and Yeomans, *Canberra Leasehold*, pp. 44, 47, 90, 97.

28 Paul Tranter and John Whitelegg, 'Children's Travel Behaviours in Canberra', *Journal of Transport Geography*, vol. 2, no. 4, 1994, pp. 269–70; Mike Kinniburgh, *Community Policing Advisory Committee: Report on Policing in the ACT* (Canberra, 1991), pp. 17–18; AFP (Canberra Region), *Annual Report*, 1999, pp. 2, 9; *Canberra Times*, 26 September 1992, 1 January 1996, 1 January 1997; Mick Palmer in *National Capital Futures*, p. 105.
29 Robbie Swan, interviewed by Daniel Connell, 11 December 2003, NAL TRC 5098, p. 222.
30 Chris Shakallis (ed.), *Head Full of Flames: Punk in the Nation's Capital* (Canberra: Robina Gugler, 2013), p. 6; Helen Garner, *Joe Cinque's Consolation* (Sydney: Picador, 2004) pp. 138–9, 223.
31 *2XX Communique*, May 2006, p. 2.
32 *Canberra Times*, 17 October 1983, 14 March 1986, 23 September 1989, 11 October 1992.
33 *Sakyamuni News*, July 1989, October 1991, October 1994; *Canberra Community Voice*, December 2003; *CIC News*, February 2001, November 2001, August 2005, April 2008.
34 Australian National University, *Annual Report*, 1990, pp. 8–9, 12; 1999, p. 2; 2008, p. 1.
35 Charlene Smith, *40: A Short History of the University of Canberra* (University of Canberra: nd), pp. 17, 23, 29–30, 32; University of Canberra, *Annual Report*, 1990, p. 3; 2000, p. 10; *InCITe*, no. 1, 2004, p. 3.
36 Iain McIntyre, *Always Look on the Bright Side of Life; The AIDEX 91 Story* (Homebrew: Melbourne, 2008); Mark Dapin, *Strange Country: Travels in a Very Different Australia* (Sydney: Macmillan, 2008), p. 315; Jon Van Daal, *A History of the Summernats* (Padstow: Bookworks, 2008); *Summernats 2005: Review and Cost Benefit Analysis* (Canberra: ACT Government, 2005), pp. 1–2.
37 *Namadgi: A National Park for Canberra* (Canberra: ACT National Parks Association, 2011), pp. 8, 70; Edgar Riek, interviewed by Heather Rusden, 6 March 1988, NLA TRC 3674.
38 Stephanie Haygarth, 'In with Renew', *Bogong*, vol. 20, no. 1, 1999, pp. 6–7; 'Landcare in Canberra', *Australian Journal of Soil and Water Conservation*, vol. 7, no. 4, 1994, p. 5.
39 Robert Boden, *Favourite Canberra Trees* (Kenthurst: Kangaroo Press, 1993), pp. 7, 14.
40 Ron McLeod, *Inquiry into the Operational Response to the January 2003 Bushfires in the ACT* (ACT Government, 2003), pp. iii–vi, 15, 26, 57.
41 Chapman Residents Action Group, *Our Story* (Canberra: Ginninderra Press, 1994), p. 20; Stephen Matthews (ed.), *How Did the Fire Know We Lived Here?* (Canberra: Ginninderra Press, 2003), pp. 11, 39, 59, 179.

42 Stephen Dovers, 'Still Settling the Limestone Plains', David Headon and Andrew Mackenzie (eds), *Canberra Red: Stories for the Bush Capital* (Sydney: Allen & Unwin, 2013), pp. 254–5; Sarah Sharp, Lisa Evans, Murray Evans and Margaret Kitchin, 'Climate Change and Biodiversity: What are the Challenges for the ACT?', *Corridors for Survival in a Changing World* (ACT National Parks Association: 2008), p. 104.
43 Michael Agostino, *ANU School of Art: A History of the First 65 Years* (Canberra: ANU, 2009), p. 193; Giurgola, *National Capital Futures*, p. 201.
44 McCarthy in *National Capital Futures*, p. 108; Greg Craven, 'The New Centralism and the Collapse of the Conservative Constitution' in *Democratic Experiments: lectures in the Senate Occasional Lecture Series 2004–2005* (Canberra: Parliament House, 2006), p. 3; Lee Grant, *Belco Pride* (Canberra: Everbest, c. 2012), p. 136.

CONCLUSION

1 *Canberra Times*, 17 February 1996; 'Skywhale Price Tag Could Exceed $300 000', *ABC News*, 10 May 2013, accessed 1 December 2013, www.abc.net.au/news/2013-05-10/skywhale-could-cost-up-to-300k/4681892.
2 Paul Daley, *Canberra* (UNSW Press, 2012), pp. 9, 13; Mary Hutchison, *Shaping Canberra* (Canberra: Humanities Research Centre, 2013), p. 12.
3 Shane Breynard, Foreword, *2113: A Canberra Odyssey* (Canberra: CMAG, 2103), p. 5.
4 Merryn Gates, 'Flipside: Canberra's Underbelly', *Art Monthly*, no. 259, 2013, p. 22; Chris Hammer, 'A Secret Map of Canberra', *Meanjin*, vol. 72, no. 1, 2013, p. 84; ACT Planning Strategy, *Background Paper No. 2: Climate Change* (ACT Government, 2012), p. 2.
5 Karl Fischer, *Canberra: Myths and Models* (Hamburg: Institute of Asian Affairs, 1984), p. 16; Maria Maley, 'Australian Capital Territory', *AJPH*, vol. 59, no. 2, 2013, pp. 323–6.

INDEX

Aboriginal people, 8–10, 11–12, 23–5, 232, 238
  accounts of, 12, 24, 33, 80, 176
  activism, 183, 204–7
  assistance to settlers, 14, 24
  Birrigai site, 8
  ceremonies and customs, 9, 23
  dispossession, 33
  use of fire, 11
  impact of disease, 12, 24
  inter-group relationships, 9, 11
  languages, 9, 13
  policy, 25, 189
  population, 9, 90, 116
  resistance, 11, 24
  settlement and land use, 11, 24, 25
  sport, 27, 204
  Wreck Bay, 90, 183, 206
Aboriginal Tent Embassy, 182
Academy of Humanities, 176
Academy of Science, 157, 176
Academy of the Social Sciences in Australia, 176
Advisory Council, ACT (FCT), 87, 108, 134, 152, 171, 179
Agache, Alfred Donat, 52
agriculture, 19, 27, 90, 242
  'Federation' wheat, 32
Ainslie, James, 13–14
Albert Hall, *see* leisure
Anglicanism, 20, 34, 47, 86, 110, 154, 238
Archer, Robyn, 247
Archibald, W.H., 58
architecture, 91, 132, 137, 148, 160, 185, 189, 231
  Boyd, Robin, 134, 137, 186
  Grounds, Roy, 157
  Moir, Malcolm, 92
  Sutherland, Heather, 92
  Taglietti, Enrico, 139
Armidale, 40
Arndt, Heinz, 131, 157
Australian Capital Territory, 94
  administration, 219
  political representation, 119, 133, 169, 179, 184, 189, 195, 226, 229
  regionalism, 114, 186, 200, 204, 234
  self-government, 194, 219–21, 226
  welfare services, 202
Australian Defence Force Academy, 212
Australian Forestry School, 91
Australian Institute of Sport, 212

Index

Australian Labor Party, 64, 84, 87, 106, 116, 119, 133, 161, 171, 172, 180, 185, 191, 195, 203, 214, 216, 219, 220, 221, 226, 228, 231
Australian National Botanic Gardens, 183, 243
Australian National Review, 92
Australian National University, 114, 129–30, 141, 156, 172, 175–7, 215, 239
Australian War Memorial, 84, 107, 232
The Australian, 160

Bailey, Kenneth, 104
Barnard Eldershaw, M., 22
Bathurst, 40
Bean, C.E.W., 92
Bitumen River Gallery, 204, 210
Black Mountain tower, 183, 192
Boden, Robert, 242
Bogong moths, 9
Bombala, 35, 40, 41
Brackenreg, J.C., 46
Braidwood, 17, 19
Brennan, Frank, 117
brick production, 48, 63, 127
Bridges, Brigadier W.T., 47, 60
Brissenden, R.F., 157, 210
Brown, Allen, 103, 127
Bruce, S.M., 65, 67, 70, 84, 88
Bryant, Gordon, 190
Buddhism, 238
Building Workers' Industrial Union, *see* labour: unionism
Burgmann, E.H., 92, 154
bushrangers, 16
Butters, John, 71–2, 73, 78, 82

Campbell, Charles, 29
Campbell, Frederick, 30, 31–2, 46
Campbell, George, 20, 30
Campbell, Robert, 14, 20
Campbell family
  Duntroon station, 14, 17
Canberra, 166
  advocates for, 62, 64, 123, 143, 147, 150, 185
  critics of, 63, 64, 84, 134, 144, 155, 169, 199, 219
  images of, 88, 135, 137, 138, 159–61, 166, 241
  investment in, 58, 63, 67, 70, 72, 83, 98, 213, 219, 227
  naming ceremony, 55–6
  planning debates, 144
Canberra, choice of site, *see* national capital
Canberra and South-East Region Environment Centre, 209
  see also environment
Canberra Times, 81, 87, 95, 123, 144, 160, 216
Canberry station, 13, 15
Carnell, Kate, 227, 228, 229
casino, 199, 226
Caswell, Charles, 51
Catholicism, 18, 46, 86, 153, 238
Chapman, Austin, 63
Chifley, J.B., 112, 115, 122
children, 16, 19, 83, 110, 147, 150, 151, 169, 236
citizenship, 39
Civil Liberties Council, ACT, 204
Clark, Manning, 131, 157
climate, 8, 22, 39, 41, 60, 94
Coane, J.M., 51
Commonwealth Club, 127
Commonwealth departments and agencies
  Aboriginal Affairs, 204
  Attorney-General, 81, 104
  Australian Security and Intelligence Organisation, 141, 233

Commonwealth departments and
    agencies (*cont.*)
  Bureau of Statistics, 91, 159
  Capital Territory, 185, 200
  Commonwealth Scientific and
    Industrial Research
    Organisation, 183
  Council for Scientific and
    Industrial Research, 21, 22
  Defence, 145, 147, 233
  Employment and Youth Affairs,
    193
  External Affairs (Foreign
    Affairs), 118, 129, 142, 160,
    196
  Finance, 197, 234
  Health, 83, 91
  Home Affairs, 44, 46, 65, 67
  Home Security, 99
  Immigration, 3, 99, 115, 174
  Interior, 2, 131, 133, 140, 146,
    170
  Labour and National Service,
    174
  Post-War Reconstruction, 99,
    113, 114, 115, 120
  Prime Minister, 81, 129, 197
  Social Services, 155, 174
  Supply, 174
  Tariff Board, 155
  Territories and Local
    Government, 219
  Trade, 81, 174
  Treasury, 81, 101, 129, 146,
    161, 174, 190, 214
  Urban and Regional
    Development, 185, 190
  Works, 65, 131, 132, 136
Commonwealth Public Service
  Board, 120
community, 16–17, 120, 123, 167,
    199
  colonial characteristics of, 28, 44
  consultation, 186, 191
  diversity, 20, 136, 157, 208, 233
  early twentieth century, 48
  as factor in choice of capital, 39
  ideologies of, 78–80
  leaders, 34, 64, 86, 87, 170, 238
  organisations, 74, 152, 169,
    170, 178, 203
  perceptions of, 96, 167, 246
  as theme, 4
  welfare, 152, 202, 219, 227
  during World War II, 110
convicts
  labour, 12, 13, 15, 19
  treatment, 1, 15, 16
Cooma, 26
Coombs, H.C., 101, 102, 112,
    127, 177
Copland, D.B., 101, 102, 103, 113
Cotter, Garrett, 14
Cotter River, 14, 48, 125, 150
Coulter, Robert, 52
Coulthard-Clark, Chris, 47
Council of Social Service, ACT,
    169, 185, 227
Crace, Edward, 30
Crisp, L.F., 112, 116, 177
Croft, Joe, 204
Cunningham, Andrew, 1, 22, 26,
    29, 30
Cuppacumbalong station, 24, 29
Curtin, Elsie, 112
Curtin, John, 93, 106

Daley, C.S., 66
Daley, Paul, 3, 248
Dalgarno, Ann, 152
Dalgety, 41
Davis, William, 20, 27, 29, 30
Davison, Graeme, 162, 163
de Salis, Count Leopold, 29, 33
Denman, Lady Gertrude, 55
Denning, Warren, 81, 84, 96, 120
Deumonga, Bobby, 27
D'Hondt system, 220

diplomatic representation, 94, 107, 141
Dobson, Rosemary, 210
Dovers, Stephen, 11, 32, 245
Dowling, Owen, 238
Dowse, Sara, 197, 223
drought
 1825–28, 14
 1837–39, 22
 1841–43, 22
 1860s, 29
 1890s, 33
 1953–54, 150
 1997, 243
 see also environment
Dunk, William, 115, 116, 127, 155
Duntroon station, 14, 15, 19, 27, 29, 47
 see also Royal Military College, Duntroon

Eatock, Pat, 182
economic development, 17, 19–20, 42, 198–9, 222–4, 230, 234, 246
 depression 1840s, 22
 depression 1890s, 33
 depression 1930s, 83–5
 mining, 20, 27
education, 199, 226
 Canberra College of Advanced Education, 172, 216
 Canberra Institue of Technology, 240
 Canberra School of Music, 170, 240
 Canberra University College, 86, 92, 104, 157
 'civics', 232
 schools, 20, 26, 48, 88, 93, 119, 125, 133, 152, 153, 203, 207, 216, 230, 237, 238
 secondary colleges, 177–9, 237

 see also Australian National University; University of Canberra
electricity generation, 48, 49, 70, 73, 209, 227, 242
Ellis, Ulrich, 119
Ellyard, Peter, 183
Enderby, Kep, 184, 189, 195
Enfield, John, 219
environment, 7–8
 Aboriginal adaptation, 9
 activism, 183–4, 210, 242, 245
 characteristics, 8, 13
 climate, 8
 conservation, 150, 209, 242
 drought, 14, 22, 29, 33
 erosion, 8, 21, 23, 46, 94, 149, 242
 as factor in choice of capital, 39
 fauna, 22, 32, 34, 88
 fauna, native, 8
 flood, 22
 forestry, 85, 149, 209
 geology, 7, 8
 as ideology, 79, 224
 as landscape, 8, 150, 210, 243
 pollution, 89, 183, 193, 209
 rabbits, 32, 45
 ringbarking, 15, 32, 60
 as theme, 4, 245
 topography, 7
 vegetation, 7
 water, 42, 245
ethnic identity, 17–18, 20, 34, 203, 207, 238
 Austrian, 137, 139
 disadvantage, 152
 Estonian, 125
 German, 110, 136, 138
 Greek, 125, 138
 immigration, 125, 126, 135
 Italian, 90, 110, 135–6, 139
 Jewish, 137
 Maltese, 136

ethnic identity (*cont.*)
  'New Australian', 118, 137
  Polish, 125, 136
  Sudanese, 238
  Vietnamese, 207–8, 238
euthanasia, 229
exploration, early European, 10–11
Eyre, Edward John, 15, 23

Fairhall, Allen, 144, 145
family, 112, 119, 136
  as economic unit, 17
  migration, 26
  as social unit, 44, 150, 223
Farley, Rick, 214
Farrer, William, 32
fauna, 45
Federal Capital Advisory Committee, 65, 67–70
Federal Capital Commission, 71–3, 76, 77–80, 82, 83, 84
Federal Capital Territory
  renamed ACT, 94
  'surrender' from NSW, 42
  survey, 42
federation
  debates over, 34–5, 37
Fenner, Frank, 137
fire
  Aboriginal use of, 11
  bushfire 1939, 95
  bushfire 2003, 244
Fischer, Karl, 38, 42, 165
Fitzgerald, Alan, 171
floods
  1851–52, 23
  1925, 89
  1971, 167
  see also environment
Follett, Rosemary, 221, 226
forestry, 110
Foskett, Alan, 117, 148
Franklin, Miles, 28
Fraser, Ian, 194

Fraser, Jim, 133, 169, 173
Fraser, Malcolm, 178, 196, 197, 198, 212, 214, 217
'free selection', *see* land
Freestone, Robert, 50, 66, 69
Fry, Ken, 195, 214, 216

Gale, John, 33
Galliard Smith, Rev Pierce, 34
Gammage, Bill, 11
gardening, *see* landscape: gardening
Garran, Robert, 77, 86
Gascoigne, Rosalie, 210
George, Henry, 43, 44
  see also land: leasehold
Giblin, Eilean, 113
Giblin, L.F., 101, 102
Gibson, Trevor, 132, 133
Gilbert, Kevin, 204, 219
Ginninderra station, 14, 15, 19, 20, 25
Giurgola, Romaldo, 213, 245
Good Neighbour Council, ACT, 137, 151
Gorton, John, 172–3
Goulburn, 40, 94, 200
government, 123
  'economic rationalism', 194
  ideas of, 64
  perceptions of, 98–9, 104
  practices of, 113, 140, 155, 161, 173–4, 192, 194, 197, 214, 215, 227, 228, 230, 231
  as theme, 5
Governor-General, 94
  role of, 232
Greens Party, ACT, 226, 242
Griffin, Marion Mahony, 53, 61
Griffin, Walter Burley
  biography, 53
  competition entry, 52
  death, 61
  end of association with Canberra, 61, 65

as Federal Capital Director of
  Design, 57–8
 ideals, 6
 legacy, 61, 67, 72
 revision of design, 58
 vision of Australia, 53, 62
Groom, Littleton, 61, 65, 67
Gundaroo, 27, 35

Halloran, Henry, 72
Hamilton, Nellie, 33
Hancock, Ian, 115
Hancock, W. K., 29, 85, 156, 209
Harrison, Hector, 154
Harrison, Peter, 61, 144, 160, 165, 176
Haslem, John, 195, 201, 214
Hasluck, Paul, 100, 101, 108, 140
Hawke, Bob, 214, 217
health, 226
 Aboriginal, 238
 aged, 152, 169
 asbestos, 203
 centres, 187
 disability, 152
 doctors, 82, 110, 216
 as factor in choice of Canberra, 39, 41
 hospitals, 49, 111, 216, 226, 228
 injecting rooms, 229
 mental, 150, 169, 180, 202
 'mothercraft', 83, 90, 91
Hewitt, Hope, 152
Heydon, Peter, 174
High Court of Australia, 143, 189, 211
Hindmarsh, John, 234
HMAS *Harman*, 110
Holding, Clyde, 195
Holford, William, 145–6, 161, 165
Holt, Beatrice (Sharwood), 82
Horne, Donald, 118, 159, 240
Hotel Canberra, 76, 93

Hotel Kurrajong, 93
House, Matilda, 206
House of Assembly, ACT, *see*
  Australian Capital Territory:
  self government
housing and accommodation, 19, 134, 145, 185, 201
 camps, 46, 48, 75–6, 114
 covenants, 69, 82
 design, 69, 78, 148, 152
 homelessness, 202, 249
 hostels, 49, 76–7, 106, 110, 118, 130–1, 134, 147, 207
 low-cost, 203
 medium density, 132, 148, 167, 224, 236
 public housing, 73, 82, 117, 148, 162, 201, 207, 214
 shortages, 100, 106, 116–17, 130, 136, 235
Howard, John, 218, 229, 230
Hughes, W.M., 61, 64, 65, 67
Humphries, Gary, 225, 228
Hungerford, T.A.G., 118, 121

income levels, 85
Institute of Anatomy, 91
Islamic faith, 239

Jennings, A.V., 136, 147
Jervis Bay, 42
Jimmy the Rover, 25
Jobless Action, 202–3
Johnson, Roger, 168, 189

Kaine, Trevor, 221, 226
Karmel, Peter, 215
Keating, Paul, 5, 222, 230
Kelly, Ros, 214
Kelly, W.H., 57
Kent-Hughes, Wilfred, 131, 144
Kingsland, Richard, 171, 172
Kinleyside, Thomas, 16
Kirkpatrick, John, 51
Knight, John, 195, 199

Labor Party, Australian, *see*
    Australian Labor Party
labour
    Aboriginal workers, 24, 33
    Chinese workers, 18
    conditions, 29, 79
    construction workers, 49, 134, 136
    costs, 70
    'free' settlers, 17, 18, 19, 28
    immigrant, 118, 135–7
    rural, 89
    shortages, 117
    supply, 74
    unionism, 30, 79, 134, 136, 203, 216
    'workers' town', 73, 126
Lake Burley Griffin, 123, 133, 145, 157, 183, 208
land
    auction, 70, 72, 83, 147, 161, 198, 235
    compulsory acquisition, 46, 58, 149
    free selection, 30, 171
    leasehold, 43–4, 63, 69, 70, 83, 147, 173, 198, 200, 213
    rural leases, 90, 149
landscape
    design, 149, 169, 219
    features, 8, 19
    gardening, 79, 138, 149
    'improvement', 32, 46, 60, 77, 131
    perceptions of, 10, 11, 13, 21, 31, 46, 88, 121, 150, 241
    reforestation, 60, 70
Lane-Poole, Charles, 91, 92, 95
Lane-Poole, Ruth, 91
Langmore, John, 216
Lanyon station, 1, 15, 22, 26, 29
Latham, John, 62, 80
law, 179, 182, 185, 204, 229, 236

Lê, Marion, 207
leasehold land, *see* land: leasehold
Legislative Assembly, ACT, 220, 225, 242
    structure and composition, 221
    see also Australian Capital Territory: self-government
leisure, 44, 49, 74, 80, 86, 88, 137, 149, 169
    cinema, 88, 140, 152
    dancing, 27, 31, 88, 109, 120
    television, 238
Lend Lease Group, 147, 153
Lhotsky, Johann (John), 12–13, 14
Liberal Party of Australia, 115, 119, 127, 152, 172, 195, 196, 199, 218, 221, 225, 226
Limestone Plains
    accounts of, 12, 42
    development, 25–6
    land grants, 17
    limits of location, 11, 14, 18
    mapping, 14
    naming, 10
    political division, 28–31
    as site for capital, 35, 39, 42
    surveyed as site for capital, 42
Linde, Werners, 125
lobbyists, 155, 214
Lyons, Enid, 93
Lyons, Joseph, 93, 105

Macquoid, Thomas, 22
McCallum, J.A., 143
McKeahnie, Elizabeth, 20
McLaren, Bill, 147
McQueen, Humphrey, 48, 204
men, 110, 152
    demographic imbalance, 26, 73, 116
Menzies, R.G., 93, 100, 105, 115, 120, 122, 127, 139, 144, 145, 146, 147, 172, 174

Miller, Colonel David, 46, 49, 50, 55, 58
Mollison, James, 189
Molonglo River, 10, 14, 88
Monaro district, 7, 11, 13, 19, 22, 29, 114
Moore, John Joshua, 13, 22
  see also settlers, colonial
Mount Stromlo Observatory, 91, 108, 160, 244
Murdoch, J.S., 55, 67, 68
Murray, Terrence Aubrey, 18
Murrumbidgee River, 10, 14
Museum of Australian Democracy, 232
music, 88, 152

Naas River, 20, 42
Namadgi National Park, 8, 209, 242
National Archives of Australia, 234
national capital
  controversy over design, 55, 57
  debates over location, 38, 40–2
  design competition, 50–2
  National Capital Planning and Development Committee, 93, 117
  role of, 98–9, 102, 106, 146, 155
  role of land nationalisation, see land: leasehold
  Senate Select Committee on the Development of Canberra, 144
National Capital Development Commission, 145, 146–8, 150, 155, 159, 161–9, 170, 184, 186, 189, 190, 198–9, 200, 208, 213, 216, 219, 220, 222
National Capital Planning Authority (National Capital Authority), 220, 224, 233
National Council of Women, ACT, 152, 185

National Gallery of Australia, 189, 211
National Folk Festival, 241
National Library of Australia, 143, 162
National Museum of Australia, 211, 230, 231
National Parks Association, ACT, 150
  see also environment
National Press Club, 214
National Science and Technology Centre, 234
Nationalist Party, 64, 65
New Delhi, 39, 45
Ngambri people, 9, 24, 33, 206
Ngunawal people, 3, 9, 90, 206
No Self-Government Party, 221
Nott, Lewis, 86, 120
Nugent, Ann, 207

O'Brien, Eris, 153
Oliphant, Marcus, 130, 156
Oliver, Alexander, 35, 38, 39, 40
O'Malley, King, 40, 44, 45, 50, 51, 52, 55, 60
Onyong (Hong Kong), 24
opinion polling, 218
O'Sullivan, E.W., 31, 34, 35
Overall, John, 146–7
Owen, Percy, 65

Page, Geoff, 210
Palmerville station, 19
Parliament, Commonwealth, 80, 93, 105, 116, 119, 187, 192, 195, 197
  Public Works Committee, 68, 70
  transfer, 65, 67, 80
Parliament House, 145
  design competitions, 59, 67
  permanent, 167–8, 189, 191, 198, 212, 218
  provisional, 67, 80, 84, 212

pastoralism, 1, 11, 12, 13–16,
　17–19, 23, 26, 46, 109, 242
　modernisation, 31–2, 44
　politics of, 29–31
performing arts
　music, 170, 183, 203, 206, 218
　theatre, 86, 152, 162, 193, 204,
　　237
Perkins, Charles, 188, 206
Petrov defection, 141–2
poetry, 209–10
policing, 82, 177, 180, 202, 236
political representation, 28
　loss of franchise in FCT, 14
　NSW Legislative Assembly, 28
　NSW Legislative Council, 18
　see also Australian Capital
　　Territory
politics
　Cold War, 141–2, 154
　environmental, 183–4
　federation, 34–6
　free selection, 28–30
　state aid, 153
　unionism, 30–1
　Vietnam War, 172, 177, 180, 233
　women's movement, 180
population, 62, 67, 73, 94, 97,
　　123, 147, 155, 160, 161, 187,
　　198, 201, 222, 223, 241
　1828 census, 15
　1841 census, 18
　1891 census, 33
　1933 census, 85
　1947 census, 116, 125
Powell, Tony, 190, 198, 235
Power, Pat, 238
Presbyterianism, 17, 86, 154
press gallery, 81, 105, 106, 107,
　　127, 156, 175, 187, 217
Prime Minister's Lodge, 78, 93
private enterprise, 70, 117, 147,
　　153, 155, 162, 167, 191, 193,
　　198, 199, 200, 213, 216, 217,
　　219, 224, 233, 234

prohibition, 44, 77
protests, 93, 172, 176–7, 183–4,
　　240
Pryor, Lindsay, 95, 144, 149
Public Service, ACT, 220, 225, 227,
　　228
Public Service, Commonwealth,
　　87, 98, 173–5, 188, 224
　accommodation for, 68, 115,
　　231
　'Canberra outlook', 101–4
　cuts, 128, 196, 231
　'economic rationalism', 214
　graduate recruitment, 91–2, 98,
　　101
　perceptions of, 68, 155, 160
　political advisers, 188
　Public Service Board, 77, 82,
　　127, 196, 197, 215
　transfer, 68, 73, 80, 81, 127,
　　133, 145, 148, 155, 187, 197

Queanbeyan, 10, 15, 19, 26, 28,
　　35, 41, 48, 77, 130, 200

rabbits, see environment
radio, 88, 106, 116, 203, 237
　2XX, 203, 237
Read, Peter, 11
Reconciliation Place, 232
refugees, 138, 207, 232, 238, 239
　see also ethnic identity:
　　Vietnamese
regionalism, 114
Reid, Alan, 105
Reid, Elizabeth, 182, 188
religion, 17, 18, 20, 44, 86, 136,
　　138, 153–5, 199, 238–9
　see also denominations
Reps, John, 40
Residents Rally, 221, 226
Returned and Services League, 110,
　　156
Robinson, George, 17
Rowse, Tim, 98, 104

Royal Australian Mint, 162
Royal Military College, Duntroon, 47–8, 60, 85, 111, 212
royal tour 1954, 140–1
Rudd, Kevin, 231
Rural Lessees Association, 90
Ryan, Susan, 180, 195, 216

Saarinen, Eliel, 52
Schreiner, Karl, 137
Scrivener, Charles, 41, 42, 46, 50
Scullin, James, 84
self-government, *see* Australian Capital Territory
Senate Select Committee on the Development of Canberra, *see* national capital
Service, Jim, 234
settlers, colonial, 1, 17–19
sexuality
  homosexuality, 180
  prostitution, 137
  same sex marriage, 229
  sex industry, 229, 236
Shumack, Samuel, 17, 29
Sitsky, Larry, 170
Skywhale, 247
Snow, Terry, 235
social hierarchy, 77–80
  in housing, 49, 70, 130, 134
  rank, 16, 117
  'social mix', 148, 167, 194, 201, 236
  status, 3, 26
  trends, 201, 202
Society for Social Responsibility in Science, 183
soldier settler farming, 116
Southwell, Thomas, 26
Southwell family, 30
sport, 44, 74, 79, 94, 119, 139, 169, 204, 217
  Australian Rules football, 49, 139
  basketball, 217

Canberra Brumbies, 217
Canberra Cannons, 217
Canberra Capitals, 217
Canberra Raiders, 217
cricket, 20, 27, 217
golf, 133
horse racing, 27
Rugby Union, 49
skiing, 149
soccer, 139
swimming, 49, 85, 133
Staley, Tony, 199
Stanhope, Jon, 228, 229
Stretton, Hugh, 123, 132, 147, 148, 162
suburbs
  Acton, 49
  Ainslie, 69, 93, 119, 201
  Barton, 69, 81, 214
  Braddon, 69, 70
  Campbell, 148
  Causeway, 76, 79
  Civic, 69, 216
  Curtin, 148
  Deakin, 93, 119
  Dickson, 148
  Downer, 148, 201
  Forrest (Blandfordia), 70, 77
  Fyshwick, 187
  Griffith, 3, 93, 119, 201
  Hughes, 148
  Kingston, 69, 72, 73, 186, 201
  Manuka, 69
  Narrabundah, 3, 117, 134, 138, 201, 203, 204, 238
  O'Connor, 131, 201
  Palmerston, 235
  Pialligo, 10
  Red Hill, 148
  Reid, 69, 201
  Russell, 148
  Swinger Hill, 186
  Turner, 119
  Watson, 148
  Westlake, 75, 90, 138

Sulman, John, 65–7, 69, 72
Summernats, 241
Swan, Robbie, 218

Tange, Arthur, 119, 212
Taylor, George, 45
Taylor, Griffith, 42, 46
Throsby Smith, Charles, 10
  see also exploration, early European
Throsby, Charles, 10
  see also exploration, early European
Tillyard, Patricia, 91
Tillyard, Robin, 90, 92
Tooma, 41
towns, 'new', 'satellite', 'centre', 217, 235
  Belconnen, 166, 187, 199, 201
  Gunghalin, 217, 235, 242
  Tuggeranong, 10, 166, 187, 199, 201
  Weston Creek, 163, 201
  Woden, 149, 163, 167, 187, 201
tracking stations, space, 175
Trades and Labour Council, ACT, 134, 203, 216
transport
  air, 93, 100, 111
  automobiles, 44, 89, 109, 145, 147, 149, 162, 165, 209
  bicycles, 44, 89, 109, 208
  horses, 44
  public, 89, 165, 167, 186, 208, 226
  railway, 26, 41, 43, 48, 81, 84, 100, 235
  roads, 16, 17, 30, 31, 70, 89, 163–5, 242
Troy, Patrick, 165
Tucker, Kerrie, 242
Tuggeranong station, 26, 31
Tuggeranong station (Isabella Plains), 14

Tumut, 41
Twofold Bay, 40

unemployment, 84, 93, 194, 202–3
United States–Australian War Memorial, 141
University of Canberra, 216, 240
urban planning, 114, 133, 145, 146, 160, 162, 176, 201, 233, 246
  in Canberra, 66
  'city beautiful' ideals, 38, 52
  debates within, 50
  'garden city', 69–70, 149
  medium density, 199
  'neighbourhood unit', 148, 162, 187, 194
  'open space', 208
  professionalisation, 39, 50
  'renewal', 186, 203, 213
  'sustainable development', 224
  'territorial unit', 187
  'Y-plan', 163–5, 166, 186, 199
Uren, Tom, 185

Voorhees, Alan, 163

Walsh, Gordon, 171
war, see World War I; World War II
War Memorial, see Australian War Memorial
Ward, Frederick, 129
Washington D.C., 40
water
  role in selection of Canberra, 42
  sewerage, 227
  supplies, 48, 70, 73, 150, 243, 245
Waterford, Jack, 216
Watson, Frederick, 12, 25
Watt, Alan, 102, 108
Weirick, James, 53
Weston, Charles, 46, 70, 79
Weston, Thomas, 49, 60

Wheeler, Frederick, 103, 173
Wheeler, Peggy, 119
White, George, 213
Whitlam, Gough, 88, 161, 172, 185, 188, 190, 192, 195
Wild, Joseph, 10
Williams, Harry, 33
Wilson, Roland, 91, 101, 102, 127
wine industry, 242
Wiradjuri people, 11
  see also Aboriginal people
women, 86, 91, 152, 223, 236
  activism, 180–2, 188, 198, 204
  demographic imbalance, 16, 18, 26, 73
  employment, 110, 115, 155, 170, 215
  networks, 44, 74, 83, 109, 112, 152, 169
  role of, 79, 82–3

World War I, 58, 62, 63
  local impact, 59–60
  Molonglo internment camp, 59
  Tuggeranong armaments factory, 59
World War II, 96, 99, 107–10
Wreck Bay, *see* Aboriginal people
Wright, Davis, 22, 23, 24
Wright, James, 1, 15, 22
  see also settlers, colonial
Wright, Judith, 209

Yarralumla (official residence), 76, 94, 232
Yarralumla station, 18, 19, 30, 31–2, 46
Yass, 33, 35, 40, 90, 200
YMCA, 86, 110
YWCA, 110

For EU product safety concerns, contact us at Calle de José Abascal, 56–1°,
28003 Madrid, Spain or eugpsr@cambridge.org.

www.ingramcontent.com/pod-product-compliance
Lightning Source LLC
LaVergne TN
LVHW010254260326
834688LV00044B/1279